Pro Microsoft Teams Development

A Hands-on Guide to Building Custom Solutions for the Teams Platform

Rick Van Rousselt

Pro Microsoft Teams Development: A Hands-on Guide to Building Custom Solutions for the Teams Platform

Rick Van Rousselt
Pelt, Belgium

ISBN-13 (pbk): 978-1-4842-6363-1   ISBN-13 (electronic): 978-1-4842-6364-8
https://doi.org/10.1007/978-1-4842-6364-8

Managing Director, Apress Media LLC: Welmoed Spahr
Acquisitions Editor: Joan Murray
Development Editor: Laura Berendson
Coordinating Editor: Jill Balzano

Cover image designed by Freepik (www.freepik.com)

Distributed to the book trade worldwide by Springer Science+Business Media LLC, 1 New York Plaza, Suite 4600, New York, NY 10004. Phone 1-800-SPRINGER, fax (201) 348-4505, e-mail orders-ny@springer-sbm. com, or visit www.springeronline.com. Apress Media, LLC is a California LLC and the sole member (owner) is Springer Science + Business Media Finance Inc (SSBM Finance Inc). SSBM Finance Inc is a **Delaware** corporation.

For information on translations, please e-mail booktranslations@springernature.com; for reprint, paperback, or audio rights, please e-mail bookpermissions@springernature.com.

Apress titles may be purchased in bulk for academic, corporate, or promotional use. eBook versions and licenses are also available for most titles. For more information, reference our Print and eBook Bulk Sales web page at http://www.apress.com/bulk-sales.

Any source code or other supplementary material referenced by the author in this book is available to readers on GitHub via the book's product page, located at www.apress.com/9781484263631. For more detailed information, please visit http://www.apress.com/source-code.

Printed on acid-free paper

For my wife Joke and my partner in crime Yves.

Table of Contents

About the Author

Rick Van Rousselt is a managing partner at Advantive, a Microsoft Gold Partner. He is an Office Apps and Services Microsoft MVP who has been working with SharePoint since 2007, eventually transitioning to Microsoft 365. With a strong focus on development, his current position has given him a diverse skillset and expertise in Microsoft 365, Azure, and all related technologies. His inquisitive disposition motivates him to continuously gain knowledge and share what he learns with those interested in learning the same technologies. He is often pounding pavement in the global tech community, speaking at events such as Microsoft Ignite, ESPC, Collaboration Summit, SharePoint Saturdays, and more, most recently on the topic of Teams development.

About the Technical Reviewers

Thomas Gölles leads the Modern Workplace Solutions team at Solvion in Graz, Austria. He has worked as a developer, architect, consultant, and team lead through his career. As an active member of the Microsoft 365 community and Microsoft MVP for Office Development, he is a co-organizer of SharePoint Saturday Vienna, Office 365 Meetup Graz, and Office 365 Meetup Vienna. Together with a group of friends, he is also part of two podcasts, selectedtech.show and at365.de. Read more about him on his blog at `https://thomy.tech`.

Albert-Jan Schot, also known as Appie, is someone who lives and breathes Microsoft 365 to such a degree that it has become second nature to him. He has numerous certifications to his name. With his extensive knowledge, Albert-Jan is a valuable source of information for colleagues. He not only enjoys stepping up to the challenge of designing, developing, and building innovative cloud solutions, he also has consultancy and training experience. He is active on a range of forums, blogs, as well as on Twitter where he shares his knowledge and passion with others. Over the years, he had the opportunity to present at several national and international user groups and events.

Acknowledgments

First, I would like to thank Apress and especially Joan Murray and Jill Balzano for allowing me to write this book and helping me accomplish this goal. In these uncertain times of COVID-19 and the world coming to a sudden stop with lockdowns, events canceled, schools and restaurants closed, writing in a structured fashion on this book has not been easy. But thanks to Jill and Joan and their continuous support and guidance, this was possible.

Additionally, I would like to thank my two technical reviewers Albert-Jan Schot and Thomy Gölles. They not only reviewed my book but were excellent sparring partners together with Stephan Bisser. They helped me to bounce ideas off each other during our biweekly webinars for Selected Tech. This is the power of the community; not only did we meet and got to know each other at different tech events, but I consider them not only fellow MVPs but friends as well.

A special kind of gratitude goes out to Yves Vuurstaek, who is my friend and business partner. While we both have equal weight to pull in our company Advantive, he always made sure that I did not get too much on my plate so that I could invest more time in my book.

This book would not have been possible without the corporate organizations—large and small—that allowed me to develop and test insight-related ideas in projects, workshops, and consulting engagements over the last 10+ years.

Finally, I want to thank my wife, Joke, and my children Daan and Romy, for tolerating my incessant disappearances into my home office. Joke, thank you for always being supportive and patient.

Introduction

Microsoft Teams is the new and exciting chat-based workspace in Microsoft 365. This new tool offers a whole new experience to collaborate and is the new standard for how people get their work done, both in the office and on the go with the mobile app. Because Microsoft Teams is a hub for teamwork, it's only natural that people using the tool would want their other tools integrated into this hub, whether it is an existing application or a brand-new one that's developed. For us developers, this is an excellent opportunity. Our applications can get more visibility and are easier to use for people if we integrate them into the Teams developer platform.

There are lots of different ways that we can integrate our applications with Microsoft Teams, from surfacing our data so that it's easily searchable to having a direct communication against the Microsoft Teams platform so that people perform better in their day-to-day jobs with the automatic creation of channels or teams.

Intended audience

This book is for developers and architects who want to know how the developer story for the Microsoft Teams platform unfolds and who wish to master developing apps inside and against Microsoft Teams. Existing Microsoft 365 developers who are already developing against one of the other services like SharePoint, Office, Dynamics, and so on can use this book to upgrade their existing skills and knowledge so that they can also develop on top of and against Microsoft Teams.

Organization of this book

This book is divided into seven major sections, each focusing on a different type of extension we can build on top of Teams, except for Part 1. Part 1 is a set of tips and tricks that extend your knowledge and make your development experience smoother and more manageable. The purpose of this book was not to help you get started with development for Microsoft Teams, because there is enough documentation, videos, and webinars out there to help you take the first baby steps into Teams development. This book starts in the first section with what to do after those first steps and how to make it easier on yourself and gives insights on how other people are developing against the platform. In Part 2, we deep dive into tabs in Teams and see how this seemingly simple extension can get a lot of visibility for your already existing apps. Part 3 is all about Bots and more specific chatbots in Teams. We will discuss general best practices when building bots and then go all the way into calling and media bots in Teams. Part 4 covers webhooks in Teams and how we can get data in and out of Teams with them. In Part 5, we discuss the ins and outs of messaging extensions and how they can be used to build fully integrated applications in Teams. In Part 6, we stop building on top of the Teams platform but start coding against it. We see how we can leverage the power of the Microsoft Graph and the power of PowerShell to have our Teams environment behave in an automated fashion. Finally, in Appendix, we discuss things to consider when you are building on top of the Teams platform such as adding your app to the Teams app store or on how to advance your techniques even further.

Code samples accompany most chapters of this book. They are targeted against Node or C# developers and explain the various topics we cover. Throughout this book, I try to keep the same example application and to build further and further along with it, so that at the end of the book, you get an example solution that covers everything. In every chapter, there is a starting solution and a completed solution. You can follow along from the starting solution through the chapter to get to the same result as the completed solution, or you can open up the completed solution and work your way from there. Also, don't forget that these solutions are not production-ready. Most keys and secrets are hard coded inside of the solution so that you can easily swap them out with your own. This is, of course, not a best practice. Therefore, these solutions are prepared for you to cherry-pick the pieces out that you can use in your applications.

PART 1

Before You Can Start Building

CHAPTER 1

What's required

Before we can start developing Microsoft Teams apps, we need to understand the inner workings of a Teams app. In this chapter, we will dive into the different parts of a Teams app, and we will walk you through the various steps to set up your development environment.

The basics

A basic Microsoft Teams application only consists of two parts. One is a place where your code can run and execute; the other is the Teams app package.

Microsoft Teams is built in the cloud and, therefore, an online platform. You will not be able to install your code in the data centers of Microsoft that host Teams. This implies that we cannot install our code there, and therefore we need to bring our own infrastructure. If you take a closer look at the architecture of Teams, you will find that Teams is built on top of existing services like Exchange Online and SharePoint Online. The other services that the Teams team needed to create Teams were built on top of Microsoft Azure (see Figure 1-1). For this reason, we are going to use Azure services to host our code.

© Rick Van Rousselt 2021
R. Van Rousselt, *Pro Microsoft Teams Development*, https://doi.org/10.1007/978-1-4842-6364-8_1

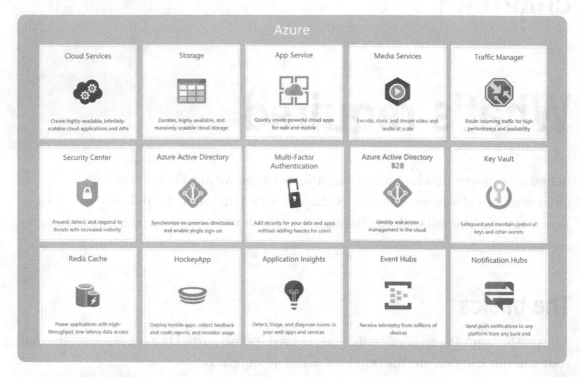

Figure 1-1.   *Azure services used by Microsoft Teams (`https://myignite.
techcommunity.microsoft.com/sessions/83471?source=sessions`) Ignite 2019
session by Bill Bliss*

The other part of a Teams application is called a Teams app package. A Teams
app package is a zip file that contains three files: two image files that Teams needs to
visualize your app and a manifest file. The images consist of a large icon and a small
icon. They will show up, for example, when installing your app from the store or when
activating your app in the Teams client. You don't need them when starting with Teams
development in the beginning. Microsoft provides two default icons. It's only when you
want to install your app in a production tenant or when you want to make it available
for download from the app store that these are required to give that extra final touch to
your app. The third file is called the manifest file and is the most essential part of the app
package. It tells Microsoft Teams what you have built, how Teams needs to surface it, and
where the code resides that Teams needs to call. Let's take a closer look at this manifest
file.

Manifest file

The manifest file is a JSON-formatted file that contains the metadata about the app you created and which Teams extensibility points it uses, cf. so it describes basically, what functionality did you build.

In its most basic form, it looks like this:

```
{
    "$schema": "https://developer.microsoft.com/en-us/json-schemas/teams/
    v1.5/MicrosoftTeams.schema.json",
    "manifestVersion": "1.5",
    "version": "1.0.0",
    "id": "665cae8e-6956-4dc1-8292-d675c018691d",
    "packageName": "ProTeamsDevelopment",
    "developer": {
        "name": "Rick Van Rousselt",
        "websiteUrl": "https://www.rickvanrousselt.com",
        "privacyUrl": "https://www.rickvanrousselt.com/privacy",
        "termsOfUseUrl": "https://www.rickvanrousselt.com/termsofuse"
    },
    "icons": {
        "color": "color.png",
        "outline": "outline.png"
    },
    "name": {
        "short": "My Teams app",
        "full": "my own teams app"
    },
    "description": {
        "short": "My first manifest",
        "full": "This is the most basic form of a manifest"
    },
    "accentColor": "#FFFFFF"
}
```

This manifest, of course, is defined by a schema created by Microsoft and has different versions. There is always the latest version that is ready for production use. Currently, at the time of writing, this is version 1.7 (`https://developer.microsoft.com/en-us/json-schemas/teams/v1.7/MicrosoftTeams.schema.json`), and a developer preview version is also available (`https://raw.githubusercontent.com/OfficeDev/microsoft-teams-app-schema/preview/DevPreview/MicrosoftTeams.schema.json`). This developer preview lets you use the latest extensibility endpoints of Teams. However, a developer preview is never a production-ready material. For some examples throughout this book, we will need the developer preview manifest, but in most samples, the 1.7 version is perfect. If we need the dev preview version, I will explicitly mention it.

The metadata about your app are also required fields. These parts are

- Schema: The HTTPS schema URL where this JSON is validated against.

- Manifest version: The version of the manifest you are using.

- Version: The version number of your app. This is semantic versioning, so MAJOR.MINOR.PATCH.

- Id: The ID of your app. A unique GUID.

- Developer information which contains

  - Name

  - Website URI

  - Privacy URI

  - Terms of service URI

- Name: The name of your application.

- Description: Describe your application.

- Icons: The filenames of the two icons you are going to include in the zip package.

- Accent colors: An accent color for your app.

- Package name: A unique identifier for this app in reverse domain notation, for example, com.example.myapp.

Now, these fields are only metadata, so while it's possible, you just create an app package with only this information in the manifest, this app would not do much, except for being installed in your environment. Because Microsoft doesn't want you to pollute your environment with nonworking apps, your Teams client will block the upload of apps like this. The app will validate against the schema, but the Teams client will notice that there is no functionality, so we need to add something that extends teams. This can be one or multiple or a combination of the following items:

- Tabs: More info in Chapter 5

- Bots: More info in Chapter 8

- Connectors: More info in Chapter 13

- Compose extensions: More info in Chapter 15

Our Teams app also needs to be installed somewhere; therefore, we are going to need a Microsoft 365 tenant to test our solution, and some developer tooling to create our code. This book has both examples for C# and Node.js in it, and they will be clearly marked. So, whatever is your poison of choice, you can choose which path to follow. The result will be 99% the same. The only part that is explicitly not available for Node.js is calling and media bots (Chapter 12).

Your environment

To get started with Microsoft Teams development, you need a Microsoft 365 tenant. You can easily register for a development tenant by joining the Microsoft 365 developer program (`https://developer.microsoft.com/en-us/office/dev-program`). Fill in all the information required and set up a fresh Microsoft 365 tenant. I would recommend that you also install the sample packs of data. This can be done in the main screen where you assigned yourself a license. This will make sure that you have some test data to work with while developing. You don't need this for developing solutions for Teams, but it saves time. That way, you don't waste time creating test accounts and filling in their profiles. Currently, there are only sample packs with user accounts, including emails and events for those users. When the sample packs have finished installing, then we still need to create a Team as a starting point for our tests. Go to the Teams web client and create a new public Team called development and add an additional user to it. In my case, I added Megan Bowen which is part of the user sample pack I installed (see Figure 1-2). Also, go to `https://portal.azure.com` and create a free subscription. You will need this to create your Bot Framework entries and other services connected to bots.

Figure 1-2. *A fresh new Team in my development tenant and Megan Bowen was just added*

App Studio

Next, install *App Studio* from Microsoft into Teams. App Studio is a free Teams app that is for starters, an excellent example of the things you can create with Teams development, but it's also an app specially designed for Teams developers. It will assist you with the creation of your manifest and help you create adaptive cards, and it also includes a bot that will answer your questions about Teams development. I usually use it when I start a new project. It's great for setting up a proof of concept or creating a rough version of the manifest I need. We are going to start out with this app later to get to know the basics (see Figure 1-3).

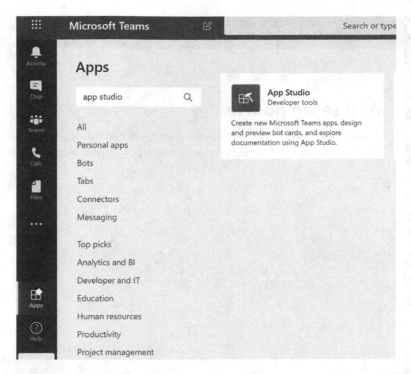

Figure 1-3. *Install App Studio from the Teams app store to aid with your Teams development*

Sideloading

Now there is only one more thing left to do, and that is to activate the sideloading of apps in your new developer environment. This setting determines if users in your tenant can upload custom Teams app packages. Since we are going to create custom Teams apps, let's turn this on. Head over to the Teams admin portal (`https://admin.teams.microsoft.com/`), and under setup policies (Figure 1-4), click the global policy. In a new tenant, everybody falls under the global policy. If you ever need to test out custom apps in a production environment, an administrator can easily create a different policy for you and your Team and give you other settings than the rest of the organization.

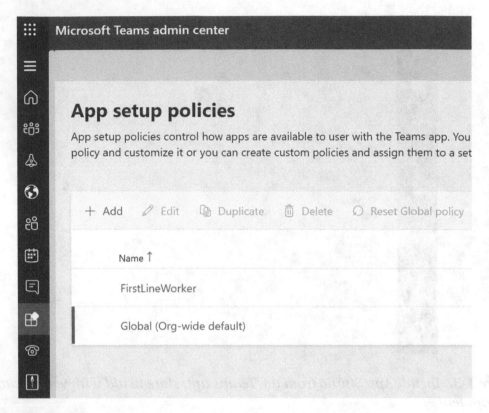

Figure 1-4. *App setup policies in the Teams admin center*

Now activate the *Upload custom apps* setting (Figure 1-5). Or if you create an app that's needed for the entire company, then you can pin it here so that it shows up in everyone's Team client. Don't forget that turning this on in a production environment for everyone can have serious implications. Everybody can simply create and upload packages as they please, which is not such a good idea for production environments.

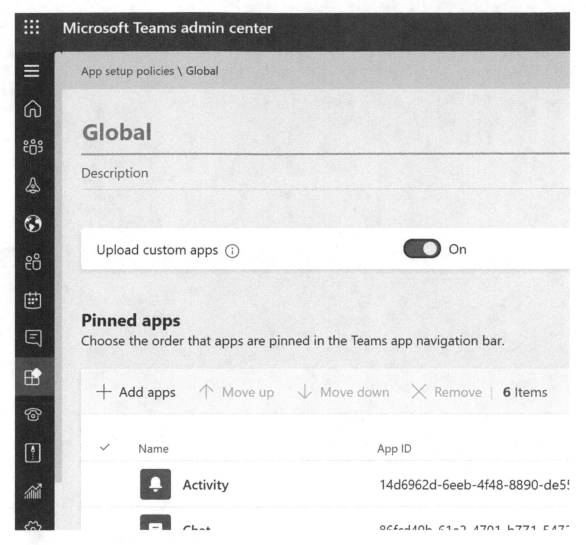

Figure 1-5. *The Upload custom apps switch turned on for the global policy*

Now that your online environment is configured for Microsoft Teams development, the one thing that remains is your offline environment. Let's take a more in-depth look at what to install on our development machine in our next chapter.

Final thoughts

In our first chapter, we covered the basics of a Teams app package and what it consists of. We discussed sideloading and App Studio and how they make our life as a Teams developer easier.

CHAPTER 2

Additional tools

Developing against Microsoft Teams does require you to get to know some other tools as well. So, in this chapter, we will first go a little deeper into the additional tools that are available so that your development experience will be more comfortable. This chapter will not have any Teams-related information, but it will help in making our Teams development experience as smooth as possible.

Additional tools on your belt

One major downside (if you want to call it that way) while developing against the Microsoft Teams platform is that it's an online tool. The days that we could do offline work on applications are long gone. This also means that because "it's in the cloud," your code should also be accessible from the cloud. Otherwise, Teams cannot find the logic you are willing to execute. To aid in this, we can use a tunneling tool. ngrok, for instance, is one of them. There are more competitors in the market, and you are free to use the one you like, but for further reference, we will use ngrok. This tool is free (until a certain point) and does an excellent job of its simple task. It will provide you with a URL that you can place in your manifest, and when Teams calls this URL, ngrok will forward all traffic through the tunnel to your local development machine. This way, you can still debug your code locally.

© Rick Van Rousselt 2021
R. Van Rousselt, *Pro Microsoft Teams Development*, https://doi.org/10.1007/978-1-4842-6364-8_2

ngrok

ngrok is a tunneling software. What it does is, when you start the program, it requests a subdomain of their domain. So, they own *.ngrok.com and they will give you a random subdomain "something.ngrok.com" for you to use. Their servers will then act as a reverse proxy and will set up SSH (Secure Shell) remote forwarding to forward all requests that come into the URL you just got back to the executable you are running and therefore making your application available to the world. You can download the executable here: `https://ngrok.com/`. I recommend that you also sign up for the service. Signing up makes it easier to create a configuration file. If you ever find yourself in an enterprise environment where ngrok is not allowed, then I encourage you to check out the Tunnel Relay (`https://github.com/OfficeDev/microsoft-teams-tunnelrelay`). This solution gets the same results but uses Azure Relay, which, in an enterprise context, gets more trust.

Getting started with ngrok is simple. The most basic command will be: `ngrok http 80.` This starts up the ngrok.exe file and gives it two parameters. The "http" one will tell ngrok that we will be using the HTTP protocol. ngrok can also be used for other protocols like TCP, as you will see later in this book when we are handling media bots. The other one will tell ngrok that it will need to connect the public URL it generates to whatever is running on port 80 of your local machine. This can be anything from a website to a bot.

Configuration file

ngrok works with YAML-based configuration files, and a config file makes it easier to get started in the morning when you start your day. But beware of YAML files; if you have never worked with them, then remember something that I learned the hard way. It does matter where you put a space or an indentation. A wrong space somewhere can make the file not correct, and you spend hours searching what you did wrong.

Download the executable and extract it into a folder. I have a tools folder on my hard drive where I put all those small tools I need. Then run the following in command line while located in the directory where you placed the executable:

```
$ ./ngrok authtoken <here is your authtoken>
```

This command is listed on the website that you see when you create your account but targeted against Linux users. If you are on a Windows machine, use the following command:

```
ngrok authtoken <here is your authtoken>
```

This command will create a configuration file for you. In my case, it looks like the one in Figure 2-1.

Figure 2-1. *Creating an ngrok YAML configuration file with the authentication code*

The configuration file's location is in your Windows user profile. For me, that's "C:\Users\RickVanRousselt\.ngrok2".

The contents of the file are still empty except for the authentication token. We will need to add information from our applications in there.

Testing ngrok

Now that we have our configuration file available, let's test out the capabilities of ngrok. While still inside the folder where the executable resides, run the following command:

Ngrok http 80

Executing this command will start up your tunnel, and you will receive a random URL (see Figure 2-2).

```
C:\Windows\System32\cmd.exe - ngrok  http 80

ngrok by @inconshreveable

Session Status                online
Account                       Rick Van Rousselt (Plan: Free)
Version                       2.3.35
Region                        United States (us)
Web Interface                 http://127.0.0.1:4040
Forwarding                    http://6eb5dda0.ngrok.io -> http://localhost:80
Forwarding                    https://6eb5dda0.ngrok.io -> http://localhost:80

Connections                   ttl     opn     rt1     rt5     p50     p90
                              0       0       0.00    0.00    0.00    0.00
```

Figure 2-2. *ngrok started with the most basic command*

If you now browse to this URL, either HTTP or HTTPS, you will receive an error. This is normal because we don't have anything running at port 80 that can be served as seen in Figure 2-3.

Failed to complete tunnel connection

The connection to **http://6eb5dda0.ngrok.io** was successfully tunneled to your ngrok client, but the client failed to establish a connection to the local address **localhost:80**.

Make sure that a web service is running on **localhost:80** and that it is a valid address.

The error encountered was: **dial tcp [::1]:80: connectex: No connection could be made because the target machine actively refused it.**

```
Select C:\Windows\System32\cmd.exe - ngrok  http 80

ngrok by @inconshreveable

Session Status                online
Account                       Rick Van Rousselt (Plan: Free)
Version                       2.3.35
Region                        United States (us)
Web Interface                 http://127.0.0.1:4040
Forwarding                    http://6eb5dda0.ngrok.io -> http://localhost:80
Forwarding                    https://6eb5dda0.ngrok.io -> http://localhost:80

Connections                   ttl     opn     rt1     rt5     p50     p90
                              6       0       0.04    0.02    2.31    2.32

HTTP Requests
-------------

GET /favicon.ico              502 Bad Gateway
GET /                         502 Bad Gateway
GET /favicon.ico              502 Bad Gateway
GET /                         502 Bad Gateway
```

Figure 2-3. *Error because there is nothing available at port 80 on your local machine*

If you return to the command line, you can see that ngrok received an HTTP 502 (bad gateway error), which indicates that there is something wrong with the web server. There is also an entry above the public URLs that's named web interface and that points to a 127.0.0.1 address. So this is something running on our machine. Browse to that URL, and you will see a small Fiddler-like web page provided by ngrok (see Figure 2-4). Here, you can see all the requests that were passed through by ngrok, along with their contents and headers. Inspecting requests can be convenient when developing for Microsoft Teams. Sometimes, you want to see what is going over the wire. And with this page, you can inspect every request going back and forward between your custom application and Microsoft Teams. There is even the possibility to replay a request. Replaying requests is going to make your life a lot easier. Because, for example, when you are developing a bot for Teams, then you are going to need to do a lot of typing to test the bot. And after you have typed the same testing sentence for the sixth time, you will be happy that this button exists, which will enable you to replay the last test while debugging your code.

Figure 2-4. *ngrok UI where you can inspect the traffic going through the tunnel*

Linking your hard drive to Teams

One of the cool things you can do with ngrok is to create a public URL that's linked to your hard drive. By doing this, you can immediately see the power but also the dangers of ngrok. Go back to your command-line tool and kill the ngrok process by pressing CTRL + C. Now enter the following command:

```
ngrok http "file:///C:\windows
```

The location on the C drive can be anything. I took the "Windows" folder because everybody running Windows has this folder, but it can be anything you want. As you can see in Figure 2-5, I now have a public URL where my Windows folder is accessible. But be aware, this will publicly expose your Windows folder, so don't keep it open for too long.

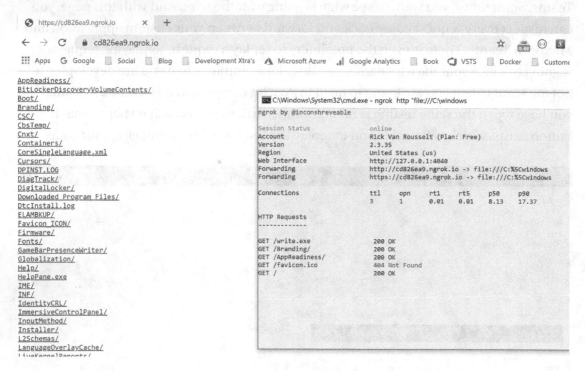

Figure 2-5. *ngrok serving my Windows folder as a web file browser*

Now to get this inside of Teams, open App Studio and create a new app. In the "manifest editor" tab, you can create a new app. Fill in the app details on the first tab, and under the "Capabilities" section, select "Tabs." Here, you can add a personal tab. Give it a unique name and entity ID, for example, FilesTab, and both URL values should point to your ngrok received URL (see Figure 2-6).

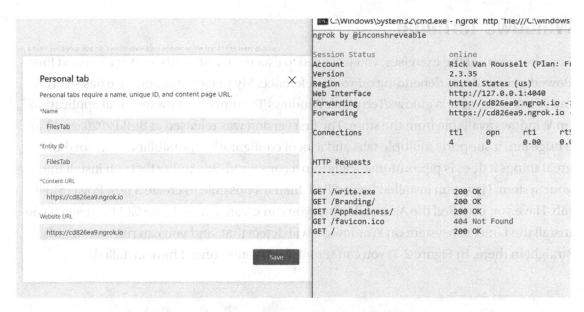

Figure 2-6. *Adding a personal tab pointing to the ngrok URL serving my Windows folder*

You can install the app directly in Teams from App Studio by clicking the Install button under the "Test and distribute" tab. The app will load, and you will see that you created a personal tab where you can browse through the files in your Windows folder. I hope that this little example demonstrates both the power and the dangers of ngrok. Next tool for our toolbelt is the Bot Framework emulator.

Bot Framework emulator

Bot's and Teams messaging extensions rely on the Microsoft Bot Framework to enable the communication and authentication between your app and Teams. To make sure you have an easy way to test these, you will need to download the Bot Framework emulator. The Bot Framework emulator is an open source project from Microsoft that allows you to debug and test your bots locally and remotely. It also displays the JSON contents (yes, a bot is just a collection of JSONs going back and forth over the wire) from each request. The Bot Framework emulator will enable you to get a more detailed view of what's going on. You can download the Bot Framework emulator at `https://github.com/microsoft/BotFramework-Emulator/releases`.

19

Windows Terminal

For some parts of the exercises, you will need to execute commands in the command line, PowerShell, or Bash, depending on your preference. My personal experience has steered me to using the new Windows Terminal. Windows Terminal is a new terminal application on Windows available from the store. The first version was released at Build 2020, and I'm a huge fan. It supports multiple tabs and a lot of configuration possibilities. One of the great things it does is pipe automatically into a command-line utility that you install into your system. Have you installed PowerShell, then it's possible to create a new PowerShell tab. Have you installed the Azure CLI, then you can create a new Azure CLI tab. Even if you install the Linux subsystem on Windows, it will detect that, and you can run commands straight in there. In Figure 2-7, you can see all the different ones I have installed.

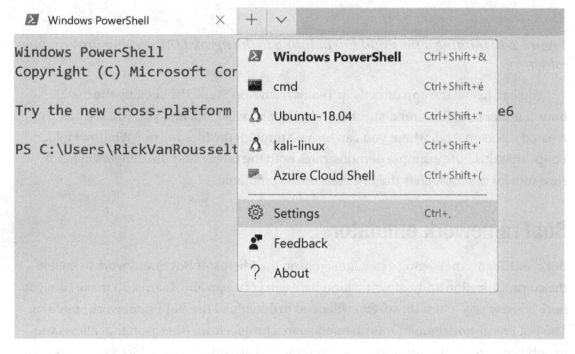

Figure 2-7. *Windows Terminal with the ability to create different tabs connected to different command-line utilities*

Summary

In this chapter, we discussed some additional tools that you can use to help you with Microsoft Teams development like ngrok and the Bot Framework emulator. These tools are independent of the development style you choose. There are more specific tools you can use, but those are more dependent on your development style. You are free to use other tools, but the ones mentioned here are, in my opinion, the most basic ones of your toolbelt.

CHAPTER 3

Make it easy on yourself

Now that we have our additional tools installed, we can start with the actual development for Microsoft Teams. Let's start with a basic application and continue to build on top of this. In this chapter, we will take our first steps into becoming a Teams developer, and when this chapter is complete, we will already have an app running in Teams.

Starting development

Like I already mentioned, you can pick your poison when building Teams applications. So, for the most part, I will explain both the Node.js way to achieve something and the .NET way to create the same. Since nothing is installed on the Teams client or in the data centers of Microsoft, you could technically even take any language or platform to develop your application. From now on, I will try to make it clear if an example is for Node.js or .NET, and in the GitHub repository that belongs to this book, you will see both labs always available. For the setup of your development environment, I'm not going too deep in detail. I will explain the requirements and some tips and tricks. Still, if you need a detailed explanation on setting up your development machine, then Microsoft has a lot of documentation around this. You can check out `http://aka.ms/teamsdev` for this. The basic setup of a development environment is very specific to your situation and especially because everybody develops in a slightly different way. Do you have a virtual machine in Azure for development or a MacBook? Then performance is not an issue. Are you on an old desktop somewhere behind a corporate firewall and proxy? Then your setup might be different.

© Rick Van Rousselt 2021
R. Van Rousselt, *Pro Microsoft Teams Development*, https://doi.org/10.1007/978-1-4842-6364-8_3

Node.js setup

Now to get started with Node.js for Teams development, you should have the following installed:

- Node.js

- npm (node package manager) or Yarn

How to install these is something I am not going to touch in this book. There are a lot of excellent tutorials that cover this online.

NVM

Notice that I don't add the version. Well, this will, of course, have changed by the time this book is three months old. The one thing I do recommend is that before you install Node, you install NVM (`https://github.com/nvm-sh/nvm`; or NVM for Windows, `https://github.com/coreybutler/nvm-windows`). NVM stands for node version manager, which allows you to switch between versions quickly. And switching between versions can be convenient because the project you create today might not have the same version anymore as the project you create three months from now. But you still need to, from time to time, maintain the first project. Well, instead of removing one version of Node and installing another, NVM will allow you to switch between versions with a simple command. NVM is also simple to use. Almost the only command you will ever need from this tool is

```
nvm use <version of Node>
```

This command will make you switch to that version of Node, and if you don't have it, it will download and install it.

Our primary working tool will, in this case, be Visual Studio Code. VS Code is a free IDE, so if you haven't used it before, download it and get familiar. If you are like me and you are coming from a C# and Visual Studio world, then a good tip is to install the Visual Studio Key Bindings extension (`https://marketplace.visualstudio.com/items?itemName=ms-vscode.vs-keybindings`). I spent years learning the keyboard shortcuts for several things in Visual Studio, and that they were missing suddenly is what annoyed me the most when changing from VS to VS Code.

Yeoman generator for Teams

Now we could start with creating a multitude of files and hooking them all together to create a web server so that we have something to show in Teams. That would take up too much time, and you would never do that in real life. So, let's get something that sets up the layout of our application for us, like a starting template. And templating, that is where Yeoman comes into play. Yeoman is a web scaffolding tool, meaning it provides, through generators, a basic model for different code variants. For us, the Teams generator is the most interesting. But should you ever consider starting a project in Vue.js or Go, then I can highly recommend this tool.

To get this working, we are going to need to install Yeoman, the generator we are using, and some dependencies (not always, but in this case, there are) so that we can use it. Go to your command-line tool and give this command:

```
npm install yo gulp-cli –global
```

This command will do two things. It will call npm to install the Yeoman generator (yo) and install the gulp-cli tooling (needed as a web server and for building the project). Both are prerequisites for our Teams generator. Then we can install the generator itself by running

```
npm install generator-teams –global
```

The -global switch you see at the end of the command will install the packages in your machine. With npm, we have two options where to install specific packages: global or local. By using global, this will become available everywhere on your device, which we are going to need for development tools like this. If we don't use this switch, it will install it locally. Meaning, in the folder, we are currently running the command. Local installations of packages are only used for a single project and are installed in the "node_modules" folder of that project, and a reference is made in the package.json file of a project.

Node.js basic app

To get our basic app working, we need to start a new project. Create an empty folder in your drive called "firstTeamsApp" and open a command window in there like in Figure 3-1.

```
md firstTeamsApp
cd firstTeamsApp
```

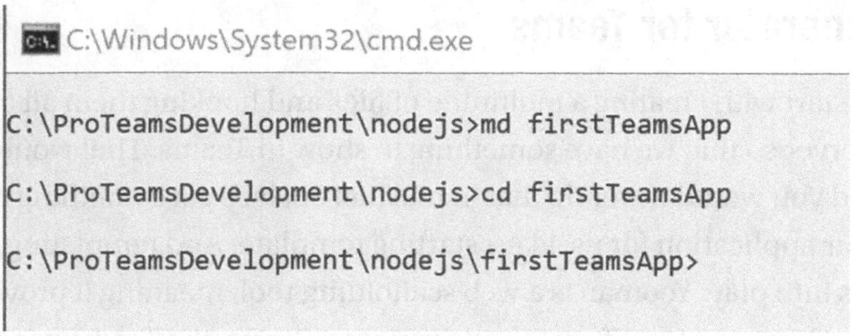

```
C:\Windows\System32\cmd.exe

C:\ProTeamsDevelopment\nodejs>md firstTeamsApp

C:\ProTeamsDevelopment\nodejs>cd firstTeamsApp

C:\ProTeamsDevelopment\nodejs\firstTeamsApp>
```

Figure 3-1. *Create an empty folder for our first Teams app*

Now we can run our generator in here to start templating out our project by using the command

Yo teams

The generator will ask us a few different questions:

- What is your solution name? You can give your solution a different name if you want. The default option is to use the parent folder name. For this first app, this is OK, so press enter.

- Where do you want to place the files? Again, you can choose something different, for instance, when you are running the generator from a higher folder than where you want your project files to end up. For now, again press enter because we are already in the correct folder.

- Title of your Microsoft Teams app project: If you want another title, then this is the moment to change it, but we are good with the title derived from the folder name.

- Optionally, you can enter your company name.

- And then the manifest version: The manifest version depends on what you are going to build, so it's a crucial question. As stated in Chapter 1, you cannot use a feature if it's not in the schema of your manifest. The latest version (not the devPreview) will be fine for this small app.

- If you have an MS Partner ID, it will also ask for it. Just leave this blank. It's only important when you want to publish your app to the public app store. But that's more explained in Appendix B.

- And then the features we are going to build: For this first app, we will start very simple with only a tab, so press enter again.

- And then the URL to host the solution: Also, press enter because we don't have an online website somewhere.

- We also don't want to include test frameworks because this starter app will work on the first time ☺ so press N.

- We also don't want to use application insights. So again press N.

- The default tab name will be a little too long so it's best to change it to "firstTab".

- And we are going to create a static tab for the first time, so select "Static tab."

Your answers should be something similar to Figure 3-2.

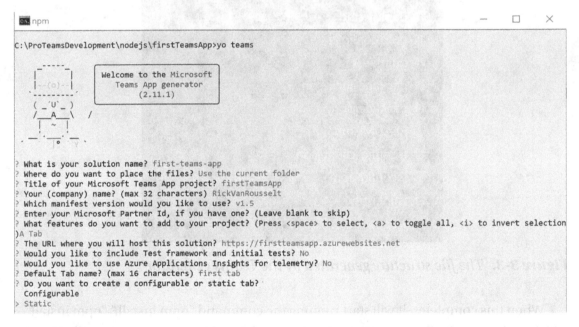

Figure 3-2. *Our first Teams app questions by the Yeoman generator*

Once you press enter, you will see a whole lot going on. What the generator is doing is creating a file and folder structure (see Figure 3-3). Using your input, it will apply a scaffolding logic to name those files and folders. It will also enable the features that you selected in the configuration files of the project. One of the most important configuration files that gets generated is the package.json file. This file contains all the metadata for your project as well as a list of dependencies. These dependencies are other libraries needed to build or run your project.

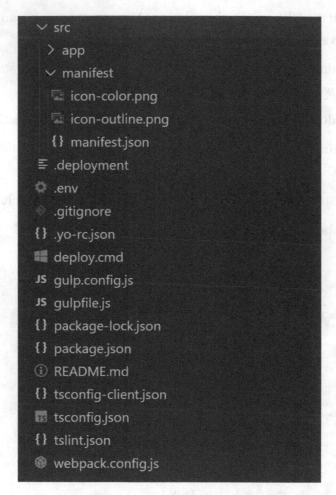

Figure 3-3. *The file structure generated by the Teams generator*

When this completes, it will start running the command "npm install." "npm install" will download all the different JavaScript libraries defined in the package.json file to a folder called "node_modules". Since it would clutter your project to have these files in your project structure, they are added to this newly created folder. This node_modules folder is also something we will not commit to our source code control system like GitHub or Azure DevOps. It will only take up a lot of space, and a peer developer working on the project can easily download the same modules again by running the "npm install" command again.

After everything has downloaded, you can start up Visual Studio Code by running the command

"code ."

For now, we are just going to get our project running so that we get our first Teams app. There is a built-in gulp task that will create our Teams package. So, it will zip the manifest JSON file and both icons inside of a zip file. Until now, we have been using a command-line tool to get our work done, but we can also use the built-in Terminal window of VS Code for this (see Figure 3-4).

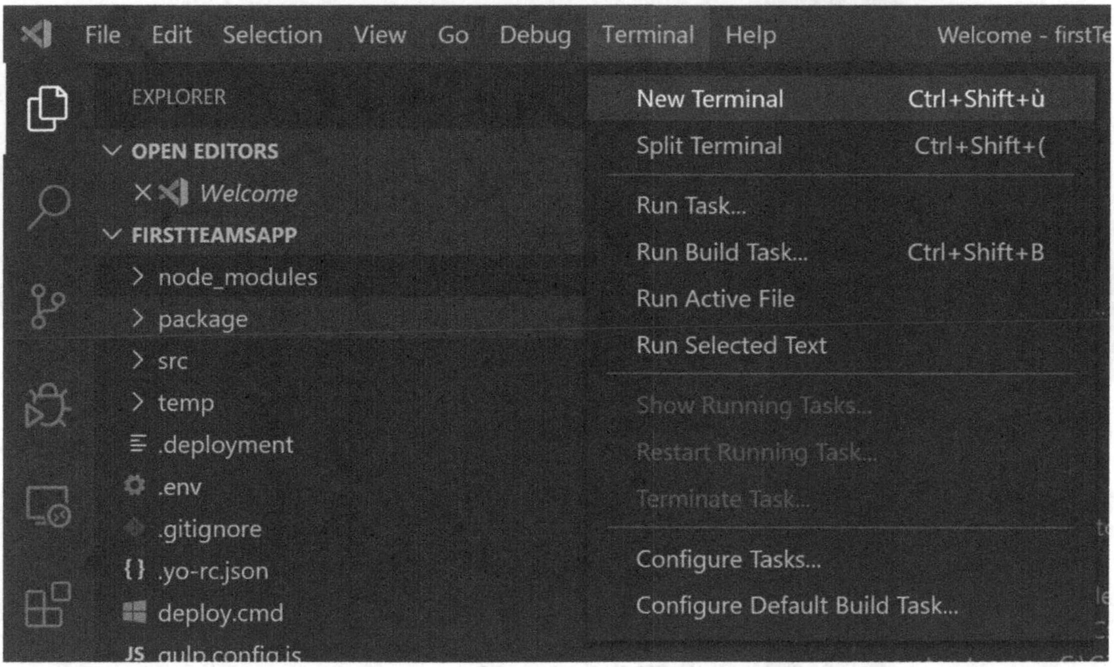

Figure 3-4. *Start a Terminal window from within VS Code*

Now, in this Terminal window, we can generate our Teams app by using the command

gulp manifest

This command will create a new folder called "package," and inside, you will find your Teams app package, which we will upload to Teams. As you know, a Teams app package is a .zip file that contains our three files, the manifest file and our two icons, as we discussed in Chapter 1. Open up your Teams environment and go at the bottom left to the "Apps" section and click the "Upload a custom app" tab (see Figure 3-5).

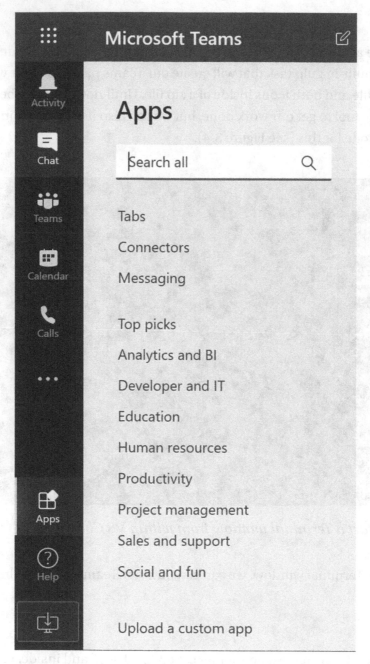

Figure 3-5. *Apps pane where the "Upload a custom app" link is*

Navigate to your code folder and upload the newly created Teams app package. As you can see, your new application is now uploaded and ready to be used (see Figure 3-6). Now when you add it, it will not render correctly. That's only normal and an expected behavior because we don't have anything running as a web server. We just told Teams to look for a web page at the default URL we set when the generator asked the questions (`https://myfirstteamstab.azurewebsites.net`).

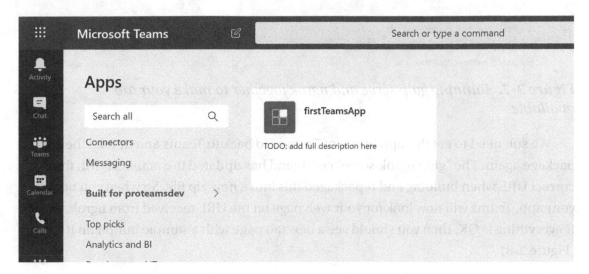

Figure 3-6. *My first Teams app added to my tenant. Ready to be added as a personal tab*

Now go back to the apps page for your organization (Figure 3-6) and click the ellipsis to delete the app you just uploaded. We need to start our web server and let Teams know that we have it running on a different URL. After you deleted the app, go back to your terminal in VS Code and use the command

```
gulp ngrok-serve
```

The Teams app generator creates the project in such a way that we don't need to create an ngrok tunnel by ourselves. This command will create a tunnel and will fill out the correct URL we receive from ngrok into the manifest file. Once the build is complete, you can scroll up a bit in the terminal to see that ngrok was started and that you received a random URL (see Figure 3-7). In my case, this time, it was `https://b141aff4.ngrok.io/`. Next time, it will be a different URL. If you open your browser and visit this URL, you will see that a web page will be rendered from this URL and is served from your local machine.

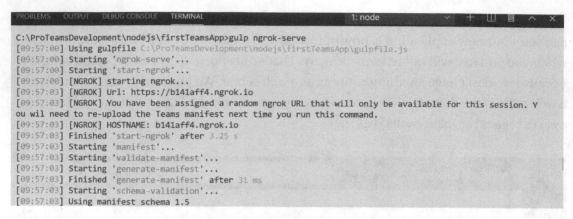

```
PROBLEMS    OUTPUT    DEBUG CONSOLE    TERMINAL                           1: node           ∨   +   ⊓   🗑   ∧   ✕

C:\ProTeamsDevelopment\nodejs\firstTeamsApp>gulp ngrok-serve
[09:57:00] Using gulpfile C:\ProTeamsDevelopment\nodejs\firstTeamsApp\gulpfile.js
[09:57:00] Starting 'ngrok-serve'...
[09:57:00] Starting 'start-ngrok'...
[09:57:00] [NGROK] starting ngrok...
[09:57:03] [NGROK] Url: https://b141aff4.ngrok.io
[09:57:03] [NGROK] You have been assigned a random ngrok URL that will only be available for this session. Y
ou wil need to re-upload the Teams manifest next time you run this command.
[09:57:03] [NGROK] HOSTNAME: b141aff4.ngrok.io
[09:57:03] Finished 'start-ngrok' after 3.25 s
[09:57:03] Starting 'manifest'...
[09:57:03] Starting 'validate-manifest'...
[09:57:03] Starting 'generate-manifest'...
[09:57:03] Finished 'generate-manifest' after 31 ms
[09:57:03] Starting 'schema-validation'...
[09:57:03] Using manifest schema 1.5
```

Figure 3-7. *Running gulp serve and ngrok together to make your tab available*

We still need to get this app inside of Teams. Go back to Teams and upload the app package again. The "gulp ngrok-serve" command has updated the manifest with the correct URL when building and repackaged this into a new zip file. So when you upload your app, Teams will now look for your web page on the URL received from ngrok. If everything is OK, then you should see a new tab page with a sample button on it (Figure 3-8).

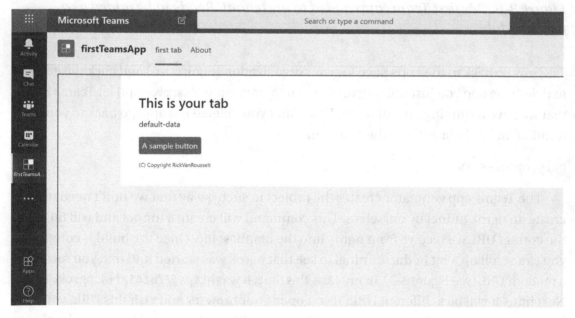

Figure 3-8. *My first Node.js Teams app with a tab running from my local web server through ngrok*

Another Node.js basic app

Another method of starting a new project with Node.js is using the Microsoft Teams
Toolkit (`https://marketplace.visualstudio.com/items?itemName=TeamsDevApp.`
`ms-teams-vscode-extension`). This is an extension for Visual Studio Code and can help
you get started. I worked with it a few times, and I like it. It provides a project base that
is a little different than the Teams generator, but you are free to use the one you enjoy
the most. Most examples in this book started by using this tool. The reason I chose this
tool is that after chatting with several people from the Teams team, I understand why
they took certain design decisions for this tool. For instance, it uses plain JavaScript
instead of TypeScript. The reasoning behind it is very straightforward. If you can code
in TypeScript, you can surely read JavaScript. But it's not always the case the other way
around.

After installing this extension, you need to select that you want to create a new
workspace. Triggering this will provide you with a new screen (see Figure 3-9) where you
can choose the item you would like to build.

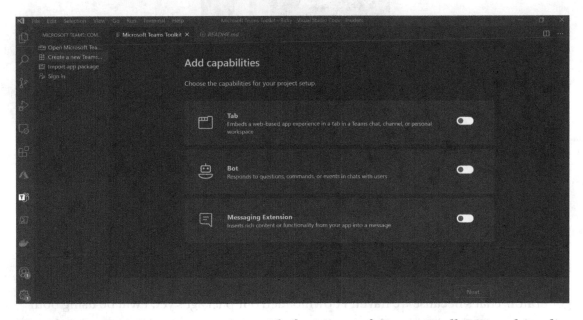

Figure 3-9. *Creating a new project with the Microsoft Teams Toolkit Visual Studio*
Code extension

Like with the Teams generator, let's create a tab. Toggle the tab switch to on and click the next button. Let's keep the personal tab option and click finish. As you can see, within a few seconds, our project layout is generated. As you can see from Figure 3-10, the structure of the project is a little different from what is generated with the Teams generator.

Figure 3-10. *Folder structure generated by the Teams Toolkit*

You probably noticed that creating this type of project was a lot faster than the Teams generator. That's because we haven't downloaded our packages yet. I will be using both yarn and npm. They both get the same results, but I find yarn to be a little faster. I also was working with a preview of this extension, so it could be that things change when it gets updated by Microsoft. So be sure to check out the readme file if you create your solution. If you start from the provided template, you can follow along here. To get our packages, execute the following commands:

```
yarn install
yarn start
```

After the installation of the packages is complete and our solution is running, we can navigate to the development server which is running on `http://localhost:3000/personal`. When you browse to this page, you will receive a notification that the Teams client is not found. So, we need to run this from within Teams.

The first thing we need to do is, of course, fire up our ngrok. Execute the following command from within the Windows terminal or the command line.

```
ngrok http -host-header=rewrite 3000
```

The way this solution works is that it updates the manifest automatically with some values for us. If you go to the file Development.env, you can see that there are specific parameters that get replaced in your manifest. Update the "baseUrl0" value with the public URL you received from ngrok, as in Figure 3-11.

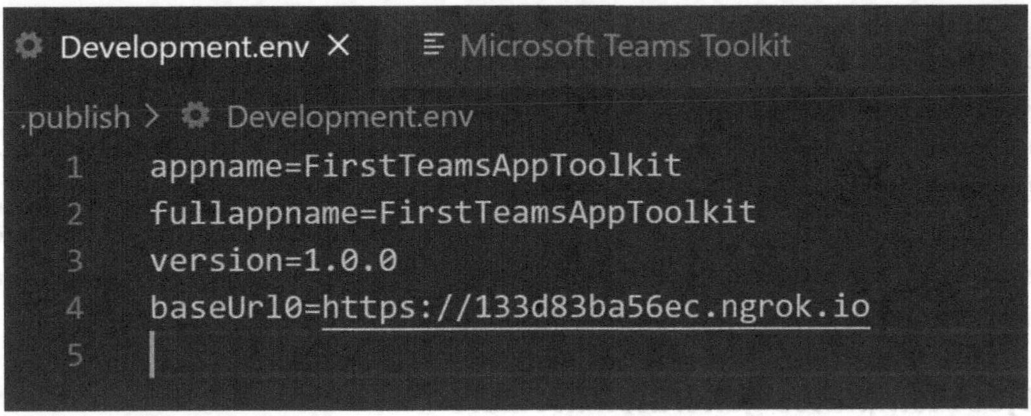

```
⚙ Development.env  ✕       ≡ Microsoft Teams Toolkit

.publish >  ⚙ Development.env
    1      appname=FirstTeamsAppToolkit
    2      fullappname=FirstTeamsAppToolkit
    3      version=1.0.0
    4      baseUrl0=https://133d83ba56ec.ngrok.io
    5      |
```

Figure 3-11.   *Update the base URL to match your ngrok URL*

After this change, we can upload our package to Microsoft Teams. Follow the same steps as we did with the package from the Teams generator. The Teams app package can be found in the folder \firstTeamsAppTeamsToolkit\.publish. Once you have uploaded the package and added it as a personal app, you will get a basic app running in Teams like in Figure 3-12.

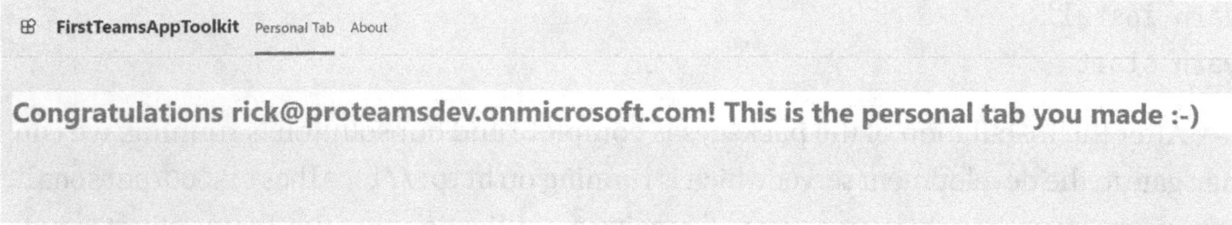

⊞ **FirstTeamsAppToolkit** Personal Tab About

Congratulations rick@proteamsdev.onmicrosoft.com! This is the personal tab you made :-)

Figure 3-12. *Our Teams app generated with the Teams Toolkit extension running*

C# basic app

For C#, there are multiple ways to do development. I'm still a fan of Visual Studio, so I will be using that as my IDE. You could also use VS Code for C# development or another IDE. Now for C#, things are a little different. There are no real templates yet for Visual Studio so we need to reuse another template or start from scratch. We could also use the Teams Toolkit for Visual Studio for this (`https://docs.microsoft.com/en-us/microsoftteams/platform/toolkit/visual-studio-code-overview`), but at the time of writing, this was not released yet. Since any website in combination with a Teams app package can be a Teams app and we already created a website with Node, we are stepping our game a bit up, and we are going to create a bot. Bots are just APIs being called, and my preferred starting point is the template that Azure creates when you create a bot. You could always start from an example you find on GitHub or from the template provided in the labs. But let me show you how I start a new project. We are going to start from scratch further on in this book. But I wanted to show you how you can easily get a new project started.

Project templates generated in Azure

My typical starting point is usually Azure. If you create a new bot (which is a .NET Core project), Azure will give you a template to start from.

Go to the Azure Portal and click the "Create a resource" button. Create a new "web app bot" (see Figure 3-13).

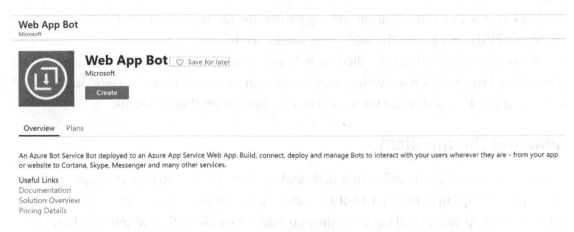

Figure 3-13. *Create a new web app bot in Azure*

After you filled in the required fields in the portal (tip: always create a new resource group, or after a while, you have no idea anymore where your resources are), select a bot template. There are several examples available. If you have never worked with Bots before, then make sure you always pick a V4 template. The differences between versions 3 and 4 of the Bot Framework are quite substantial. For this small app, the "Echo Bot" template is enough. After Azure has done its magic, you already have a perfect working bot. But that's not what we need. We need the code behind it to get going with our Teams development. Open up the web app bot resource that just got created, and in the "build" tab, you should be able to download the bot's source code (see Figure 3-14).

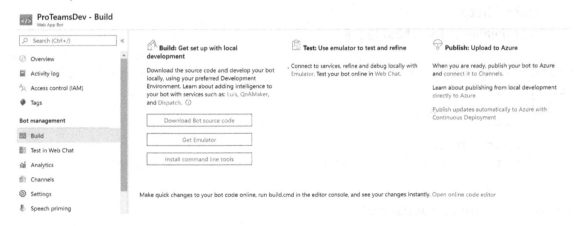

Figure 3-14. *Download a generated bot's source code from Azure*

Clicking the download button will trigger the download of a zip file. Extract the contents of this zip file into the folder you would like to work in.

Now open the solution file called "echobot.sln" and press the play button; you should see a website pop up, welcoming you to your first bot. We are not working with bots yet. But this page is what we need. Let's see how to get that in Teams.

Generate the manifest

Now we can create the manifest manually and create with the two icons the app package ourselves by zipping it. But that's not something we want to do every time; let's open App Studio. App Studio will generate the manifest for us. Go to the "Manifest editor" tab and create a new app. On the first page, we need to add some general information about ourselves and the app we are building. After doing this, go to the "tabs" tab and add a personal tab. There are three locations where a tab can surface, but we will go deeper in that in the next chapter. Enter your tab a name and a URL where it lives. Since we only have a localhost URL for our solution when we start debugging our Visual Studio solution, and we need an available online URL, let's fire up ngrok. First, we need to define where to point ngrok to, so open the configuration file (see Figure 3-15) and add the following section:

```
tunnels:
  myfirstteamsapp:
    addr: 3978
    proto: http
    host-header: localhost:3978
```

```
authtoken: 1WeYzMeUhtt44wGBJD08SFEL2i6_DZufFj3VjqmcbSBiR9RQ
tunnels:
  myfirstteamsapp:
    addr: 3978
    proto: http
    host-header: localhost:3978
```

Figure 3-15. *ngrok configuration file*

The settings entered here are quite simple. We define our entry, in this case, "myfirstteamsapp". After which, we tell ngrok that our local website is running on HTTP with port 3978. So, if your default Visual Studio setting creates this in a different port, this is where you can change it. The last entry "host-header" is specific for Visual Studio. Visual Studio is expecting that the HTTP header contains the localhost:3978 entry. When browsing locally to this URL, your browser automatically sends this information. But since we are navigating with our browser or Teams to another URL (the one we will receive from ngrok), we are sending a different host-header in our request. This entry will change that host-header while the request travels through the ngrok tunnel to your machine. Save the configuration file and start up ngrok (see Figure 3-16).

```
C:\Tools\ngrok\ngrok.exe - ngrok  start --all

ngrok by @inconshreveable

Session Status                online
Account                       Rick Van Rousselt (Plan: Free)
Version                       2.3.35
Region                        United States (us)
Web Interface                 http://127.0.0.1:4040
Forwarding                    http://ade138d1.ngrok.io -> http://localhost:3978
Forwarding                    https://ade138d1.ngrok.io -> http://localhost:3978

Connections                   ttl     opn     rt1     rt5     p50     p90
                              0       0       0.00    0.00    0.00    0.00
```

Figure 3-16. *ngrok started, and a random URL is available online for our app*

With ngrok up and running, we know our URL we need to add to the tab settings in App Studio. Fill in the URL and other parameters (see Figure 3-17).

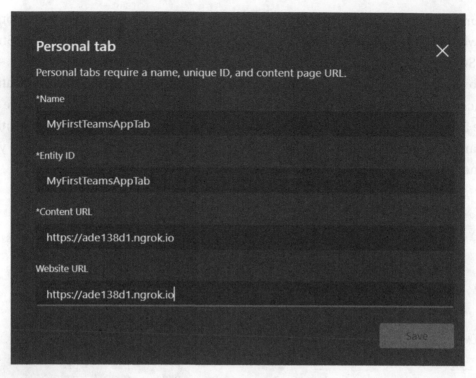

Figure 3-17. *Fill in the personal tab information with a name, ID, and the URL received from ngrok*

If you want to be sure that the tunnel is up and running, then you can (while your Visual Studio is still running in debug mode) browse to one of the URLs received from ngrok. As you can see from Figure 3-18, we can access our web page from both localhost and the random generated URL received from ngrok.

Figure 3-18. *Both localhost and the ngrok URL are serving our web page, and we can see from the ngrok output that our tunnel is online*

Back in App Studio, go to the "test and distribute" tab. You can ignore the warnings. I love that Microsoft has already built-in some hints that help you when you would want to push out your app to the store. Because then all those warnings will have to be solved. But for now, you are good to go. If you click install and add, this will immediately install the app inside of your Teams environment, which will then show your web page right inside of the Teams client (see Figure 3-19). You could also do this manually by downloading the app package and uploading it like in Figures 3-5 and 3-6.

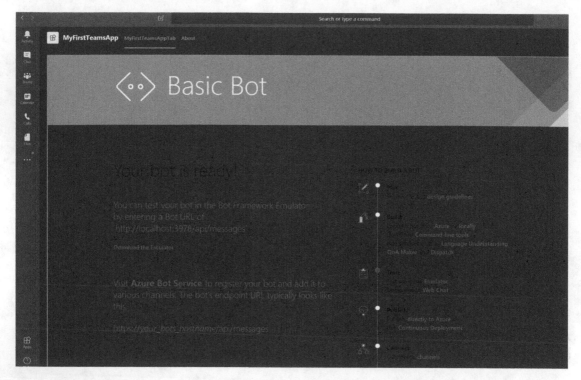

Figure 3-19. *My first C# Teams app with a tab inside of the Teams client*

Visual Studio app package generation

For the first step, creating our Teams manifest and the app package, going through App Studio is good enough. But we don't want to do this every time we change something in our code. By the time you finish this book, you will know the ins and outs of the manifest file, so why do it with a UI? The easiest way going forward is by adding the manifest and both icons in your solution. Adding these files has a bonus, that when you commit your code to source control, those essential files get saved. Let's see how we can let Visual Studio generate our app package at every new build. For this, we can use a task runner.

First, let's add our three files to our solution. Put them in a separate folder. Create a new folder in your solution and call it "TeamsManifest". In App Studio, download the package and unzip it so that you can copy the three files into the folder you just created (see Figure 3-20).

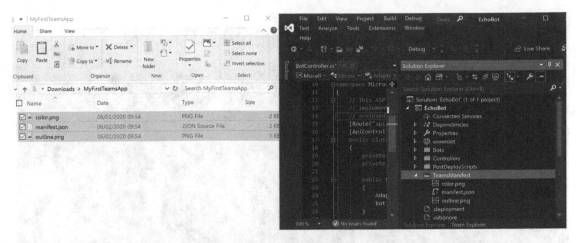

Figure 3-20. *Copy the contents of the generated zip package by App Studio to your Visual Studio solution*

Now add a new npm configuration file to the project (Figure 3-21) and add the following code to it:

```
{
  "version": "1.0.0",
  "name": "teamsproactive",
  "private": true,
  "devDependencies": {
    "gulp": "^4.0.0",
    "gulp-zip": "^4.2.0"
  }
}
```

The npm configuration file describes in this case that there are some developer dependencies needed when you build your solution. These two packages allow you to run a zip task.

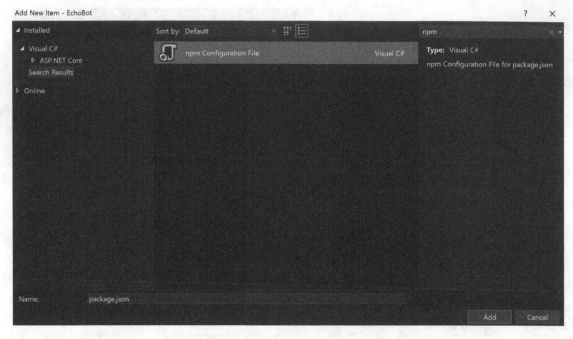

Figure 3-21. *Add an npm configuration file to your solution*

Next, add a new JavaScript file to the solution, name it gulpfile.js (see Figure 3-22), and add the following code to the file:

```
const gulp = require('gulp');
const zip = require('gulp-zip');

gulp.task('packageCreation', () =>
    gulp.src('TeamsManifest/*')
    .pipe(zip('manifest.zip'))
    .pipe(gulp.dest('bin\\debug'))
);
```

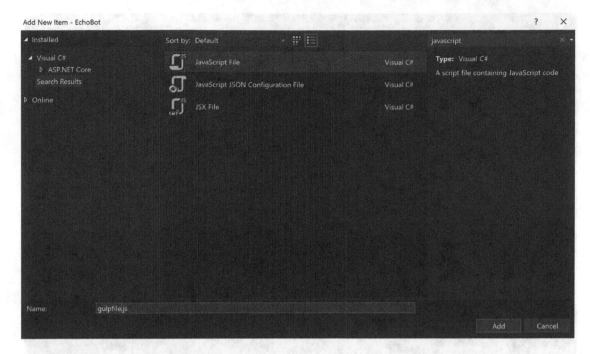

Figure 3-22. *Add a gulpfile.js to your solution*

In the gulpfile.js, you can create little JavaScript snippets that you can run. This case creates a task (snippet) that takes all files from the "TeamsManifest" folder of your solution and zips them into a file called manifest.zip. The zip file gets saved inside your "bin\debug" folder. If you name your folder different or you want your Teams package saved inside another folder, then change this file.

Now, if you fire up the task runner explorer (under View ➤ Other Windows), you can see the task you just created. And if you right-click it, you can select to have it run after every build (see Figure 3-23). Now every time you build your solution, the manifest and both image files are used to create a new Teams package. Enabling you to make changes in the manifest file, build your solution, and have your Teams package is ready to be sideloaded into Teams.

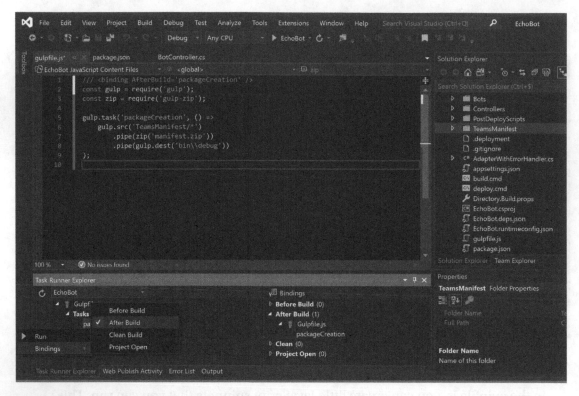

Figure 3-23. *Run a task after every build*

Summary

In this chapter, we covered the basics of how to start with a new project. Now you can create a Microsoft Teams app in both Node.js and C#. We have seen that a Teams app package is just a zip file and that it points to an endpoint somewhere. This endpoint is where our code gets executed. We discussed one way to generate the bot part for a Teams app, but as you know, there are many roads to the same goal. I suggest you take your time to get familiar with the solutions generated and invest a workflow that is best for you. Everybody works differently, and if you like to take another approach, then that is perfectly fine. These days, there are so many tools that can make our life more comfortable, and you might have found one that I don't know yet. Join me as we continue to the next chapter, where we will dive deeper into the different possibilities we have to extend Microsoft Teams.

PART 2

Tabs

CHAPTER 4

Teams Client JavaScript SDK

Now that we got some experience with the basics of building a Teams application, it's time to start digging deeper into Teams development. In the following chapters, we will begin building a company app that has every possible way to extend Microsoft Teams. This chapter will be all about the Teams Client JavaScript SDK. Let's see how it interacts with a static tab.

Background

Almost every company in the world has an intranet. I have built a lot of them, way more than I would like to admit. So as an example, for the remaining chapters, we will start building a Teams app for our company that will replace the current intranet. Why do you ask? Because Teams is the tool where people start their day. It's a hub for Teamwork, so it's only reasonable that they also have a way to view what's going on in the company from within Teams and that they can connect and interact with the different aspects of the company.

The first requirement is straightforward. Integrate an existing web application with Microsoft Teams. This web application was already built some time ago and is publicly available. Users typically open their browser in the morning and visit this publicly accessible website to order their sandwiches for lunch.

Tabs

Since this is an already existing web application, we can easily convert this into a tab for Teams. A tab is a Teams-aware web page, which is another way of saying that this tab is just an iFrame within Teams that shows a web page. Because of this, users visiting this tab can not only see the application but that application can also have some interaction

© Rick Van Rousselt 2021
R. Van Rousselt, *Pro Microsoft Teams Development*, https://doi.org/10.1007/978-1-4842-6364-8_4

with Teams. And this interaction is where the Teams Client JavaScript SDK comes into play. Because a tab is an iFrame, there was no way that your website can know that it's shown inside of Teams. So, Microsoft created some extension points that we can talk to with JavaScript. This way, we can let our application know that it's running inside of Teams.

You should also know that two kinds of tabs exist in Teams: a channel/group scoped tab, also known as a configurable tab, and a personal scoped tab, also known as a static tab. Configurable tabs are used as a tab in a channel or a chat conversation. These can be configured before they are added (hence the name configurable tab). They are also shared by everyone in the channel or the chat; so keep into consideration when building tabs that, for example, you don't let people use login credentials in the configuration part because then the entire channel would use those credentials when viewing the tab. If you come across a use case like this, you should use a static tab or use another means of authentication when users visit your tab.

There are more considerations when thinking about tabs. For instance, your web application is always shown within the Teams client. So, don't forget that you don't have the full width of the screen at your disposal. We all know that responsive design was a hype ten years ago and that everybody, by default, does it. But it's still something to keep in mind. The other thing to keep in mind is that people are already working inside of Teams. If you then create a very complex web application, then people might get lost within the navigation of the app. Remember they also have the Teams navigation. And there's no way to open a second tab like in a web browser, so keep your functionality simple. It's better to integrate only a piece of your application inside of Teams and keep the focus on that specific piece than to try to add the entire web application to a tab. It's better to spread out the functionality across multiple tabs or even look into other integrations like bots or messaging extensions, but those are for later chapters.

Static tab

For our first requirement, viewing an existing application to order sandwiches, we are going to use the static tab functionality. We could also create a configurable tab for this, but then we would have to install the tab into multiple channels because not everyone in the company is a member of the same team. And we don't want people to order sandwiches in other people's names. A static tab works best here because it's scoped to a user.

The JavaScript Client SDK

The Teams JavaScript Client SDK is a library provided by Microsoft and enables your application (running in a tab) to communicate with the Teams client. The SDK works both in the browser and in the client application. When developing applications that appear within a Teams tab, we sometimes want Teams to do something for us, like authenticate a user. Or we want Teams to notify us when the user does a particular action, like switching between light and dark modes. The JavaScript Client SDK is publicly available on GitHub (`https://github.com/OfficeDev/microsoft-teams-library-js`), so you can see how it works, and if you experience issues with it, then this is the place to log an issue.

C#

Now to get started with our company app in C#, I have not created a web app bot like in the previous examples, but I started from a .NET Core empty template. You can do the same or you can start from the basic solution provided in the samples. Don't forget to update the NuGet packages inside your solution. The Bot Framework, .NET Core, and Teams packages are developed at a very fast pace. Usually, by the time you finish a Teams app, there is already a new update available. The reason why I'm starting with a .NET Core blank template is to show you that you can start from any template you like. Teams just calls your website or API. We do this to show you how the boilerplate code of everything works. The tip from starting from an Azure Bot Template as described in the previous chapter is to make sure that in your day-to-day job, you don't waste precious time setting up boilerplate code.

The basic solution

The basics of this solution are simple. We have an application with a basic home page and a page where we can order lunch. Translate this to an ASP.NET Core app, and this translates to two controllers. The first is a home controller to show the basic home page (see Figure 4-1). The code of this controller is basic, with only an "Index" method and an "Error" method.

```
public IActionResult Index()
    {
        return View();
    }
```

```
[ResponseCache(Duration = 0, Location = ResponseCacheLocation.None,
NoStore = true)]
public IActionResult Error()
{
    return View(new ErrorViewModel { RequestId = Activity.Current?.
    Id ?? HttpContext.TraceIdentifier });
}
```

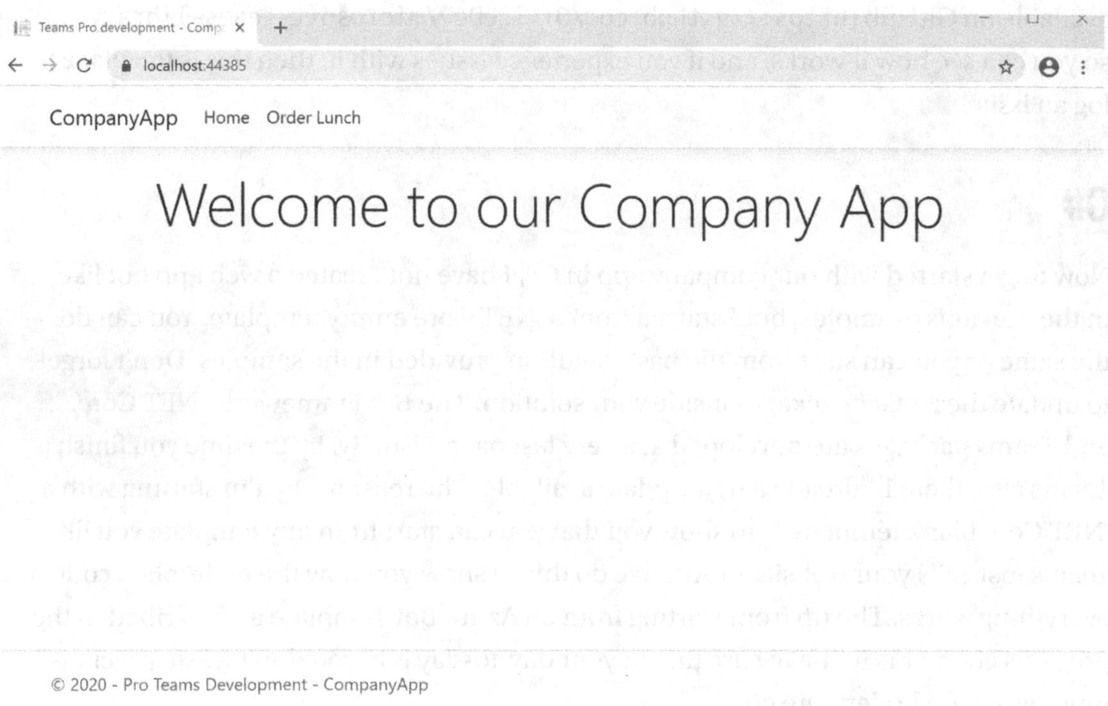

Figure 4-1. *Our company app's home page*

As you can see, the basic stuff is already provided by the template. The second controller we need to create ourselves is the "lunch" controller with an "index" method to show the possible lunch options and an "Order" method to handle the click event when somebody orders a sandwich.

```
public class LunchController : Controller
  {
    public readonly List<Lunch> LunchOptions = new List<Lunch>()
    {
```

```
            new Lunch(1,"BLT"),
            new Lunch(2,"Cheese"),
            new Lunch(3,"Ham")
        };

        public ActionResult Index()
        {
            return View(LunchOptions);
        }

        // GET: Lunch/Create
        public ActionResult Order(int id)
        {
            ViewBag.Ordermessage = $"Thanks for ordering a
            {LunchOptions[id].Name} sandwich.";
            return View();
        }

    }
```

Together with the index view of our lunch controller, we have a basic app where we can order lunch as you can see in Figure 4-2. As you might notice, we are not using any database or authentication yet, just to keep it simple.

```
<h1>Your Lunch Options</h1>

<table class="table">
    <thead>
        <tr>
            <th>
                @Html.DisplayNameFor(model => model.Id)
            </th>
            <th>
                @Html.DisplayNameFor(model => model.Name)
            </th>
            <th></th>
        </tr>
    </thead>
```

```
    <tbody>
        @foreach (var item in Model)
        {
            <tr>
                <td>

                    @Html.DisplayFor(modelItem => item.Id)
                </td>
                <td>
                    @Html.DisplayFor(modelItem => item.Name)
                </td>
                <td>
                    @Html.ActionLink("Order", "Order", new {  id=item.
                    Id  })
                </td>
            </tr>
        }
    </tbody>
</table>
```

Figure 4-2. *Order page to order sandwiches*

Now that we have a basic application, we can start to integrate this inside of Microsoft Teams. We created a basic application to serve as an example, but this could easily be an already existing application. To get this inside of Teams, we need to create our manifest. As described in previous chapters, App Studio would be an excellent way to start. This way, you have some help filling out the basic requirements of the manifest. I've already added a manifest to the solution including a gulp task to create a Teams package after every build. If we now upload our manifest to Teams, we get the result as in Figure 4-3.

Figure 4-3. *The company app, order lunch section inside of Teams*

The most important part of getting this application inside of Teams is the description of the static tab that we want to add.

```
"staticTabs": [
    {
        "entityId": "LunchTab",
        "name": "Lunch",
        "contentUrl": "https://proteamsdev.ngrok.io/lunch?context=teams",
        "websiteUrl": "https://proteamsdev.ngrok.io/lunch",
        "scopes": [
```

```
            "personal"
        ]
    }
],
```

As you can see, I've added a different URL for the "contentUrl" setting as for the "websiteUrl" setting. The content URL is the URL that Teams will use to show the web page; the website URL is when you click the "open website" icon inside of Teams, and this opens the browser with this link (see Figure 4-4).

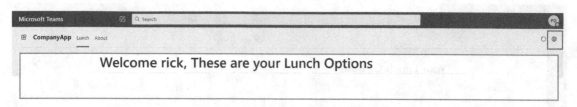

Figure 4-4. *The blue area is my static tab URL defined with the contentUrl property. The red area is the icon that uses the websiteUrl property to open up the browser and navigate to the URL defined*

Now, what's the benefit of this? The advantage of this is that you can start to differentiate in your app whether a user visits you through Microsoft Teams or a normal browser. For this, we can easily update the code to check in our controller if somebody is coming from Teams.

```
public ActionResult Index()
{
    string context = HttpContext.Request.Query["context"].ToString();
    HttpContext.Session.SetString("context", context);
    if (context == "teams")
    {
        ViewBag.Layout = "_LayoutForLunch";
    }
    else
    {
        ViewBag.Layout = "_Layout";
    }
```

```
        return View(LunchOptions);
    }

    // GET: Lunch/Create
    public ActionResult Order(int id)
    {
        var context = HttpContext.Session.GetString("context");
        if (context == "teams")
        {
            ViewBag.Layout = "_LayoutForLunch";
        }
        else
        {
            ViewBag.Layout = "_Layout";
        }

        ViewBag.Ordermessage = $"Thanks for ordering a
        {LunchOptions[id].Name} sandwich.";
        return View();
    }
```

As you can see in the "Index" method, we can get the additional query string from
the URL. Because in Teams we configured the manifest with that extra query string, we
can separate if a user is coming directly to our application or via the Teams app. By doing
so, we can use a different layouts page inside of Teams. As discussed at the beginning of
this chapter is that we need to make the navigation inside of Teams simple. We already
have a Teams navigation, and then our own navigation only makes it more confusing
for a user. So, in our new layouts page, let's call it "_LayoutForLunch.cshtml" we disable
the top navigation and only show the lunch section as in Figure 4-5. Basically, copy the
default _layouts page and remove some of the navigational components.

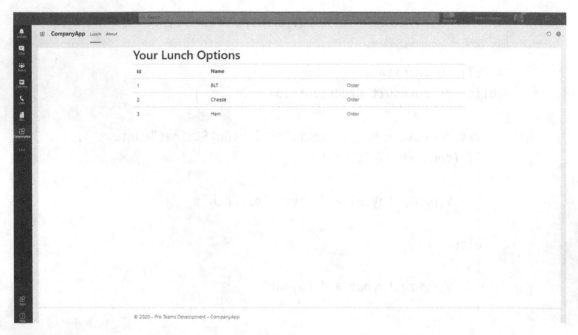

Figure 4-5. *The company app, order lunch section inside of Teams but without navigation*

The default _layouts page looks like this:

```
<!DOCTYPE html>
<html lang="en">
<head>
    <meta charset="utf-8" />
    <meta name="viewport" content="width=device-width, initial-scale=1.0" />
    <title>Teams Pro development - CompanyApp</title>
    <link rel="stylesheet" href="~/lib/bootstrap/dist/css/bootstrap.min.css" />
    <link rel="stylesheet" href="~/css/site.css" />
</head>
<body>
    <header> ! this part we remove
        <nav class="navbar navbar-expand-sm navbar-toggleable-sm navbar-
        light bg-white border-bottom box-shadow mb-3">
            <div class="container">
                <a class="navbar-brand" asp-area="" asp-controller="Home"
                asp-action="Index">CompanyApp</a>
```

```
        <button class="navbar-toggler" type="button" data-
        toggle="collapse" data-target=".navbar-collapse" aria-
        controls="navbarSupportedContent"
                aria-expanded="false" aria-label="Toggle navigation">
            <span class="navbar-toggler-icon"></span>
        </button>
        <div class="navbar-collapse collapse d-sm-inline-flex flex-
        sm-row-reverse">
            <ul class="navbar-nav flex-grow-1">
                <li class="nav-item">
                    <a class="nav-link text-dark" asp-area="" asp-
                    controller="Home" asp-action="Index">Home</a>
                </li>
                <li class="nav-item">
                    <a class="nav-link text-dark" asp-area="" asp-
                    controller="Lunch" asp-action="Index">Order
                    Lunch</a>
                </li>
            </ul>
        </div>
    </div>
    </nav>
</header>
<div class="container">
    <main role="main" class="pb-3">
        @RenderBody()
    </main>
</div>

<footer class="border-top footer text-muted">
    <div class="container">
        &copy; 2020 - Pro Teams Development - CompanyApp
    </div>
</footer>
<script src="~/lib/jquery/dist/jquery.min.js"></script>
<script src="~/lib/bootstrap/dist/js/bootstrap.bundle.min.js"></script>
```

```
    <script src="~/js/site.js" asp-append-version="true"></script>
    @RenderSection("Scripts", required: false)
</body>
</html>
```

And the _layoutsForLunch page looks like this:

```
<!DOCTYPE html>
<html lang="en">
<head>
    <meta charset="utf-8" />
    <meta name="viewport" content="width=device-width, initial-scale=1.0" />
    <title>Teams Pro development - CompanyApp</title>
    <link rel="stylesheet" href="~/lib/bootstrap/dist/css/bootstrap.min.
    css" />
    <link rel="stylesheet" href="~/css/site.css" />
</head>
<body>
    <header>
    </header>
    <div class="container">
        <main role="main" class="pb-3">
            @RenderBody()
        </main>
    </div>

    <footer class="border-top footer text-muted">
        <div class="container">
            &copy; 2020 - Pro Teams Development - CompanyApp
        </div>
    </footer>
    <script src="~/lib/jquery/dist/jquery.min.js"></script>
    <script src="~/lib/bootstrap/dist/js/bootstrap.bundle.min.js"></script>
    <script src="~/js/site.js" asp-append-version="true"></script>
    @RenderSection("Scripts", required: false)
</body>
</html>
```

To make a good integration with Teams, we also need to take into consideration the theming of Teams. If a user has selected dark mode, then our app should not do the opposite. Our app also looks best if we stick to the prescribed UI look and feel of controls and other elements on the page like Teams to make the integration seamless. For that and even more, we will need to start using the Microsoft Teams Client JavaScript SDK.

JavaScript SDK

Like always, we can either download the latest version of this package and include it in our library or reference a CDN to include the JS file. We are going to keep it simple; I usually just use the CDN because when you want to change the version, it's just a simple change of the URL, and you don't need to worry this way about optimizing the speed for the download of the JS file.

In the now customized layout for Microsoft Teams called "_LayoutForLunch.cshtml", we add the script reference to the Teams Client JavaScript SDK. Currently, we are at version 1.6, but it's always good to check, which is the latest version. I usually check directly with NPM (`www.npmjs.com/package/@microsoft/teams-js`); there is also the URL you need. Just add it below the other script tags inside of the layouts page.

Now that we have a reference to the SDK, we still need to initialize it. Initializing the SDK must be done with the following command:

```
microsoftTeams.initialize();
```

After this command, we can start the functionality of the Teams Client JavaScript SDK. So let's add a script tag with the following logic to our index page:

```
<script type="text/javascript">

    microsoftTeams.initialize();

    microsoftTeams.getContext(function (context) {
        var theme = context.theme;
        var color;
        switch(theme) {
            case "dark":
                color = "#F3F2F1";
            break;
            case "contrast":
```

```
                color = "#ffff01";
            break;
        default:
                color = "#252423";
        }
        var h1Elements = document.getElementsByTagName("h1");

        for(var i = 0; i < h1Elements.length; i++) {
            h1Elements[i].style.color = color;
        }
    });
</script>
```

This code will first initialize the Teams SDK, and then it will get the context of Teams. This context will contain all the information that Teams can provide to you about the user and the environment. If we look at the documentation from Microsoft, then we can retrieve the following information:

```
{
    "teamId": "The Microsoft Teams ID in the format 19:[id]@thread.skype",
    "teamName": "The name of the current team",
    "channelId": "The channel ID in the format 19:[id]@thread.skype",
    "channelName": "The name of the current channel",
    "chatId": "The chat ID in the in the format 19:[id]@thread.skype",
    "locale": "The current locale of the user formatted as languageId-
    countryId (for example, en-us)",
    "entityId": "The developer-defined unique ID for the entity this
    content points to",
    "subEntityId": "The developer-defined unique ID for the sub-entity this
    content points to",
    "loginHint": "A value suitable as a login hint for Azure AD. This is
    usually the login name of the current user, in their home tenant",
    "userPrincipalName": "The User Principal Name of the current user, in
    the current tenant",
    "userObjectId": "The Azure AD object id of the current user, in the
    current tenant",
    "tid": "The Azure AD tenant ID of the current user",
```

```
"groupId": "Guid identifying the current O365 Group ID",
"theme": "The current UI theme: default | dark | contrast",
"isFullScreen": "Indicates whether the tab is in full-screen mode",
"userLicenseType": "Indicates the user licence type in the given SKU
(for example, student or teacher)",
"tenantSKU": "Indicates the SKU category of the tenant (for example, EDU)",
"channelType": "microsoftTeams.ChannelType.Private | microsoftTeams.
ChannelType.Regular"
}
```

In this stage, we are just interested in the theme that the user selected. But as you can imagine, once we start with authentication, then the userObjectId and UserPrincipalName are some things we are going to need. Now specific to our piece of code, we have three types of themes, default, dark, and high-contrast. I've taken the liberty not to include some other JavaScript library or to make the CSS difficult—to keep this example simple and to show how it works. Now if we load our app inside of Teams, the color of the header should match the color we chose for the Teams theme (see Figure 4-6).

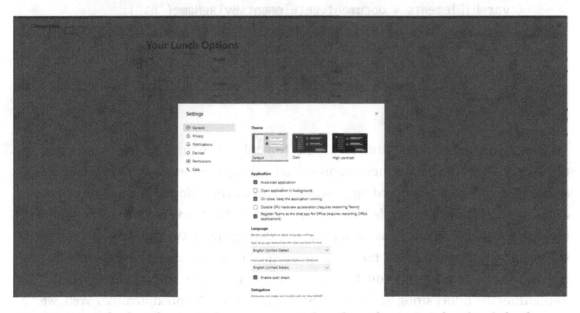

Figure 4-6. *The header text of our app matches the color we set for the default theme*

Now the problem, of course, is when people switch theme with the app open. You can try it yourself. As long as you either refresh the app or change the theme when the app is not open, the theme will match the color we picked. But when we change it when our app is open, then nothing happens. This is because there is no event or trigger fired when we change the theme. Or at least there is, but we just didn't subscribe our code to the event. To do this, we can call the following function. This function will register our code and connect it to the event handler that gets executed every time the Teams theme changes.

```
microsoftTeams.registerOnThemeChangeHandler(function(theme) {
    var color = "#252423";
    if (theme === "default") {
        color = "#252423";
    } else if (theme === "dark") {
        color = "#F3F2F1";
    } else if (theme === "contrast") {
        color = "#ffff01";
    }

    var h1Elements = document.getElementsByTagName("h1");

    for(var i = 0; i < h1Elements.length; i++) {
        h1Elements[i].style.color = color;
    }

});
```

The preceding code does the same logic. Not only when the page loads, but when the user changes the theme, then Teams will let our application know what theme was selected, and we can act accordingly. Now we have a simple app where people can order a sandwich, and the look and feel of the app are set to the theme of Teams. There is just one thing missing, and that's knowing who is ordering lunch. We could make a text box where people add their name, but since we already have the context which contains the username, we can easily add that to our page. But I want to show a different way. Remember the query string in the manifest that contained "context=teams"? Well, we can add Teams-specific query strings here. These are the following (taken from the

documentation from MS, https://docs.microsoft.com/en-us/microsoftteams/
platform/tabs/how-to/access-teams-context):

- {entityId}: The ID you supplied for the item in this tab when first configuring the tab.

- {subEntityId}: The ID you supplied when generating a deep link for a specific item within this tab. This should be used to restore to a specific state within an entity, for example, scrolling to or activating a specific piece of content.

- {loginHint}: A value suitable as a login hint for Azure AD. This is usually the login name of the current user, in their home tenant.

- {userPrincipalName}: The User Principal Name of the current user, in the current tenant.

- {userObjectId}: The Azure AD object ID of the current user, in the current tenant.

- {theme}: The current UI theme such as default, dark, or contrast.

- {groupId}: The ID of the Office 365 Group in which the tab resides.

- {tid}: The Azure AD tenant ID of the current user.

- {locale}: The current locale of the user formatted as languageId-countryId (e.g., en-us).

So in our case, we can use the userPrincipalName. So let us update our manifest URL from

```
"contentUrl": "https://proteamsdev.ngrok.io/lunch?context=teams",
```

to

```
"contentUrl": "https://proteamsdev.ngrok.io/lunch?context=teams&nam
e={userPrincipalName}",
```

If we then update our LunchController's Index method also to read this query string, remove everything after the @ sign, and pass it on to the view, we can show a nice welcome message on the screen.

```
ViewBag.UserName = HttpContext.Request.Query["name"].ToString().Split("@")[0];
```

You can place this line anywhere you want in the method as long as it's before the return statement. In the view, we can then change our welcome message to

```
<h1>Welcome @ViewBag.UserName, These are your Lunch Options</h1>
```

This will show a nice welcome message for the user as you can see in Figure 4-7.

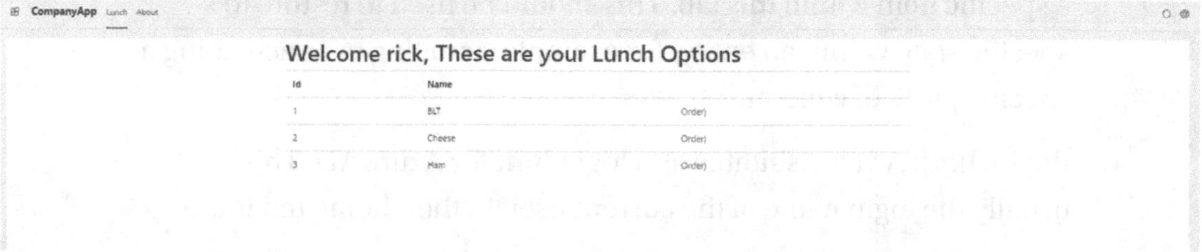

Figure 4-7. *A nice welcome message for our user when opening up the application*

Summary

We are at the end of the chapter for the C# part. In this chapter, you got your first contact with static tabs and with the Teams JavaScript Client SDK. You are more than welcome to follow along for the Node.js version, or you can skip to the next chapter, where we will dive deeper into tabs and the SDK.

Node.js

To get started with our company app in Node.js, we can use the Teams generator to create a new project like in the previous chapter, use the Microsoft Teams Toolkit extension in Visual Studio Code, or you can start from the basic solution provided in the examples. As with C#, the development of the generator, the Teams Toolkit, and both the Teams and Bot Framework SDKs are moving at such a fast pace that there are numerous updates by the time you reach this chapter. Since Microsoft always commits to giving support on older versions, you should be good. The newer versions just might have an easier way to accomplish the same goals or have more integration with the Teams environment. The basic app was created with the Teams Toolkit, and only a static tab was selected as a scaffolding option.

If you have been following along with the C# part of the chapter, the story is similar. We have a simple app to order lunch. Now when using the Teams generator or the

Teams Toolkit, things are a little easier. For one, we don't need to reference the Teams Client JavaScript SDK ourselves. This is already included in the template. The main difference with going for one of these options is that you are free to use what kind of front-end framework you bring to the table. Do you like React? Or prefer Vue.js? TypeScript vs. JavaScript? The choices are endless. The main choice you see everywhere in the Microsoft ecosphere is React. So, we are going to stick with that. But here's a fair bit of warning. The examples provided by Microsoft for Node.js are all different. Some use React, while others don't. So, always take a good look at a sample first. Now for this sample, you can follow along with the start template provided or look at the result in the completed application.

The basic solution

Once again, this will be a basic solution. We have a page where we can order lunch. Translate this to our Node.js solution, and we have a PersonalTab.js file, which is located under the components folder. The PersonalTab.js file was already generated for us. But we need to modify it a little so that we can show the different lunch options. Let us create a JSON file that holds the lunch options data. Add a folder called data and create a new file called lunchOptions.json. The contents of the file are the following:

```
[
    {
      "id": "1",
      "name": "BLT"
    },
    {
      "id": "2",
      "name": "Cheese"
    },
    {
      "id": "3",
      "name": "Ham"
    }
  ]
```

Now we need to include this data inside of our tab so that we can use it. Reference the JSON file by adding the following line to the top of the PersonalTab.js file:

```
import lunchOptions from "../data/lunchOptions.json";
```

This allows us to render the information of the JSON file on the page.

If you look at the standard render() function, then you might already notice that the Teams context is already loaded for us. That's convenient. If you were following along for the C#, you know that it already took a few steps to get the context added to a page, and here it's already provided for us. Now leave that piece of code for now. We are just going to add our lunch order options. Right below, you can add the following code:

```
<table class="table">
<thead><tr><th>ID</th><th>Name</th></tr> </thead>
  {lunchOptions.map(function (item) {
    return <tr><td>{item.id}</td><td>{item.name}</td><td><Button
    onClick={() => orderLunch(item.name)}>Order</Button></td></tr>;
  })}
</table>
```

The code itself is quite straightforward. If you are a React specialist, you probably have a lot of remarks by now. But let's just keep it simple. This code will read the lunchOptions, and the "map" function will loop each lunch item and add a row to the table for it. At the end of the row, there is also a button added, and when you click it, the "orderLunch" function is executed. Now we still need to add this function. After the return function of the render method, add the following method:

```
function orderLunch(name) {
  alert(`Thanks for ordering a ${name} sandwich.!`);
}
```

For now, we are just going to show an alert when we click the order button. But you could easily push this back to a database. This code should work just fine, and you should be able to run this. But let's make it a little prettier, and to do that, we are going to use a package that is already included in the template, the FluentUI package. FluentUI is a platform-independent collection of UX components announced by Microsoft at Build 2020. More information can be found at https://developer.microsoft.com/en-us/ fluentui#/, and it's a nice way to style your application in the same styles as the other Microsoft products like Microsoft Teams. Add the following line to the top of the file again below all the other "import" statements:

```
import { Button, Flex } from '@fluentui/react-northstar';
```

And change the render method to this:

```
render() {

    let userName = Object.keys(this.state.context).length > 0 ? this.state.
context['upn'] : "";
    return (
      <div>
        <Flex>
        <div>
          <h1>Congratulations {userName}! This is the personal tab you made
          :-)</h1>
        </div>
        </Flex>
        <Flex>
        <h1>Your Lunch Options</h1>
        </Flex>
        <Flex>
        <table class="table">
        <thead><tr><th>ID</th><th>Name</th></tr> </thead>
          {lunchOptions.map(function (item) {
            return <tr><td>{item.id}</td><td>{item.name}</td><td><Button
            onClick={() => orderLunch(item.name)}>Order</Button></td></tr>;
          })}
        </table>
        </Flex>
      </div>
    );

  function orderLunch(name) {
    alert(`Thanks for ordering a ${name} sandwich.!`);
  }
}
```

Now the only thing left for us to do is to test our solution. Don't forget to update the manifest file with the correct information, build the solution, and set up ngrok. If all goes well, you should end up with something similar to Figure 4-8. And let's not forget that if you have trouble adjusting the manifest, you can always use App Studio from inside Teams or use the Microsoft Teams Developer Toolkit in Visual Studio.

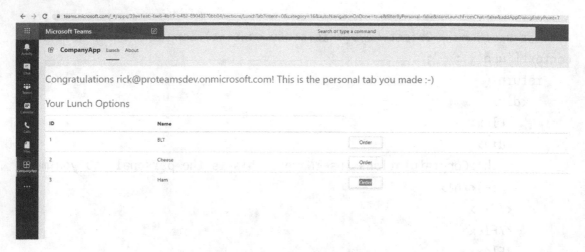

Figure 4-8. *Our Node.js company app running as a static tab*

Now we have a very basic app working, but this could easily be an existing application. If we were editing an existing application, we would need to differentiate whether a user uses our application through Teams or the browser. This can easily be done if you look at the boilerplate code. If we look at the app.js file, we can see that the Teams Client SDK package is added through the import statement. Of course, make sure that this is defined in your package.json file or you are going to have trouble referencing it. Then we can easily say

```
if (microsoftTeams) {*execute logic here in Teams*}
```

I hope you agree with me that this is a lot easier than in C#, where we needed to add this ourselves. Now let's see what else we can do with the Teams JavaScript Client SDK in the next section, like changing the theme of our application accordingly to Teams.

Next steps

As I stated before, using a template, whether it is the Yo Teams generator or the MS Teams Toolkit from within Visual Studio Code, the Client SDK is already provided for us. Including the package ourselves is also a possibility. Now let's see what else we can do with this SDK.

As with C#, one of the first things we want to have is that when a user selects another mode in Teams, like dark mode, our app reflects this. Now we are in a bit of luck because in the FluentUI, the themes are already defined, so less work for us. Let's first add a function to our personal tab that will update the theme for us.

```
updateTheme = (themeStr) =>{
  switch (themeStr) {
      case "dark":
          var theme = themes.teamsDark;
          break;
      case "contrast":
          var theme = themes.teamsHighContrast;
          break;
      case "default":
      default:
          var theme = themes.teams;
  }
  this.setState({ theme:theme });
}
```

As you can see in this piece of code, which I added right below the constructor of our PersonalTab class, we take a string with the theme name as input and set the theme accordingly. Now we only need to get that string somewhere. This is where the SDK comes into play. If we add the following code to the ComponentDidMount method

```
microsoftTeams.registerOnThemeChangeHandler(this.updateTheme);
```

then this will give us that string every time a user changes their theme settings. Well, the only thing missing now is the first time the user opens our application. Because then there will not be an event fired that will let our code know that the theme is not the default one. To get this going, we can get the information out of the query string of the page. We are going to dive deeper into the different options with query strings in the next chapter. But for now, you only need to add the one for a theme. So go over to your manifest and change the "ContentUrl" of the static LunchTab to

```
"contentUrl": "{baseUrl0}/personal?theme={theme}",
```

This will tell Microsoft Teams not only to load our web page but also to add the name of the theme that the user has selected to the URL. The only thing we need to do is to extract it and set the colors of our app accordingly.

In our PersonalTab.js file, add another function. This one will strip the query string from the URL.

```
getQueryVariable = (variable) =>{
  const query = window.location.search.substring(1);
  const vars = query.split("&");
  for (const varPairs of vars) {
      const pair = varPairs.split("=");
      if (decodeURIComponent(pair[0]) === variable) {
          return decodeURIComponent(pair[1]);
      }
  }
  return undefined;
}
```

And add the execution of this function as well to the "ComponentDidMount" method like the following:

```
 componentDidMount() {
    // Get the user context from Teams and set it in the state
    microsoftTeams.getContext((context, error) => {
      this.setState({
        context: context
      });
    });
    this.updateTheme(this.getQueryVariable('theme'));
    microsoftTeams.registerOnThemeChangeHandler(this.updateTheme);
  }
```

Now even when we start in a different theme mode, our code is aware of the correct theme, and as a bonus for using the FluentUI library, we don't need to write the CSS for the HTML elements, like the buttons, ourselves. Just change the theme setting, and our app will follow the Teams design like in Figure 4-9.

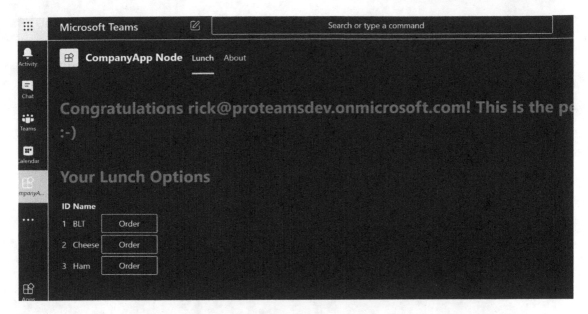

Figure 4-9. In high contrast, our buttons are styled the same as the rest of Teams

Now there are a lot more functions available in the Teams library. A simple one but very powerful is the enable print capability. Have you ever tried to make a page print-ready in SharePoint? If you haven't tried this before, then trust me, it's a pain, because you need to strip out all the navigation and additional items that aren't from your application but come with the product itself, like the navigation; try when you have our app open to print with the `"Ctrl+P"` command. Your page is going to be littered with the navigation of Teams. We can solve this using the SDK by adding the following statement to the "ComponentDidMount" method.

```
microsoftTeams.enablePrintCapability()
```

Test it out yourself and see what happens to the application. This makes our development work a lot easier.

Summary

This brings us to the end of this chapter, where we started off with a simple application to see that integrating existing applications can be done in Teams with the use of tabs. In those tabs, we have the power of the Teams JavaScript Client SDK at our disposal.

The SDK allows us to have an interaction with Microsoft Teams and integrate our app seemingly. We discussed that with only a few minor tweaks, we could update the look and feel of our app to mimic Teams, and this will improve the usability and adoption for end users. Join me in the next chapter, where we will explore the possibilities of tabs even further, and this, of course, goes hand in hand with the client SDK.

CHAPTER 5

Static and configurable tabs

In the previous chapter, we created a static tab to get hands-on experience with the Teams Client JavaScript SDK. In this chapter, we will explore more of the different tab options. We will see what specific items we need to take into consideration when creating our own tabs. Let us navigate through the inner workings of Teams tabs starting with how they are constructed.

A web page

As you might have noticed, tabs are just web pages; we can use C# or Node.js, an SPFx web part, a PowerApp, or whatever technology we want, but it all boils down to a web page we want to show inside of Microsoft Teams. There are, however, some requirements that your web page must fulfill to get hosted inside of Teams. Those requirements are especially around headers used for iFrames and Same-Origin policies. These requirements are mainly around security because tabs can be made context aware. We can find out a lot of information inside of a tab about the user, channel, and team like we have seen in the previous chapter. This means that the web page that is shown as a tab is inside an iFrame and must be safe to use.

Iframing is a technology that has been around for a long time. It has its perks but also its drawbacks. A well-known drawback is let's say your web page has a username, password, and login button. Well, if you then allow your page inside of an iFrame, somebody, with not so good intentions, could take your page, put it inside of an iFrame on their page, and have, for instance, JavaScript running on their page that acts as a keylogger. This way, users think that they are just logging in to your system, but their credentials are being logged to another system. This is called "clickjacking." Another way to do this is to iFrame your web page and overlay the input fields with other input fields. This way, when a user enters their credentials, the input fields and login button are not

75

yours, so the information is not going to your website, and they have effectively stolen the credentials of the user.

To mitigate this, browsers implemented a security feature a long time ago where you can add a header to your web page called "X-Frame-Options." This one is a little outdated; modern browsers have evolved more into using "Content-Security-Policy," but the concept remains the same. It prevents other people from just placing your page as an iFrame anywhere they want. Because of this, and Teams uses iFrames, you do need to specify that Teams can iFrame your page. This can be done by setting your headers as the following:

- Content-Security-Policy: frame-ancestors teams.microsoft.com *. teams.microsoft.com *.skype.com

- X-Frame-Options: ALLOW-FROM `https://teams.microsoft.com/`

- And for Internet Explorer 11 compatibility, you need to set X-Content-Security-Policy

If you ever want to see how this security feature works, then I can recommend you try to iFrame the login page of Microsoft 365. This page is protected in this way so that malicious users cannot iFrame Microsoft's Office 365 login page. Therefore, if you ever need somebody to log in to Microsoft 365, then you need to use a different method. But more on that in a later chapter. The same goes for Google vs. Bing. If you try to add Google as an embedded web page in a tab, then you will get an error; if you do this for Bing (which has been adjusted by Microsoft to allow IFraming with the Teams app), then you won't get this error.

Another security feature implemented by browsers that might get in the way is the "Same-Origin" policy. This policy prevents a web page from making requests to a different domain than where the content is served from. This is very specific to scripts. As an example, let's say you are hosting your Teams tab inside of `www.proteamsdev.com`. Well, if you then get some data with JavaScript from another website like `www.teamsdevpro.com`, then this is by default not allowed. There are numerous ways around this, mainly because otherwise, the Internet would just not work anymore if everybody had to host all scripts by themselves. A good example of this is CDNs (content delivery networks) which are optimized to serve the same JavaScript file to lots of people. An example of this is the Teams JavaScript SDK itself which we load from a CDN from Microsoft.

Some methods are suitable and secure, and others a little less. I do recommend that you read up on these topics. You don't have to be an expert on these topics, but a basic understanding will get you a long way. The Teams client also implements this security feature. We must describe in the manifest what URLs we are going to be using inside of our code. The "validDomains" section holds the URLs you are using.

```
"validDomains": [
    "proteamsdev.ngrok.io"
]
```

If you ever get stuck with developing tabs and you are getting strange errors, then double-check if the validDomains setting is correct. It already bit me several times that I have forgotten this and took me several hours of searching to find the issue. But enough security for now. Let's get back to building tabs for Teams.

Types of pages

As you know, we have two types of tabs in Teams. A personal-scoped custom tab (aka a static tab) and a channel/group custom tab (aka a configurable tab). But with the configurable tab, we need some additional pages. This is because the configurable tab first needs to be configured and afterward can be removed, we need to implement those extra steps. In Teams, we can have three types of pages:

- A content page: This is the page where the contents are shown inside of the tab similar to a static page

- A configuration page: When setting up a tab, this page is shown first. This page sets the content's page URL. This URL is where the tab gets the content page from because this is not something you configure in the manifest for a configurable tab.

- A removal page: When removing a tab, this page is optionally shown so that we have a way to clean data from our system if needed. If you don't implement it or it doesn't work, then Teams will still allow the user to remove the tab. Otherwise, the tab would be stuck and the user would never be able to remove it.

We already created a content page in the previous chapter, but let's extend it with something that defaults to most modern browsers these days. In HTML5, we got the capability to use the native device functionality like

- Camera

- Microphone

- Location

- Notifications

Be aware that not all these features are equally implemented across the Teams client's landscape. Some are not implemented in the Teams mobile app; in the browser client, it then depends again on which type of browser the user has. Therefore, if you need this kind of functionality in your application, then test first what is possible and what not. I could give you a list of the clients with their particular features, but that changes so much that this list would always be wrong.

Feedback and Location

Let's extend our static lunch ordering application with a little more functionality. We would like people to view the Location of our sandwich shop. But since the Location is always at the office, and people order their lunches when they are in the office, we can assume that we just need to pinpoint their current Location. We also want a way to give feedback. Users should be able to take a picture while eating their delicious sandwiches. For this, we are going to use some Google Maps integrations to show a map, and we are going to access the webcam feed to get a picture. Both the current Location and access to the webcam can be requested with HTML5. So, we are going to implement these features and activate them in the Teams client as well. You will also be needing a Google Maps key. Google recently changed their policy. It used to be that you could get a free key to use the Google Maps API. Getting free keys is no longer possible. Nowadays, you must pay for it, but when you create a developer account on Google, you get a free-spending budget of $200 every month. So that's good enough for some development with the Google APIs, and basically, it's still free. You could also use Bing Maps or any other map tool; I just like the Google Maps one. To create your API key, create an account on `https://developers.google.com/`, and activate the "Maps JavaScript API." A more detailed step-by-step guide is found here: `https://developers.google.com/maps/documentation/javascript/get-api-key`.

C#

You can follow along if you start from the Chapter 5 start solution. If you want to look at the completed solution, then see the "CompanyApp – Completed" folder. Since most of the logic is going to be in JavaScript, we just need to create two additional methods inside of our LunchController. Let's call them GiveFeedback and Location. Add the following code:

```
public ActionResult GiveFeedback()
{
    return View();

}

public ActionResult Location()
{
    return View();
}
```

Also, create views for them. Inside the Lunch folder under Views, create two new files "GiveFeedback.cshtml" and "Location.cshtml" or do as I do and right-click view and select the "CreateView" option.

In the "Location.cshtml", we will add some default HTML that will hold our Google map. And we need to import a script from Google Maps that will help with the rendering.

```
@{
    ViewData["Title"] = "Visit our location";
    Layout = "_LayoutForLunch";
}

<h1>Visit our location</h1>
<script src="~/js/location.js" asp-append-version="true"></script>
<script async defer src="https://maps.googleapis.com/maps/api/
js?key=<INSERT_API_KEY>&callback=initMap"></script>

<div id="map" style="height: 300px;"></div>

<div>
    <a href='@Url.Action("Index", "Lunch")' class="btn btn-
    primary">Return</a>
</div>
```

As you can see, not much is going on here—a little header, a div to hold the map, and a link to return to our home page. Don't forget to add your API key, or you will not be able to access the Google Maps API. The real logic is going to be in our location.js file. Add this file to your JS folder and add the following JavaScript code:

```
var map, infoWindow;
function initMap() {
    navigator.permissions.query({ name: 'geolocation' });

    map = new google.maps.Map(document.getElementById('map'), {
        center: { lat: -34.397, lng: 150.644 },
        zoom: 6
    });
    infoWindow = new google.maps.InfoWindow;

    // Try HTML5 geolocation.
    if (navigator.geolocation) {
        navigator.geolocation.getCurrentPosition(function (position) {
            var pos = {
                lat: position.coords.latitude,
                lng: position.coords.longitude
            };

            infoWindow.setPosition(pos);
            infoWindow.setContent('Pro Teams development.');
            infoWindow.open(map);
            map.setCenter(pos);
        }, function () {
            handleLocationError(true, infoWindow, map.getCenter());
        });
    } else {
        // Browser doesn't support Geolocation
        handleLocationError(false, infoWindow, map.getCenter());
    }
}

function handleLocationError(browserHasGeolocation, infoWindow, pos) {
    infoWindow.setPosition(pos);
```

```
infoWindow.setContent(browserHasGeolocation ?
    'Error: The Geolocation service failed.' :
    'Error: Your browser doesn\'t support geolocation.');
infoWindow.open(map);
}
```

Now, what's happening here? Well, first, you notice that the initMap function is never called—not in this file or in the view. That's because the Google Maps script takes some time to load. Google solves this by adding the possibility to add a callback function. As you can see in the script URL, it ends with "&callback=initMap". This means when the script gets loaded, our initMap function is called. In the initMap function, we call on the HTML5 geolocation function. First, we create the Google map, with some random coordinates. Then we invoke the request for the Location. This will ask the browser to share the Location of the user. It could be that when you are developing for Teams in the browser, you get a pop-up. It also could be that if you are using the client, this is not working. Why is that? That's because we didn't ask permission in our manifest to utilize this functionality. So, Teams will block this by default. Add the following statement to the manifest:

```
"devicePermissions": [
  "geolocation"
],
```

This manifest entry will let Teams know that your app is going to need this functionality and will allow you to request the Location. Once we have the current Location, we can adjust the map and place a marker onto it. We are now able to upload the latest version of our Teams package, open our static lunch app, and get the result as in Figure 5-1.

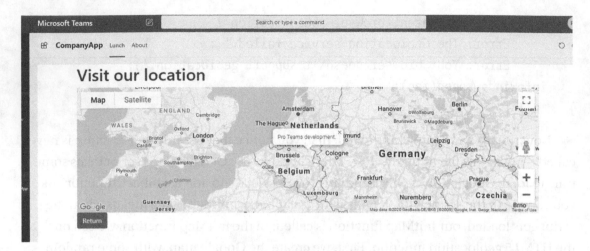

Figure 5-1. *Our current Location from within a static Teams tab in C#*

Node

We are going to continue with the solution where we left off. If you take the start solution, then you can follow along or look at the completed solution in the "02. Company App Lunch - static pages" folder. To get started with our Google map, first, we need to create a "Location.js" file under the components folder. This is going to hold our location component, which is responsible for showing the map. As with the previous components, we know by now what to do to keep our app in sync with the selected Theme of Teams. So, let's add that logic already. Later, we will see how to get this logic in one place because duplicating code is not such a good idea. But for now, it will do. So let us start by creating our Location class and adding a constructor.

```
class Location extends React.Component {
  constructor(props) {
    super(props)
    this.state = {
      context: {},
      theme: {}
    }
  }
}
```

The context and the Theme are properties that we already used before. Let us add some methods like before that will allow us to change the Theme.

```
updateTheme = (themeStr) => {
  switch (themeStr) {
    case "dark":
      var theme = themes.teamsDark;
      break;
    case "contrast":
      var theme = themes.teamsHighContrast;
      break;
    case "default":
    default:
      var theme = themes.teams;
  }
  this.setState({ theme: theme });
}

getQueryVariable = (variable) => {
  const query = window.location.search.substring(1);
  const vars = query.split("&");
  for (const varPairs of vars) {
    const pair = varPairs.split("=");
    if (decodeURIComponent(pair[0]) === variable) {
      return decodeURIComponent(pair[1]);
    }
  }
  return undefined;
}
```

And of course, add the "componentDidMount" so that it will load our context and Theme.

```
componentDidMount() {
  // Get the user context from Teams and set it in the state
  microsoftTeams.getContext((context, error) => {
    this.setState({
      context: context
    });
  });
```

```
    this.updateTheme(this.getQueryVariable('theme'));
    microsoftTeams.registerOnThemeChangeHandler(this.updateTheme);
}
```

Basically, we have got the plumbing of a basic Teams tab ready. But we don't show anything yet. Let's add the render method.

```
render() {
  return (
    <div>
      <Provider theme={this.state.theme}>
        <Flex><div style={{ height: '350px', width: '500px' }}>
          < MapShower
            centerAroundCurrentLocation
            google={this.props.google}
          >
          </ MapShower>
        </div>
        </Flex>
        <Flex>
          <div>
            <Link to="/personal">
              <Button icon={<EditIcon />} text primary content="Back" />
            </Link>
            <Link to="/Feedback">
              <Button icon={<ChatIcon />} text primary content="Give
              Feedback" />
            </Link>
          </div>
        </Flex>
      </Provider>
    </div>
  );
}
```

As you can see, we start with adding the Fluent UI provider to enable the Theming and add a new component to it called "CurrentLocation". We don't have this component yet, so let's add that. The reason I'm adding this as a separate component is because this is already a lot of code, and I want to keep it straightforward. This part will contain our entire Teams page, and the subcomponent "CurrentLocation" will be solely responsible for rendering out the Google map. Now before we create the new component, add the following piece of code to the bottom of the file:

```
export default GoogleApiWrapper({
  apiKey: '<INSERT_API_KEY>'
})(Location);
```

This export statement will set our API key to that we want to use for the Google Maps API. You should now get an error, because we didn't add the Google Maps npm package to our solution. We could reference it as a script entry like in C#. But with Node, it is much easier to add a package. Run the following command inside your terminal:

```
yarn add google-maps-react
```

This will add the npm package to your solution and will add it as a reference to your package.json file. The only thing left to do is to add it to our import statements. For reference, here are all the import statements:

```
import React from 'react';
import './App.css';
import { Link } from "react-router-dom";
import * as microsoftTeams from "@microsoft/teams-js";
import { Button, Flex, Provider, themes, EditIcon, ChatIcon } from '@
fluentui/react-northstar';
import { GoogleApiWrapper } from 'google-maps-react';
import MapShower from '../data/map';
```

As you can see, I've already added a reference to a map.js file under the data folder. This is the one that will hold our CurrentLocation component. Create a file under the data folder and create another React component. Let's start with the beginning. First, import React and add a constant that will configure the size of the map.

```
import React from 'react';
import ReactDOM from 'react-dom';

const mapStyles = {
```

```
  map: {
    width: '100%',
    height: '300px',
  }
};
```

Again, you can write this a lot better, but for reference, I like to keep it in this file. The rest of the class looks like this:

```
export class MapShower extends React.Component {
  constructor(props) {
    super(props);

    const { lat, lng } = this.props.initialCenter;
    this.state = {
      currentLocation: {
        lat: lat,
        lng: lng
      }
    };
  }

  componentDidUpdate(prevProps, prevState) {
    if (prevProps.google !== this.props.google) {
      this.loadMap();
    }
    if (prevState.currentLocation !== this.state.currentLocation) {
      this.newerMap();
    }
  }

  newerMap() {
    const map = this.map;
    const current = this.state.currentLocation;

    const google = this.props.google;
    const maps = google.maps;
```

```
    if (map) {
      let center = new maps.LatLng(current.lat, current.lng);
      map.panTo(center);
    }
  }
  componentDidMount() {
    if (this.props.centerAroundCurrentLocation) {
      if (navigator && navigator.geolocation) {
        navigator.geolocation.getCurrentPosition(pos => {
          const coords = pos.coords;
          this.setState({
            currentLocation: {
              lat: coords.latitude,
              lng: coords.longitude
            }
          });
        });
      }
    }
    this.loadMap();
  }
  loadMap() {
    if (this.props && this.props.google) {
      // checks if google is available
      const { google } = this.props;
      const maps = google.maps;

      const mapRef = this.refs.map;

      // reference to the actual DOM element
      const node = ReactDOM.findDOMNode(mapRef);

      let { zoom } = this.props;
      const { lat, lng } = this.state.currentLocation;
      const center = new maps.LatLng(lat, lng);
      const mapConfig = Object.assign(
        {},
```

```
          {
            center: center,
            zoom: zoom,
          }
        );

        // maps.Map() is constructor that instantiates the map
        this.map = new maps.Map(node, mapConfig);
      }
    }

    render() {
      const style = Object.assign({}, mapStyles.map);
      return (
        <div>
          <div style={style} ref="map">
            Loading map...
          </div>
        </div>
      );
    }
  }
export default MapShower;

MapShower.defaultProps = {
  zoom: 14,
  initialCenter: {
    lat: -1.2884,
    lng: 36.8233
  },
  centerAroundCurrentLocation: false,
  visible: true
};
```

A lot is happening inside of this code. Let's start with the render method. We are setting a default value so that if everything goes super slow, we still show a "loading map" text. You also notice that at the bottom, we set some default settings. There could always be something wrong with our request to the Google Maps API, so we have to set a default value. These default values must be added to the constructor as well; otherwise, our app would have no idea what those properties are. Now, if you look at our componentDidUpdate method, you will notice that we check again if the Google Maps API is loaded and if we can access the current location. The newerMap method is responsible for updating the map to the correct location if we can get the location from the browser or Teams. This location is requested inside of the componentDidMount, where afterward we execute the logic of the loadMap function, which will update the map, so it's centered on the correct location. Don't forget to update your manifest with the "devicePermissions" setting so that Teams allows your app to read the current location.

```
"devicePermissions": [
    "geolocation"
],
```

If we now upload a new version of our Teams package and go to our app, we should be able to retrieve our current location and show it on a Google map as seen in Figure 5-2.

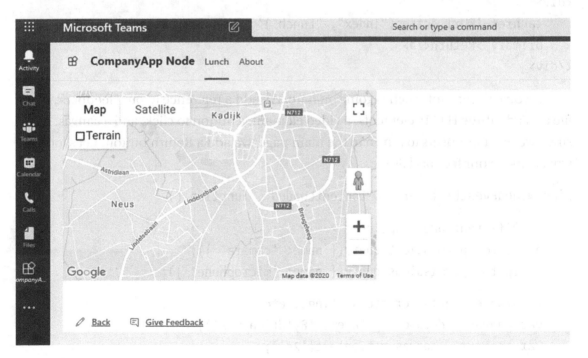

Figure 5-2. Our current Location from within a static Teams tab in Node

C#

The next action we haven't discussed yet is our feedback mechanism. If you haven't added the view for the Feedback method, then you can do this now. The logic here is again going to be more in JavaScript than in C#, so the view is rather simple.

```
@{
    ViewData["Title"] = "Please give some feedback about your lunch";
    Layout = "_LayoutForLunch";

}


<h1>Please give some feedback about your lunch</h1>
<script src="~/js/feedback.js" asp-append-version="true"></script>

<video id="video" width="640" height="480" autoplay></video>
<button id="snap" class="">Snap Photo</button>
<canvas id="canvas" width="640" height="480"></canvas>

<div>
    <a href='@Url.Action("Index", "Lunch")' class="btn btn-
    primary">Return</a>
</div>
```

As you can see, not much is going on here. We add a reference to our "feedback.js" file and add three HTML elements: a video element, a button to click, and a canvas. And since we want our users to return to the main page, we add a Return button. Let's look at what's inside our feedback.js file.

```
window.addEventListener("DOMContentLoaded", function () {

    // Different query options:
    navigator.permissions.query({ name: 'camera' });
    navigator.permissions.query({ name: 'microphone' });

    // Grab elements, create settings, etc.
    var canvas = document.getElementById('canvas');
    var context = canvas.getContext('2d');
    var video = document.getElementById('video');
```

```
    // Put video listeners into place
    if (navigator.mediaDevices && navigator.mediaDevices.getUserMedia) {
        navigator.mediaDevices.getUserMedia({ audio: false, video: true
        }).then(function (stream) {
            //video.src = window.URL.createObjectURL(stream);
            video.srcObject = stream;
            video.play();
        }).catch(error => {

            console.log(error);
        });
    }

    // Trigger photo take
    document.getElementById('snap').addEventListener('click', function () {
        context.drawImage(video, 0, 0, 640, 480);
    });

}, false);
```

To keep it simple, I've reverted to the vanilla JavaScript way of waiting until the DOM is loaded. Once this is completed, we ask for permission from the browser to use the webcam and the microphone. Now, we aren't using the microphone anywhere else in the code, but I kept this reference so that you can see that it's also possible to get the audio feed of a user. This way, it would even be possible to set up a Teams call from your application running in a tab. But that would be a lot of work and would create a kind of inception feeling for the end user. But there are other use cases that do make sense. We could, for instance, use the Speech-To-Text API (https://azure.microsoft.com/en-us/services/cognitive-services/speech-to-text/) to enable our user to use voice commands in our tab.

After we get permission, we start by getting references to the HTML elements we created in our view. Once we have these, we fill up the video HTML element with the stream we start receiving from the browser or Teams. The button is just there so that we can get the picture from the stream and put that next to the video. Again, don't forget to add the additional requests for device permissions in the manifest.

```
"devicePermissions": [
  "geolocation",
  "media"
],
```

If we now upload our new manifest and test this code, we should be able to see a video stream of ourselves and take a picture as you can see in Figure 5-3.

Figure 5-3. *Getting the video stream in a static Teams tab*

As you can see, you can do a lot with device permissions, and it's a good thing that Teams allows developers to utilize those different options.

Node

For our feedback page, we are going to need another component. Let's add another file called "FeedBack.js" to our components folder. This will again hold our basic "set theme logic" but also the option to use the webcam. The main logic will be in our componentDidMount method.

```
componentDidMount() {
  // Get the user context from Teams and set it in the state
  microsoftTeams.getContext((context, error) => {
    this.setState({
      context: context
    });
  });
  this.updateTheme(this.getQueryVariable('theme'));
  microsoftTeams.registerOnThemeChangeHandler(this.updateTheme);
  microsoftTeams.enablePrintCapability()
  var canvas = document.getElementById('canvas');
  var context = canvas.getContext('2d');
  var video = document.getElementById('video');
  if (navigator.mediaDevices && navigator.mediaDevices.getUserMedia) {
    navigator.mediaDevices
      .getUserMedia({ video: { facingMode: "environment" } })
      .then(stream => {
        const video = this.videoTag.current;
        video.srcObject = stream;
        video.setAttribute("playsinline", true);
        video.play();
      });
  }
}
```

Here, we are getting a reference to again the canvas element and the video element. When this is executed, it will get the media stream of our device and insert that into the video element. Now, the only thing remaining is to be able to take a picture. So in the takePicture function, we get the stream and create an image out of it.

```
takePicture = () => {
  const video = this.videoTag.current;
  const canvasElement = this.canvas.current;
  const canvas = canvasElement.getContext("2d");

  canvasElement.height = video.videoHeight;
  canvasElement.width = video.videoWidth;
  canvas.drawImage(
    video,
    0,
    0,
    canvasElement.width,
    canvasElement.height
  );
}
```

The only thing that is left is to add the three elements—video, button, and canvas—to our page. Let's do that in the render section.

```
render() {
  return (
    <div>
      <Provider theme={this.state.theme}>
        <Flex>
          <div>
            <video ref={this.videoTag} width="400" height="400" autoPlay />
          </div>
          <button id="snap" class="" onClick={() => this.
          takePicture()}>Snap Photo</button>
          <canvas id="canvas" width="640" height="480" ref={this.
          canvas}></canvas>
        </Flex>
        <Flex>
          <div>

            <Link to="/personal">
              <Button icon={<EditIcon />} text primary content="Back" />
            </Link>
```

```
        <Link to="/Location">
          <Button icon={<ChatIcon />} text primary content="Location" />
        </Link>
      </div>
    </Flex>
  </Provider>
</div>
  );
}
```

I've taken the liberty to style it a little bit and to add links that will enable us to move between pages. If all goes well, then you should, after uploading the new Teams package, see a video feed rendering, and you should be able to take a picture like in Figure 5-4. Don't forget to also add the files to the app.js file. This will enable the react-router to find your pages.

```
<Router>
    <Route exact path="/personal" component={PersonalTab} />
    <Route exact path="/location" component={Location} />
    <Route exact path="/feedback" component={FeedBack} />
</Router>
```

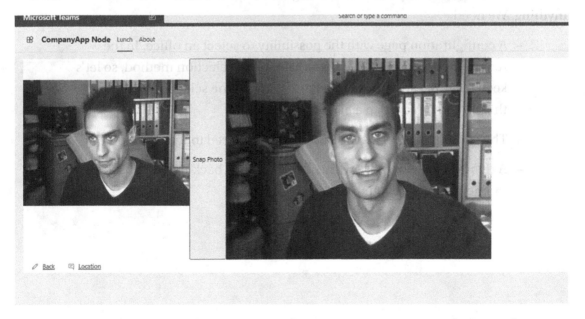

Figure 5-4. *Getting the video stream and creating a picture out of it in Node*

Configurable tabs
Our company app

Now that we have mastered the power of static tabs inside of Microsoft Teams, it's time to take it one step further. Let's go back to the original requirements of replacing our intranet with a company Teams' application. Something that every intranet has is news items. Well, we want to show those news items inside of Microsoft Teams, and to start with this, we are going to show them inside of a tab that can be added to a chat or a channel. This is because our global company has offices in different parts of the world. And those offices all have different news. Each of those offices has a Team, and in the general channel, they would like the news in a separate tab but only for that specific office. So, we are going to need to filter our news first before we show it. The configuration of the filter will be done by the owner of the team who sets up the tab. And because this is manually set, as an additional bonus, people can set up this tab in private chats and change the filter there according to their needs. We will build other features in later chapters; therefore, we also need to save the information about what Team/chat has what the news tab and what filter they selected.

These requirements are quite straightforward, but just to be on the safe side, let's break them down so that we don't miss anything. You don't specifically need to do this, but it is something I usually do when starting a new feature so that I'm sure I don't miss anything. We need

– A configuration page with the possibility to select an office. In the requirements, it's not specified what kind of selection method, so let's keep it simple and use a radio button. When the selection is made, this should be saved to a back-end database.

– The content page that shows us the news filtered to that location.

– A removal page because we need to clean our back-end database the moment someone removes the tab.

The config page

First things first. We need to tell Microsoft Teams that we are going to add a configuration page. This is done in the manifest file by adding a configurableTabs section.

```
"configurableTabs": [
  {
    "configurationUrl": "https://proteamsdev.ngrok.io/news/configure",
    "canUpdateConfiguration": true,
    "scopes": [ "team", "groupchat" ]
  }
],
```

As you can see, this takes three parameters. First is the URL of our configuration page. You should notice that it's not like with a static page that you also set the URL of the content page where the tab points to. In a configurable tab, this is done with the Teams SDK on your configuration page. The second parameter enables the user to recall the configuration page again. If you look at Figure 5-5, you can see that there is an additional item in the menu that says "Settings." If you put this setting to false, then that would not appear. By default, this is already set to true, so I didn't need to set it here, but I prefer to set the setting than to rely on a default setting. Setting all the parameters makes it easier for another developer to see what's happening in your code and configuration. The third setting is the scopes. A configurable tab can be used inside a channel tab or inside a groupchat. If you ever need to have it only in a channel tab and not in a groupchat, then you can specify that here. There are two more settings that you don't see here, and those are specific if you ever want to host your Teams application inside of SharePoint. But more on those in a later chapter. Now, let us add our configuration page.

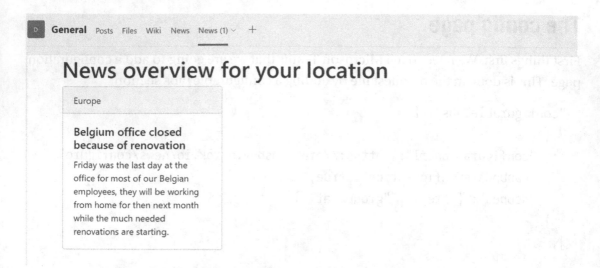

Figure 5-5. *Our configurable tab with company news filtered on Location*

C#

First, we are going to add another Controller to hold our logic. Let's call this our NewsController. In this NewsController, we are going to need to do four things—show our configuration page, save the information in our configuration page, show our page that will be visible in the tab with our news, and lastly, show a removal page for when our tab gets removed. So let's create four methods for this. We also are going to need a class to represent our news. This NewsItem class is pretty simple; we can add more properties later on, but for now, an id, title, location, and contents should suffice.

```csharp
public class NewsItem
{
    public int Id { get; set; }
    public Location Location { get; set; }
    public string Title { get; set; }
    public string Contents { get; set; }

    public NewsItem(int id, Location location, string title, string
    contents)
    {
        Id = id;
        Title = title;
```

```
        Contents = contents;
        Location = location;
    }
}
```

Back to our NewsController. Here, we first specify the Configure method because that's the method we defined to be called in our manifest.

```
public IActionResult Configure()
{
    LocationModel m = new LocationModel();
    return View(m);
}
```

With writing this method, I noticed I hadn't mentioned the locations. One of the requirements was to filter on the correct office location, so let's just create an enumerable for the different office locations.

```
public enum Location
{
    America,
    Europe,
    Asia
}
public class LocationModel
{
    public Location Location { get; set; }
}
```

Now for the view of our configuration page, we are going to show a drop-down that shows the locations.

```
@model LocationModel
@{
    ViewData["Title"] = "Configure";
    Layout = "_LayoutForLunch";
}
```

```html
<script src="https://code.jquery.com/jquery-3.5.1.min.js"
        integrity="sha256-9/aliU8dGd2tb6OSsuzixeV4y/faTqgFtohetphbbj0="
        crossorigin="anonymous"></script>
<script src="~/js/newsConfiguration.js" asp-append-version="true"></script>

<h1>Welcome to our Company news app</h1>

<div>Please select your office location</div>

@foreach (var value in Enum.GetValues(typeof(Location)))
{
<div>
    @Html.RadioButtonFor(m => m.Location, value, new { @class = "e-primary" })
    @Html.Label(value.ToString())
</div>
}

<button type="button" class="btn btn-info btn-xs">Submit Order</button>
```

As you can see here, I have resorted to jQuery. I know it's outdated, and nobody uses it anymore, but you will see later on that we need to save the location to our back end, and I find the jQuery code still more readable than plain JavaScript. As you noticed again, there is almost no logic in the actual C# part of this code. Most of the logic is in the newsconfiguration.js file. It's because we need to access the Teams Client JavaScript SDK. Create the newsconfiguration.js file and add the following code:

```javascript
const locationSaveButtonSuccess = (location) => {
    microsoftTeams.settings.setValidityState(true);
    saveTab(location);
}

let saveTab = (location) => {
    microsoftTeams.settings.registerOnSaveHandler((saveEvent) => {
        microsoftTeams.settings.setSettings({
            websiteUrl: "https://proteamsdev.ngrok.io/news",
            contentUrl: "https://proteamsdev.ngrok.io/news?location=" +
            location,
            entityId: "CompanyNews",
            suggestedDisplayName: "News",
```

```
            removeUrl: "https://proteamsdev.ngrok.io/news/remove"
        });
        saveEvent.notifySuccess();
    });
}
$(document).ready(function () {
    $('.btn').on('click', function (event) {

        var selectedLocationTypeVal = $('[name=Location]:checked').val();

        $.ajax({
            url: '/SaveConfiguration',
            data: selectedLocationTypeVal,
            contentType: 'application/json',
            dataType: 'json',
            type: 'POST',
            cache: false,
            success: function (data) {
                locationSaveButtonSuccess(selectedLocationTypeVal);
            },
            error: function (jqXHR, textStatus) {
                alert('jqXHR.statusCode');
            }
        });
    });
});
```

As you can see, we don't do a whole lot. Just when the user has selected their location and presses the save button, we send it to our API that stores the location for the channel. Now, we are not going to do a whole lot with this information just yet. This is for later, but we are already doing some plumbing work. Currently, the only thing we need is what's in the locationSaveButtonSuccess function. And we could also just trigger this when a user selects a value in the drop-down. This is what we are doing in the Node. js solution. The locationSaveButtonSuccess is first going to set the microsoftTeams. settings.setValidityState to true. Setting the validity state tells Teams to enable the save button. If you remove this line, then the configuration page will load, but the save button will never be enabled. So always add this line of code after your configuration logic has been done. The next saveTab function will tell teams what settings it needs to set when this save button is clicked. And this holds similar configuration parameters to the manifest when you create a static tab. This is where you finally configure the URL of the tab pointing to your page. As you can see, we are using the querystring to define what location has been selected. You set the tab URL with the contentUrl property, Teams remembers this, and when a user opens the tab, it will always call that URL. This is a whole lot easier than having to create our own save logic and storing the channel ID and selection in a database, which depending on the complexity of your app will still be required sometimes. The rest of the properties speak for themselves; just don't forget to always add the saveEvent.notifySuccess() function. This tells Teams that everything has been set and that it can proceed with creating the tab. In case you are wondering, there is also a notifyFailure function if you ever should need it to stop Teams from creating the tab. This can be used, for instance, when something fails that you can stop the creation or even roll back certain configuration settings that you already executed in your back-end code. The only thing that is left now is to add a view for our news tab and some logic to filter, and we have a custom tab in Teams that shows us specific news.

For reference, here is the entire NewsController:

```
public class NewsController : Controller
    {
        public readonly List<NewsItem> NewsItems = new List<NewsItem>()
        {
            new NewsItem(1,Location.America, "Seattle office voted best in
            sales","This month our Seattle Office was voted best in sales
            at the Seattle Small and Medium Business Owners Convention. Also
            known as SSMBOC"),
            new NewsItem(2,Location.Europe, "Belgium office closed because
            of renovation","Friday was the last day at the office for
            most of our Belgian employees, they will be working from home
            for then next month while the much needed renovations are
            starting."),
            new NewsItem(3,Location.Asia, "Japan office move is getting
            started","Since the purchase of the new highrise for our Japas
            office, our co-workers there have started with preparing
            everything for the big move. They are happy and sad at the
            same time while they prepare to leave our original starting
            location"),
        };
```

```
    public IActionResult Index([FromQuery] string location)
    {
        Enum.TryParse(location, out Location submittedLocation);
        return View(NewsItems.Where(x => x.Location == submittedLocation));
    }
    public IActionResult Configure()
    {
        LocationModel m = new LocationModel();
        return View(m);
    }

    [HttpPost("SaveConfiguration")]
    public HttpResponseMessage SaveConfiguration()
    {
        using (StreamReader reader = new StreamReader(Request.Body,
        Encoding.UTF8))
        {
            var locationString = reader.ReadToEndAsync().Result;
            Enum.TryParse(locationString, out Location submittedLocation);

            return new HttpResponseMessage(HttpStatusCode.OK);
        }
    }

    public IActionResult Remove()
    {
        return View();
    }
  }
}
```

And here's the index view:

```
@model IEnumerable<NewsItem>
@{
    ViewData["Title"] = "Index";
    Layout = "_LayoutForLunch";
}
```

```
<h1>News overview for your location</h1>

@foreach (var item in Model)
{
    <div class="card" style="width: 18rem;">
        <div class="card-header">
            @item.Location
        </div>
        <div class="card-body">
            <h5 class="card-title">@item.Title</h5>
            <p class="card-text">@item.Contents</p>
        </div>
    </div>

}
```

Node

For Node, if you look inside the last solution available, "Company App Lunch - Configurable Tab," you will see that I've cleaned it up a bit by placing the static tab items in a different folder, just to keep it a little tidy. So, don't startle when you notice that the structure is a little bit different. We are going to need a configuration page to get started by adding a new component in a new file called NewsTabConfig.js.

```
import React from 'react';
import '../App.css';
import * as microsoftTeams from "@microsoft/teams-js";
import { Dropdown } from '@fluentui/react-northstar';

const inputItems = [
    'America',
    'Europe',
    'Asia'
];

class NewsTabConfig extends React.Component {
    constructor(props) {
        super(props)
```

```
        this.state = {
            context: {}
        }
    }

    componentDidMount() {
        // Get the user context from Teams and set it in the state
        microsoftTeams.getContext((context, error) => {
            this.setState({
                context: context
            });
        });
    }

    enableSave = (key) => {
        var contentUrl = "https://proteamsdev2.ngrok.io/news?location=" +
        key.value;
        microsoftTeams.settings.setValidityState(true);
        microsoftTeams.settings.registerOnSaveHandler((saveEvent) => {
            microsoftTeams.settings.setSettings({
                contentUrl: contentUrl,
                entityId: "CompanyNews",
                suggestedDisplayName: "News"
            });
            saveEvent.notifySuccess();
        });
    }

D

        </div>
        );
    }
}

export default NewsTabConfig;
```

The component renders a drop-down in the render method with the data of the locations. To keep it simple, I've added the locations as a constant to the file. When the Location is selected, or rather every time a different one is selected, the onChange method is activated. This method is where we tell Teams to which URL our tab should point. As with C#, the first thing we do is to enable the save button. By default, this is grayed out and cannot be clicked until you call this line:

```
microsoftTeams.settings.setValidityState(true);
```

Now we only need to register what happens when a user clicks the save button. Here, we set our contentUrl, which is the URL our tab will go to, and we add as a query string our Location. This is saved by Teams and will always be the URL that this tab uses for its life span. The entityId and suggestedDisplayName are some things we can choose. entityId is more for developers because the end user doesn't see this and can be compared to the name of a class. It needs to be unique so that we can always find our tab if needed. The display name doesn't have to be unique and can be a user-friendly name. As you can see, we are going to point to a news page, this one we still need to create, so let's create a new file called NewsTab.js.

```
import React from 'react';
import '../App.css';
import * as microsoftTeams from "@microsoft/teams-js";
import {
    Flex,
    Text,
    Card,
    Provider,
    Grid,
    cardsContainerBehavior,
} from '@fluentui/react-northstar';
import news from "../../data/news.json"

class NewsTab extends React.Component {
    constructor(props) {
        super(props)
        this.state = {
            context: {},
```

```
            location: ""
        }
    }

    componentDidMount() {
        // Get the user context from Teams and set it in the state
        microsoftTeams.getContext((context, error) => {
            this.setState({
                context: context
            });
        });
        this.updateLocation(this.getQueryVariable('location'));
    }

    updateLocation = (location) => {
        this.setState({ location: location });
    }

    getQueryVariable = (variable) => {
        const query = window.location.search.substring(1);
        const vars = query.split("&");
        for (const varPairs of vars) {
            const pair = varPairs.split("=");
            if (decodeURIComponent(pair[0]) === variable) {
                return decodeURIComponent(pair[1]);
            }
        }
        return undefined;
    }

    render() {
        let loc = this.state.location;
        return (
            <Provider>
            <h1>Welcome to the news of the {this.state.location} office</h1>
                <Grid accessibility={cardsContainerBehavior} columns="2">
                    {news.map(function (item) {
```

```
                        if (item.location === loc) {
                            return <Card
                                key={item.id}
                                aria-roledescription="user card">
                                <Card.Header>
                                    <Text content={`${item.title}`}
                                    weight="bold" />
                                </Card.Header>
                                <Card.Body>
                                    <Flex column gap="gap.small">
                                        <Text content={item.contents} />
                                    </Flex>
                                </Card.Body>
                            </Card>
                        }
                    })}
                </Grid></Provider>
        );
    }
}
export default NewsTab;
```

In our NewsTab component, we will render the information for news items filtered on Location. The information in my example is coming from a JSON file in the data folder. I could as easily create an API and call that one to get the information. The main logic here is again in the componentDidMount function. It will get the Location that we get from the query string and that was placed there by our configuration page and set in on the state of our component. When our component renders the information, it will get the Location from the state and will filter the news items accordingly. As you can see, I used again pieces of the Fluent UI framework to enhance my application visually. With just an import statement, I can create an application that seems native to Teams. Now the only thing left is to add our components to our app.js file. This way, the router knows where to send the user when they hit the /news or /config URL.

```
if (window.parent === window.self) {
    return (
```

```
    <Router>
      <Route exact path="/personal" component={TeamsHostError} />
      <Route exact path="/news" component={TeamsHostError} />
      <Route exact path="/config" component={TeamsHostError} />
    </Router>
  );
}

// Initialize the Microsoft Teams SDK
microsoftTeams.initialize(window);

// Display the app home page hosted in Teams
return (
  <Router>
    <Route exact path="/personal" component={PersonalTab} />
    <Route exact path="/location" component={Location} />
    <Route exact path="/feedback" component={FeedBack} />
    <Route exact path="/news" component={NewsTab} />
    <Route exact path="/config" component={NewsTabConfig} />
  </Router>
);
```

Now, when you start up the development server and upload the latest version of the manifest file, you should be able to configure the tab and get the result like in Figure 5-6.

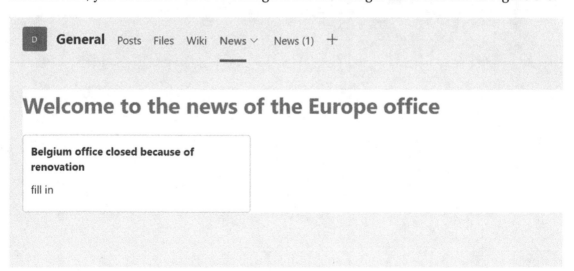

Figure 5-6. *Our configurable tab with company news filtered on location*

Perspective

In this chapter, we discovered the ins and outs of Teams tabs. If you have made it this far, then you can say with confidence that Teams tabs don't hold any more secrets for you. We created the foundation for our Teams company app that we will keep on using throughout this book. We looked at the different types of tabs, implemented configuration settings, and applied custom logic to work with those configuration settings. With this solid foundation, we can set up any kind of tab in Teams. Still hungry for more? In the next chapter, we will see how we can authenticate users inside of our tab.

CHAPTER 6

Authentication inside tabs

In the previous chapters, we created static and configurable tabs and used the JavaScript SDK to integrate our application with Teams. Now, this brings us a little further in our step to create a company application that will replace our intranet, but there is still one major component missing: authentication. There are numerous use cases where we need to know who the user is that is using our application. We can always ask the user to identify themselves, but that's not user-friendly or secure. For this, we need authentication.

Introduction

Authentication is, in my view, one of the hardest concepts to understand in software development. There are so many components that come into play, and if you accidentally mess up one of them, then there is a flaw in your authentication flow. This can mean that users just cannot log in to your application, or even worse is that malicious users can compromise their accounts.

One advice I give all the developers I work with is take some time off and learn the different flows and components that have to do with authentication. It's tough to get your head around in the beginning, but once you understand the concepts, your life will be so much easier. We could fill this entire book about authentication alone, so we are going to try to keep it simple. We are going to use Azure Active Directory as an authentication provider for us, which means that users will need to authenticate against Azure Active Directory with their corporate account. For the context of this book, it's also straightforward because when testing, you can just use the account you use to develop Teams. Authorization and authentication are platform and language independent. It doesn't matter if you are writing C#, Node, or Java; they all must play by the same standards.

© Rick Van Rousselt 2021
R. Van Rousselt, *Pro Microsoft Teams Development*, https://doi.org/10.1007/978-1-4842-6364-8_6

For tabs in Teams, we have got three different ways of authentication:

- Authenticate with a pop-up

- Authenticate using silent authentication

- Authenticate using single sign-on

And this is already where it gets tricky. They all use the same OAuth 2.0 implicit grant flow. The implicit flow is one of several OAuth flows available. I think the most well recognized one is the Client Credentials grant flow. That's the flow where you need a client ID and a Secret in your code, and you can exchange that against Azure AD for an authentication token, which you must have seen in numerous other examples. In Teams, we are using the implicit grant flow. This flow is initially designed for single-page applications. Those are typically built with client-side frameworks like Angular, React, and Vue, meaning they are JavaScript based. If I would use a secret to authenticate, then everybody who has minimal experience with browsers can open the developer tools and extract that secret from the JavaScript files downloaded to make the web page run. Therefore, another type of authentication flow needed to exist. This is the implicit grant flow. The main advantage of this flow is that you don't need some back-end server performing additional tasks. By this, I mean that you can have the user login. In combination with the client ID that you provide in code, which is public, they can receive a token that you can then use in your JavaScript code to get information out of various APIs like the Microsoft Graph. But as you might have guessed, this also has some security implications. That token lives inside of your JavaScript code, meaning that a user can open up the browser and can get that token and use it to make their own requests to APIs. Well, if the user does it with their own token that's something we allow, we just make it simple for them and do this in our own JavaScript code. The problem is when somebody else's code gets that token and starts making requests in the user's name that the user doesn't know about. So using this flow is not without its dangers. Make sure that you treat this token as a secret that nobody can know about, don't save it in the browser's local storage or cookies, and it's better to make an additional request for authentication than to expose a user's token to the outside world. To help you with this, one of the features of this flow is that the token received is not valid for an extended period. It usually expires after an hour, in which case you need to do the authentication flow again.

The implicit grant flow has its drawbacks, but it also has its benefits. As you can see in Figure 6-1, the flow is straightforward, and it is easy to understand.

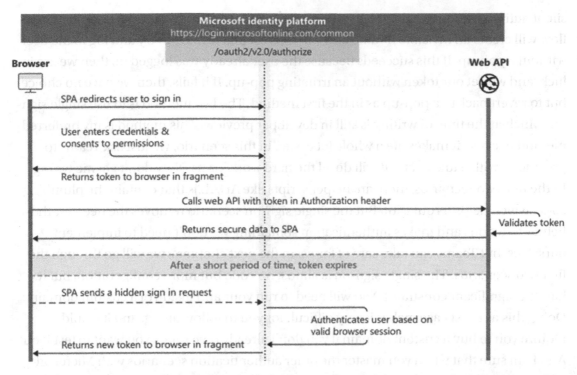

Figure 6-1. *OAuth implicit grant flow (source: Microsoft* `https://docs.microsoft.com/en-us/azure/active-directory/develop/v2-oauth2-implicit-grant-flow`)

We initiate the implicat grant flow and the endpoint that Microsoft, in this case, but it could also be Google or another provider, specifies is `https://login.microsoftonline.com/{tenant}/oauth2/v2/authorize`. This will provide us with a pop-up where the user can enter their credentials. We don't get access to this pop-up; that way, we cannot intercept the user's password. The endpoint will, however, after a successful login, redirect the user back to a page of us. Inside of this redirect, a token will be added to the query string or the fragment, and this is your auth token that you can subsequently use in your requests to the various Microsoft APIs.

Now back to our Teams tab authentication. As already stated, we have three types of authentication. And we can do these using the preceding flow. We can do it as the standard described earlier, with a pop-up. But that's not always fun for the user to log in several times a day into the same system, especially because they are already logged in to Teams and probably in a corporate environment in to Windows as well; therefore, we can also revert to the silent authentication, where the authentication will try to take place without the need for the user to log in. Now, you might get a little confused with this because earlier I stated that with this login method, you should not save the token. In the silent authentication, we don't keep the token. It utilizes the power of the browser. This flow will create an invisible iFrame and will redirect that iFrame to try and log in the user without a pop-up. If this succeeds because the user already was logged in, then we are in luck, and we get our token without an irritating pop-up. If it fails, then we have no choice but to revert back to a pop-up as in the first method. The last method is to use single sign-on, which at the time of writing is still in developer preview. This method is my preferred method because it makes life a whole lot easier. In this scenario, we just ask Teams to provide us with a token, and it will do all the hard work for us. Now don't get me wrong. In the first two scenarios, there are helper scripts like ADAL.js that contain the plumbing code, which helps us out a lot. But the single sign-on scenario removes the need for those helper functions and makes authentication something we don't need to implement ourselves, but Teams can take care of for us. In the next chapters, we will go through the first two scenarios. The single sign-on is almost no code but more configuration, but it has one significant constraint. You will need to run your app inside of a custom domain. Doing this as a test case makes it very difficult for you to follow along, and it would require you to buy a custom domain if you don't already own one if you want to test it out. And I am sure that when you master the other authentication scenarios with Microsoft Teams, the single sign-on is going to be a walk in the park for you.

There is, however, a caveat; things change over time, and so does authentication. To make it even more complicated, there are two different endpoints that Microsoft provides that can give you an authentication token back: the V1 endpoint and the V2 endpoint. If you ever look online for examples on how to do authentication, then you might see differences in the examples you find. This is one of the reasons why those differences exist. The new V2 endpoint can work with not only Azure AD accounts but also with personal Microsoft accounts. So depending on your needs, you might want to go for the V2 endpoint. The easiest way to recognize which of the endpoints is used is by looking at the URL they call. In the V2 endpoint, there is a V2.0 in the URL. So usually, you will see something like "oauth2/v2.0/authorize" at the end. Then to make things even more confusing, Microsoft have also two versions of helper classes available for you to use to make the authentication flow a little bit easier. One is called ADAL.js (Active Directory Authentication Library), and the other one is called MSAL.js (Microsoft Authentication Library for JavaScript). ADAL.js is the oldest one, which you might have guessed by its name. It's also recently been marked as deprecated, meaning that Microsoft will only add security fixes to it but no more new features. Now don't panic if this is starting to look like a very complicated situation. They do the same thing. Some things are, of course, different, but the authentication flows remain the same; they are web standards, so a helper library is bound to the same rules. The new MSAL was mainly created because the changes that needed to be done to ADAL to allow for additional features were way too high and would have broken the library. They are both supported (for now), and you can use any one of them. It just depends on the use case. I mainly work in big enterprises, so there we still rely on ADAL.js because that one works best with ADFS servers, which are still heavy used in most corporations. If you are thinking about making an application and allowing people to log in with their personal account, then MSAL is a much better choice.

Pop-up authentication

In our first scenario, we are going to have a button to log in. Usually, you would hide the rest of the page and let the user log in first and then show everything, but we are going to add the button so that you can see how it works. Be careful that you always use a button or some other kind of user-initiated action. Logging in automatically could confuse the user or trigger an error from Teams because you are navigating in between pages automatically, which can be considered as malicious code. Not showing a pop-up is for the next section.

But first things first. We need to authenticate against Azure Active Directory if we want to get any data out of Microsoft 365. No matter what the product is we are getting that data out of, it can be SharePoint, Exchange, Teams, and so on. So it's time to open up the Azure Portal.

Open the portal by navigating to `https://portal.azure.com` (or if you are like me and you want to see all the cool new stuff and don't care that sometimes there are some bugs, then navigate to `https://preview.portal.azure.com`). Navigate to the Azure Active Directory blade and select App registrations like in Figure 6-2.

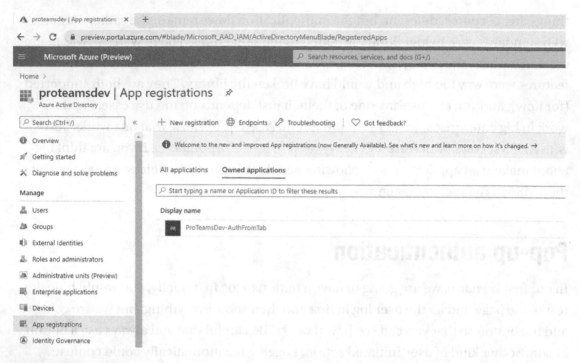

Figure 6-2. *The Azure Portal; Azure Active Directory blade App registrations*

Here, you will be able to register your apps. As you can see from Figure 6-2, I already registered mine, but let's go through the steps.

Click "New registration," and you will get a screen similar to Figure 6-3 where we can enter some basic information about our app.

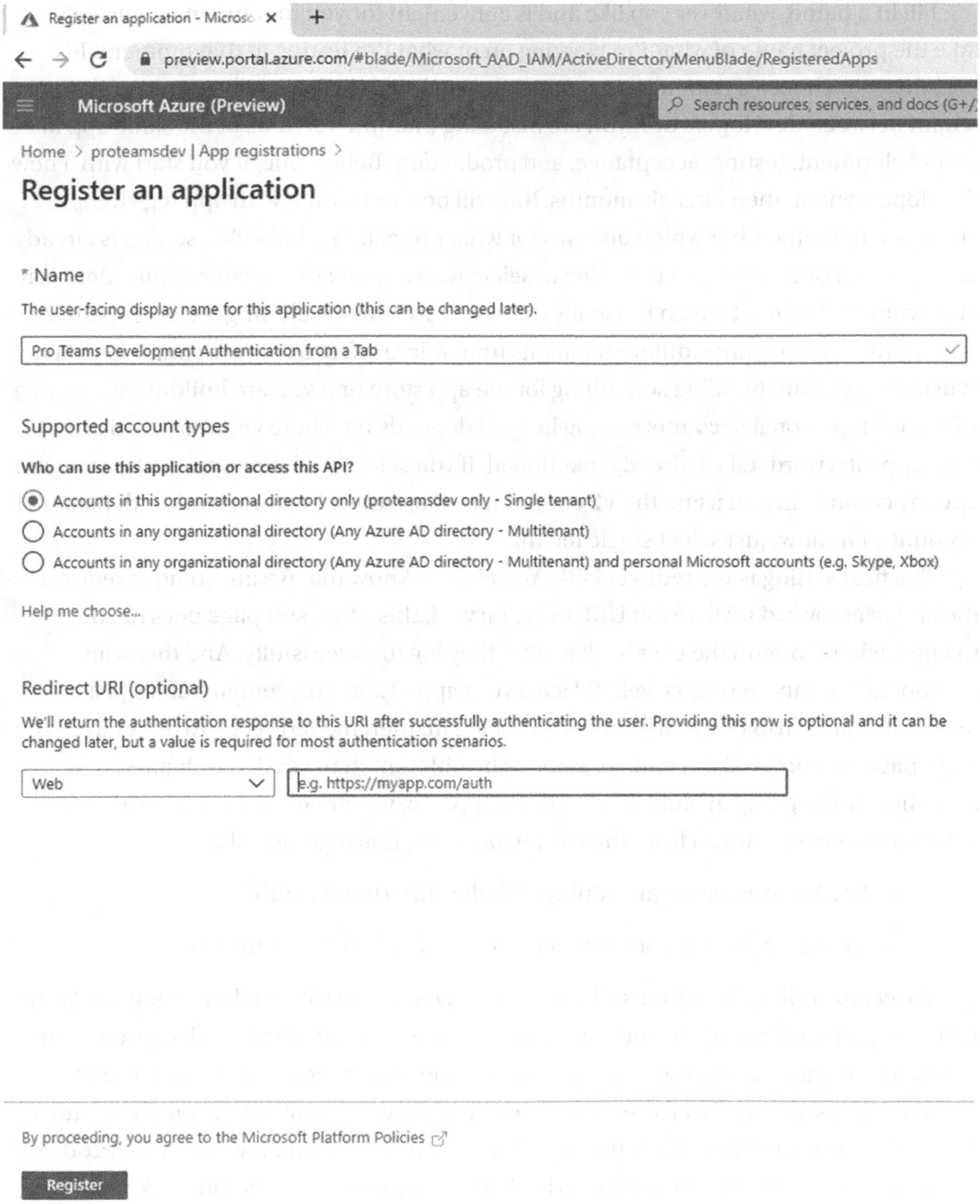

Register an application - Microso ×   +

← → C   🔒 preview.portal.azure.com/#blade/Microsoft_AAD_IAM/ActiveDirectoryMenuBlade/RegisteredApps

≡   Microsoft Azure (Preview)   🔍 Search resources, services, and docs (G+/

Home > proteamsdev | App registrations >

Register an application

* Name

The user-facing display name for this application (this can be changed later).

Pro Teams Development Authentication from a Tab   ✓

Supported account types

Who can use this application or access this API?

◉ Accounts in this organizational directory only (proteamsdev only - Single tenant)

○ Accounts in any organizational directory (Any Azure AD directory - Multitenant)

○ Accounts in any organizational directory (Any Azure AD directory - Multitenant) and personal Microsoft accounts (e.g. Skype, Xbox)

Help me choose...

Redirect URI (optional)

We'll return the authentication response to this URI after successfully authenticating the user. Providing this now is optional and it can be changed later, but a value is required for most authentication scenarios.

| Web   ∨ | e.g. https://myapp.com/auth |

By proceeding, you agree to the Microsoft Platform Policies 🗗

[Register]

Figure 6-3.   Registering a new app in Azure Active Directory

Fill in a name, whatever you like and is convenient for you to remember. I usually take the project name of what I'm working on or what I'm testing at that moment. It's best that you choose a naming convention and stick with it, especially if you are sharing a tenant between developers or if you are installing multiple versions of the same app like for development, testing, acceptance, and production. Believe me, if you start with a new developer tenant, then after six months, this will be overflowing with app registrations, and you can't remember which one was for what project. The following setting is already an important one. Here, you are going to select who is going to use your application. Is it only within this tenant which is usually the case if you are developing for a company, or is it multitenant, meaning different tenants from Microsoft 365 can use your app which is usually if you are building something for the app store or if you are building something where even personal accounts can log in. It all depends on where you want to distribute your app afterward. Like I already mentioned, if you select the latter option, then you are already committing on using the V2 endpoint because the V1 cannot work with personal accounts. For now, just select single tenant.

The next setting is the redirect URL. You already know that we are going to redirect the end user toward a Microsoft URL to log in; well, this Microsoft page does need to know where to send the user back to after they log in successfully. And this is an additional security setting as well. If I steal your app's Client ID, remember it's just JavaScript. And I use that to try and let a user log in; then the redirect URL that I want the login page to return to is, of course, going to be different than what's configured here, and Microsoft is going to block that login attempt. So, we already know we need a page where to receive the token from the user. In our case, this is going to be for

- C#: A new page we are adding with the URL /lunch/auth

- Node: A new component that resides under the URL /authclose

We get to adding these items a little bit later. Don't worry if you don't know the URL at the beginning of a project. You can change these afterward. If you click register, your app will be created. In the overview page of our app registration that we then see are several GUID's, we need to write these down because we are going to need them later. The main one is the Client ID of the app. That's the unique ID that will allow our code to tell Azure AD that we are requesting to log in to that specific application. Make sure you take the GUID with the label "Application (client) ID." The one that says "Object ID" is another GUID that Azure uses to identify it internally. We don't need that one, but I must admit, I've written down the wrong GUID a few times already, and it takes hours for you to find why your code is not working.

The next item on our list is to configure that we are going to use the OAuth implicit grant flow. Navigate to the "Authentication" blade. Here, you can see that if you didn't specify a redirect URL, you can add one here, or edit an existing one, or even have multiple. If you scroll a little bit down, you can see under the "Implicit Grant" header two checkboxes. Checking these and saving will mark your app registration to be used for the implicit grant flow. Now you should only check the box that you need. I know it's easy to just mark them both and be done with it, but from a security standpoint, you should always think before you just give out permissions. In this case, we just need the "Access Tokens" checkbox, because we are going to need an access token to authenticate our request to the Microsoft Graph to get the location from the user. With the "ID Tokens," we can receive not only an access token but also additional claims. The access token is for authorization, while the ID token is for both authentication and authorization. In this case, we are not interested if the user is authenticated. If he's not, then we just don't get our data. But there are many use cases where your app also needs to know if the user is authenticated and where you need those additional claims. The only task remaining is, because we are going to get a user profile property from Azure AD, is that we make sure that there is data in there. Navigate to the Users blade under Azure Active Directory and make sure that there is information filled in under the "Office" property inside your contact information.

Now that we have our authorization flow configured, the only thing left to specify is to what data do we need access. Navigate to the API Permissions page, and here you can select the required access for your application. In this case, we need to read the user's profile, and that is a default setting that is already selected and granted. Let's say as an example that we needed to get the emails from the user. Then we could choose this permission by adding a permission, selecting the Microsoft Graph, and selecting the email read permission. Now remember that this implicit grant flow is designed for single-page applications, and therefore, you have the option to select "Application Permissions," but these will never be given. It's because this flow is just not used where you can request a token as a back-end application. This flow will always use delegated permissions (a user delegates your code to get them some data from an application). Now that we have our app configured, we can start setting up our code.

Let's start by adding an additional button and a click event behind it. In the Node example, we can add it to the PersonalTab component. In C#, we can add an additional JS file to hold the code, but they both will do the same thing.

```
microsoftTeams.authentication.authenticate({
  url: "/Auth",
  width: 600,
  height: 535,
  successCallback: this.getUserProfile,
  failureCallback: function (reason) {
    console.log("Login failed: " + reason);
  }
});
```

This little piece of code calls the Teams JavaScript SDK, and we will let it know that we want to start up an authentication flow. Teams will create a pop-up page for us where this authentication flow can take place. It will also make sure that this pop-up page can communicate back to our main page. For this, we have got the successCallback and failureCallback functions. We can trigger these from our pop-up page to let our main page know if the login was a success or not. Notice that we are not doing anything that has to do with authentication yet. This is all going to happen in a separate page. In the code example, this is the Auth component, or in the C# example, this is going to be a separate method on the Lunch controller.

Let's create this page. In Node, you can create a new Auth.js file and make it a React component. In C#, we will create the Auth method and create a view for it. Once you have done this, it's time to initiate the authentication flow the moment this page opens.

Add the following code to initiate the authentication flow when the page is loaded:

```
microsoftTeams.getContext(function (context) {
        let state = Math.random();
        localStorage.setItem("auth_state", state);
        localStorage.removeItem("auth_error");
        // Go to the Azure AD authorization endpoint
        let queryParams = {
            client_id: "fcf962d3-ab8f-48ee-af6c-c6770b78e63b",
            response_type: "token",
            response_mode: "fragment",
```

```
    scope: "https://graph.microsoft.com/User.Read openid",
    redirect_uri: window.location.origin + "/lunch/index",
    nonce: "ADO3FBDE-ACA5-4AC3-A41A-3E60768CB7E3",
    state: state,
    // The context object is populated by Teams; the loginHint
    attribute
    // is used as hinting information
    login_hint: context.upn
};

let authorizeEndpoint = "https://login.microsoftonline.
com/" + context.tid + "/oauth2/v2.0/authorize?" +
toQueryString(queryParams);
window.location.assign(authorizeEndpoint);
});
```

As you can see, we first need to get the Teams context again. This is to get the tenant ID and the user ID. The Tenant ID is used for constructing the URL where we are going to send our authentication request to. You could also hard code this, but since Teams already can provide us with the tenant ID of the logged-in user, why not use this. This will also help you when you move your code from a developer tenant to a production tenant. This way, you don't need to make this configurable or change the code before deployment. The upn, or user profile name, is not a required field and is used as stated in the configuration as a login hint. This means that when a user logs in for the first time, the username is already filled in. Remember, the information that you receive from the context could be wrong. It's all just JavaScript so users can change this in the developer tools; therefore, treat them as hints or helpers and not as the absolute truth because you have no idea if they are valid. What else do we see in the request we are sending to Azure?

- – State: As you can see, I'm using a GUID to declare the state. In this
  example, it's hard coded, which is not good. This is to prevent cross-
  site request forgery attacks. That's why you need to have something
  randomly generated in your request, which you can then check
  afterward when you get the token back if this value is still the same
  and if nobody fiddled with the token or request on the way to Azure
  or back.

121

- Nonce: This is not required for this kind of request. It's more for when you are using the ID tokens. It looks like the state parameter where we need to give a random string, but, in this case, Azure will use that random string and will add that to the ID token it will send back to you. This way, you can check if what you receive is really from Azure.

- Client ID: This is the client ID we got from the Azure Portal and is the identifier for our app.

- Response type: Here, we are requesting what we need from Azure to give back, in this case, a token (the authorization token or bearer token as it's also called). If we were also using the ID tokens, we could add "id_token" here.

- Response mode: This can be fragment or query. This is how you would like the token to be returned to you when Azure redirects back to your page, in the query string or in the fragment.

- Resource: This is the resource we are requesting access to, in this case, the Microsoft Graph. If you check out the completed example, you will see that you can also change this with scope. This has to do with requesting tokens to the V1 or the V2 endpoint. In the V1 endpoint, it's resource; in the V2 endpoint, it has been changed to scope, and the values are also a little bit different. Like in the following code, notice that the endpoint is different:

```
microsoftTeams.getContext(function (context) {
        let state = "AD03FBDE-ACA5-4AC3-A41A-3E60768CB7E3";
        localStorage.setItem("auth_state", state);
        localStorage.removeItem("auth_error");
        // Go to the Azure AD authorization endpoint
        let queryParams = {
            client_id: "fcf962d3-ab8f-48ee-af6c-c6770b78e63b",
            response_type: "token",
            response_mode: "fragment",
            resource: "https://graph.microsoft.com",
            redirect_uri: window.location.origin + "/lunch/index",
            nonce: "AD03FBDE-ACA5-4AC3-A41A-3E60768CB7E3",
            state: state,
```

```
        // The context object is populated by Teams; the
        loginHint attribute
        // is used as hinting information
        login_hint: context.upn
    };

    let authorizeEndpoint = "https://login.
    microsoftonline.com/common/oauth2/authorize?" +
    toQueryString(queryParams);
    window.location.assign(authorizeEndpoint);
});
```

Now the only thing left for us to do is have a page that will receive the redirection from Azure. Now I specifically did this in two different ways to show you that there are different options. In C#, I did not create an additional page. I just added the code that will check if it is a redirect to the Index page to order lunch. This means that a pop-up will appear with the auth page; you will then get redirected to Azure, log in, and then redirected inside the pop-up back to the order page. You can see this quick flash. Now it's not that nice that people see a glimpse of that page, but it demonstrates that it's perfectly possible. You could also reuse the Auth page/component we created for this. On this receiving page, whichever it is, we are going to need some code that checks if it's a redirect and gets the token out of our fragment.

```
microsoftTeams.initialize();
    localStorage.removeItem("auth_error");

    let hashParams = getHashParameters();
    if (hashParams["error"]) {
        // Authentication/authorization failed
        localStorage.setItem("auth_error", JSON.stringify(hashParams));
        microsoftTeams.authentication.notifyFailure(hashParams["error"]);
    } else if (hashParams["access_token"]) {
        // Get the stored state parameter and compare with incoming state
        let expectedState = localStorage.getItem("auth_state");
        if (expectedState !== hashParams["state"]) {
            // State does not match, report error
            localStorage.setItem("auth_error", JSON.stringify(hashParams));
            microsoftTeams.authentication.notifyFailure("StateDoesNotMatch");
```

```
        } else {
            // Success -- return token information to the parent page
            microsoftTeams.authentication.notifySuccess({
                idToken: hashParams["id_token"],
                accessToken: hashParams["access_token"],
                tokenType: hashParams["token_type"],
                expiresIn: hashParams["expires_in"]
            });
        }
    } else {
        // Unexpected condition: hash does not contain error or access_
        token parameter
        localStorage.setItem("auth_error", JSON.stringify(hashParams));
        microsoftTeams.authentication.notifyFailure("UnexpectedFailure");
    }

    // Parse hash parameters into key-value pairs
    function getHashParameters() {
        let hashParams = {};
        location.hash.substr(1).split("&").forEach(function (item) {
            let s = item.split("="),
                k = s[0],
                v = s[1] && decodeURIComponent(s[1]);
            hashParams[k] = v;
        });
        return hashParams;
    }
```

As you can see, we get the hash parameters and check to see if we get a token or if Azure returned an error. We do this after we initialized the Teams SDK because we still need to let Teams know that the login was successful or not, so that it can close the pop-up for us, which we initiated when clicking the login button. We also get the possibility to return additional parameters to our parent page like the token. As you can see, we also do a check for the random state parameter we created and save in our local storage. If our call to Azure returns the same state parameter, we know that there wasn't tampered with the request along the way. Now the only thing left for us is to use this token in our Order page to get information about the user. When we get the value back, we set this value on the page.

```
function getUserProfile(accessToken) {
    $.ajax({
        url: "https://graph.microsoft.com/v1.0/me/",
        beforeSend: function (request) {
            request.setRequestHeader("Authorization", "Bearer " +
            accessToken);
        },
        success: function (profile) {
            $("#officeLocation").text(profile.officeLocation);

        },
        error: function (xhr, textStatus, errorThrown) {
            console.log("textStatus: " + textStatus + ", errorThrown:"
            + errorThrown);

        },
    });
}
```

As you can see in the code, we are going to make a request to the Microsoft Graph and get information about the logged-in user. Thanks to the power and uniformity of the Microsoft Graph, this is nothing more than a GET request with the bearer token we got earlier attached as a header. When this call is returned, the only thing left for us to do is to update our page. Now when you run this code for the first time, the user also must give consent that the app can do something in their name. This is again an added layer of protection. This only happens the first time an app runs, and as you can see from Figure 6-4, because I am an admin in this environment, I can also approve it for all users; this way, other users don't get this consent screen anymore.

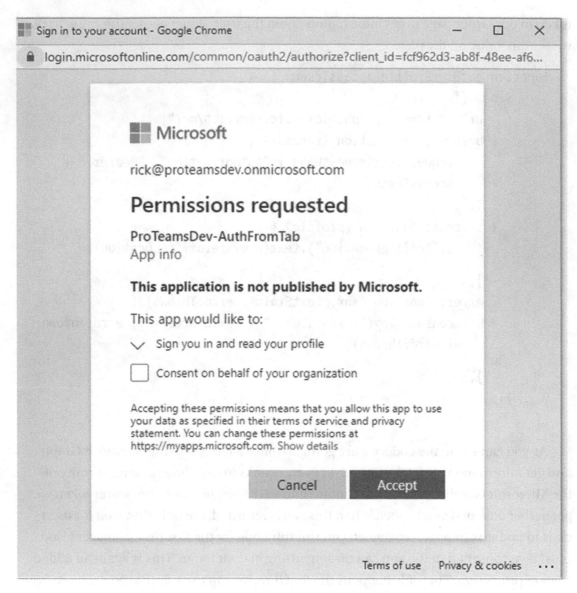

Figure 6-4. *The first time you run your application, the user must give consent*

Silent authentication

Now, as you can imagine, giving pop-ups to the user the whole time is annoying for them and not user-friendly. So, we need an alternative. Therefore, the opportunity also exists to try and log in without the user filling out their information like stated in the beginning of the chapter. Let's see how we can accomplish this. If we were going to do this all by ourselves, we would need to write a lot of code, and this is where ADAL.js or MSAL.js comes into play.

In this case, we are going to stick with ADAL.js, but you are free to experiment with both libraries.

ADAL.js

We are going to update the C# project for this one. Since this is just a JavaScript code, you could also update the Node example with this code. Now let's get started.

To keep everything a little separated so that you can tell the difference between the two flows, we are going to add a new JS file called lunchSilent.js. And instead of referencing in our Lunch index to load the lunch.js file, we are going to reference the lunchSilent.js file.

```
@* Used for Pop-up authentication*@
@*<script src="~/js/lunch.js" asp-append-version="true"></script>*@
@*Used for Silent Authentication*@
<script src="~/js/lunchSilent.js" asp-append-version="true"></script>
```

We of course are going to need to reference ADAL.js. Let's add that one to our shared layouts page used for our Lunch page. Add this next reference to our "_LayoutsForLunch. cshtml" file.

```
<script src="https://secure.aadcdn.microsoftonline-p.com/lib/1.0.17/js/
adal.min.js"></script>
```

Now, in the lunchSilent.js file, we are going to go at it a little bit different than before, because now we don't need the authenticate button. We are only going to need it when the flow fails as a last resort that users still have a way to authenticate when our flow failed. "handleAuthError" and "getUserProfile" are the two functions we are going to keep. This is because we still need to handle errors and get our user profile information. The rest is all going to be different. The first item on our list is trying to see if the silent authentication flow can just succeed. So after our page is loaded, we are going to start up the flow.

```
microsoftTeams.initialize();

    // ADAL.js configuration
    let config = {
        clientId: "fcf962d3-ab8f-48ee-af6c-c6770b78e63b",
```

```
        redirectUri: window.location.origin + "/lunch/authsilentend",
        // This should be in the list of redirect uris for the AAD app
        cacheLocation: "localStorage",
        navigateToLoginRequestUrl: false
};

let upn = undefined;
microsoftTeams.getContext(function (context) {
    upn = context.upn;
    loadData(upn);
});
```

As you can see, we are setting the configuration for our ADAL.js code, and you should notice that we are going to need a new page to end our flow. Like in the pop-up scenario, we are going to be creating pages for the flow to complete. The difference here is that they will be hidden iFrames; this is what the silent authentication does. We are using the Teams Client JavaScript SDK to get the users' ID that we can use in the configuration later on. Now the bulk of the code is in the loadData function.

```
// Loads data for the given user
    function loadData(upn) {
        // - login_hint provides the expected user name
        if (upn) {
            config.extraQueryParameters = "scope=openid&login_hint=" +
            encodeURIComponent(upn);
        } else {
            config.extraQueryParameters = "scope=openid";
        }

        let authContext = new AuthenticationContext(config);

        // See if there's a cached user and it matches the expected user
        let user = authContext.getCachedUser();
        if (user) {
            if (user.userName !== upn) {
                // User doesn't match, clear the cache
                authContext.clearCache();
            }
        }
```

```
// Get the id token (which is the access token for resource = clientId)
let token = authContext.getCachedToken(config.clientId);
if (token) {
    authContext.acquireToken(
        "https://graph.microsoft.com",
        function (error, token) {
            if (error || !token) {
                console.log(error);
                return;
            }
            // Use the access token
            getUserProfile(token);
        }
    );

} else {
    // No token, or token is expired
    authContext._renewIdToken(function (err, idToken) {
        if (err) {
            console.log("Renewal failed: " + err);

            // Failed to get the token silently; show the login button
            $("#authenticate").css({ display: "" });

            // You could attempt to launch the login popup here,
            but in browsers this could be blocked by
            // a popup blocker, in which case the login attempt
            will fail with the reason FailedToOpenWindow.
        } else {
            authContext.acquireToken(
                "https://graph.microsoft.com",
                function (error, token) {
                    if (error || !token) {
                        console.log(error);
                        // the user is going to authenticate
                        $("#authenticate").css({ display: "" });
                        return;
                    }
```

```
                    // Use the access token
                    getUserProfile(token);
                }
            );
        }
    });
  }
}
```

In this function, we are going to add the username we got from the Teams SDK and add a scope. As you notice from the scope, this is different than in the pop-up scenario. ADAL.js uses the ID tokens. So let's go back to the Azure Portal and activate that by activating the second checkbox as in Figure 6-5.

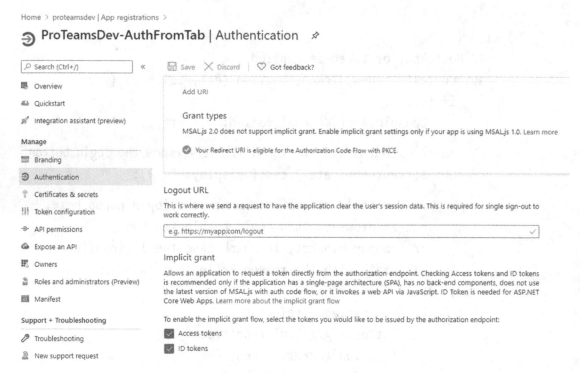

Figure 6-5. *Activate the ID tokens checkbox under the Authentication tab*

Since we are going to add a new page, we are also going to be needing a new redirect URL configured in the Azure Portal. Do this as well. We chose the /lunch/AuthSilentEnd URL, so let us add that one like in Figure 6-6.

∧ Single-page application   Quickstart   Docs

Redirect URIs

The URIs we will accept as destinations when returning authentication responses (tokens) after successfully authenticating users. Also referred to as reply URLs. Learn more about Redirect URIs and their restrictions

https://proteamsdev.ngrok.io/lunch/authsilentend

Figure 6-6. *Add the new redirect URL for our silent authentication flow*

Now looking at the code again, the part that is going to do all the work for us is going to be the "AuthenticationContext." We get this from ADAL.js, and it takes our configuration as a parameter. This will see if there is already a token in the cache for this user. As you can remember from the previous part, I said that you must be careful with caching tokens. ADAL.js can do this either in the session or in the local storage of the browser. We are going to use the localStorage, but remember that this is a risk for security by design so it depends in which context you can use this. Now, if the token is not in the cache, we are going to ask ADAL.js to renew the token for us. Once this is done, we can either get our user profile information or show a button for the user to manually initiate the authentication flow if it failed. Notice that we are required to do two calls to get a token that we can use to call the Microsoft Graph. Since ADAL.js is going to get the ID token for us, we only authenticate the user, and for the Microsoft Graph, we are going to need a token that authorizes us to do so. So in the subsequent call, we go back to Azure AD and ask it for explicit permissions to call the Microsoft Graph. We could work around this in this use case because we could also add claims to our ID token that would hold the information we need, but I wanted you to have an example of what you need to do to call the Microsoft Graph. Let's say you would need to access the user's emails; well, that would be hard to put into a claim. The next thing we need to do is create our AuthSilentEnd page. This page will be responsible for handling the response when the silent authentication fails. Create a new method on our controller and add a view onto it. The method can be empty because we are just going to add some JavaScript. The content of the view is this:

```
@{
    ViewData["Title"] = "Order";
    Layout = "_LayoutForLunch";
}
```

```
<script type="text/javascript">
    window.addEventListener("DOMContentLoaded", function () {

        microsoftTeams.initialize();

        // ADAL.js configuration
        let config = {
            clientId: "fcf962d3-ab8f-48ee-af6c-c6770b78e63b",
            redirectUri: window.location.origin + "/lunch/authsilentend",
            // This should be in the list of redirect uris for the AAD app
            cacheLocation: "localStorage",
            navigateToLoginRequestUrl: false,
        };
        let authContext = new AuthenticationContext(config);

        if (authContext.isCallback(window.location.hash)) {
            authContext.handleWindowCallback(window.location.hash);
            // Only call notifySuccess or notifyFailure if this page is in
            the authentication popup
            if (window.opener) {
                if (authContext.getCachedUser()) {
                    microsoftTeams.authentication.notifySuccess();
                } else {
                    microsoftTeams.authentication.
                    notifyFailure(authContext.getLoginError());
                }
            }
        }

    }, false);
</script>
```

As you can see, we need to configure ADAL.js again because it's a different page loading. Make sure that you use the same configuration. The rest is pretty straightforward. If this page is a pop-up, then notify Teams the authentication was successful or a failure like in the pop-up authentication. The only thing left now is that when the silent authentication fails, we make sure that we change the code in the auth.

cshtml view so that it matches the rest of our configurations. It still uses the pop-up configuration, and we cannot use two different methods. So change the code for when the DOM is loaded to the following:

```
microsoftTeams.getContext(function (context) {
            // ADAL.js configuration
            let config = {
                // Use the tenant id of the current organization. For guest
                users, we want an access token for
                // the tenant we are currently in, not the home tenant of
                the guest.
                tenant: context.tid,
                clientId: "fcf962d3-ab8f-48ee-af6c-c6770b78e63b",
                redirectUri: window.location.origin + "/lunch/
                authsilentend",        // This should be in the list of
                redirect uris for the AAD app
                cacheLocation: "localStorage",
                navigateToLoginRequestUrl: false,

                // Setup extra query parameters for ADAL
                // - openid and profile scope adds profile information to
                the id_token
                // - login_hint provides the expected user name
                extraQueryParameter: "scope=openid+profile&login_hint=" +
                encodeURIComponent(context.loginHint),
            };

            // Navigate to the AzureAD login page
            let authContext = new AuthenticationContext(config);
            authContext.login();
        });
```

As you can see, this is a similar code as the lunchSilent.js page. We configure our AuthenticationContext the same way. Only this time, we force a login by calling the login() method of ADAL.js. The only thing remaining is to hide the button when the page loads; so in our lunch index page, add a display:none to the authenticate button like so:

```
<button id="authenticate" style="display: none" class="btn btn-
primary">Authenticate</button>
```

Once you added everything, you can run your code again, and the button should be invisible now. If the silent authentication succeeds, you should see your office location get filled in. If you want to play around with the different use cases, then open up your browser developer tools and clear your localStorage with the command in the console tab.

```
localStorage.clear()
```

This way, when you refresh your page, you will not have any token in your cache, and you can see what happens. If you then refresh the tab, you can see that the flow is running different, and a little faster as well, because you already have a token available.

Final thoughts

As you probably know, there is a lot more to tell about authentication and authorization. In this chapter, we went through the necessary steps you need to authenticate your users inside a tab in Microsoft Teams. But we haven't discussed all the OAuth flows that exist; for tabs, those are not applicable, but when we go deeper into Bots for Teams, we will hit this topic again. We now created an easier way for us to identify which user is using our application, and we can even retrieve additional information from the user by accessing APIs like the Microsoft Graph. In the next chapter, we will finalize the starting point of our intranet's replacement by adding our Teams application into SharePoint.

CHAPTER 7

Integrating Teams and SharePoint

While we are building applications for Microsoft Teams, you will be pleased to know that Teams and SharePoint are good friends. Microsoft has made it easier for people who are developing against SharePoint to have their apps surface in Teams, and they have made it easier for us to develop against Teams to have our app surface in SharePoint. This is, in my opinion, a win-win situation, because we now have multiple platforms where we can run the same app, with no changes required. In this topic, we will go a little deeper into getting our app surfaced in SharePoint.

Preparing our app

Now that we are ready to have our app deployed, we can decide where to place it. For our company app, we are going to make it pinned to the top of the Teams client navigation bar, and we are going to show it inside a SharePoint page. Now for the SharePoint part, we can only show our configurable tab. Showing static tabs in SharePoint is on the road map, so for this feature, we will have to be patient. To have our configurable tab available in SharePoint, we should adjust the manifest first. Open your manifest and update the version number. It's always a good practice to update the version number whenever you do changes to the manifest. This way, you are sure that you can update the app. Otherwise, you might need to delete it and upload it again. Then in the configurable tab section, add the following:

```
"supportedSharePointHosts": [
   "sharePointFullPage",
   "sharePointWebPart"
]
```

© Rick Van Rousselt 2021
R. Van Rousselt, *Pro Microsoft Teams Development*, https://doi.org/10.1007/978-1-4842-6364-8_7

This will, when we deploy our app to SharePoint, tell it how to show our app, as a full-page experience or in a web part. Depending on what you want as a user experience, you can select one or both. Your configurable tab section of the manifest should now look something like this:

```
"configurableTabs": [
  {
    "configurationUrl": "https://proteamsdev.ngrok.io/news/configure",
    "canUpdateConfiguration": true,
    "scopes": [ "team", "groupchat" ],
    "supportedSharePointHosts": [
      "sharePointFullPage",
      "sharePointWebPart"
    ]
  }
],
```

Notice that we still have a reference to our ngrok URL in here. When deploying your app to production, this should be changed to the URL of where your app is installed. Depending on the sort of technology or your choice in cloud vendor, this can be anything. I'm keeping my ngrok reference, but be aware that for this to work, ngrok should be running as well as your development IDE web server (IIS in Visual Studio or Yarn in Visual Studio Code).

Deploying our app

Until now, we have been deploying our application through sideloading. This is perfect for development, but now that we have a first working version, we would like to deploy that into our production tenant. Generally, in most production tenants, sideloading is turned off. If this is not the case in your company Tenant, then you should speak to an administrator because having this activated means that users can just upload apps freely and who knows where they downloaded the app from. Apps that are pushed from the Microsoft App store must go through a certification process, so those you can trust. But randomly downloaded apps have not been verified to safeguard your data. To have your app uploaded to your tenant catalog, the person doing the upload should be a global admin or a Teams service admin. If they upload an app, they have the possibility to select that this app is placed in the Tenant app catalog, as you can see in Figure 7-1. This is done directly from the Teams client. If sideloading would have been active, I could immediately select to upload to a specific Team or for myself. Now, as a developer, you should typically not be the one installing the application, but I thought let's add a quick how-to guide for you so that you have an understanding of the process.

With the app now available inside the Tenant app catalog, our end users can go to the Tenant location and install it. As you can also see in Figure 7-1, there is this "Built for..." section. This is your Tenant app catalog and is always named after your Tenant's name. Another way to upload the app is directly from the Teams admin center. If you navigate your browser to `https://admin.teams.microsoft.com/policies/manage-apps`, then you get the option to add an app. This page also allows you to specify for each app available for Teams from the store if users can install it.

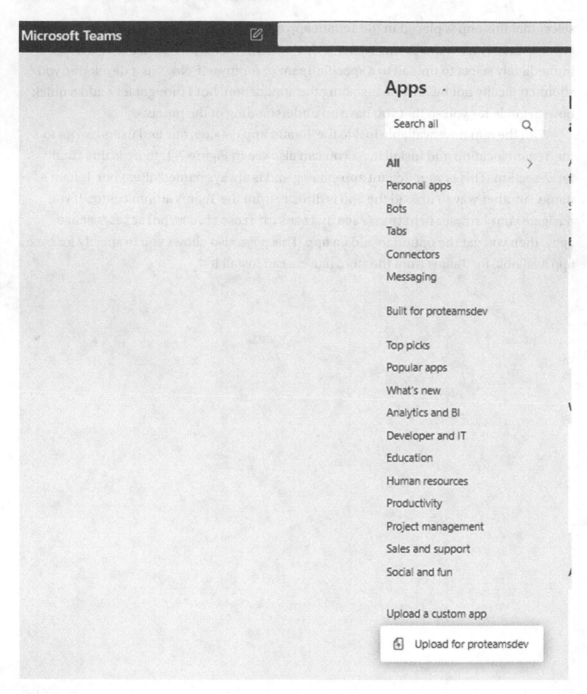

Figure 7-1. Upload an app for my company called proteamsdev

Installing the app for each user can be cumbersome. How are we going to persuade users to install our company app? Well, we can also install and pin it for them. This is very useful when we want to go live on, for example, a Monday morning. Then we install and pin the app, and all users should see it in their Teams client on Monday morning. For this, we can create app setup policies in the Teams admin center. On this page (`https://admin.teams.microsoft.com/policies/app-setup`), we can create different policies for different users. Let's say we have built an app for the finance department. Then we could create a separate policy for them and install this app only for the finance department. Now for our company application, we want it installed for everybody, so click the global policy, and you should see something like Figure 7-2.

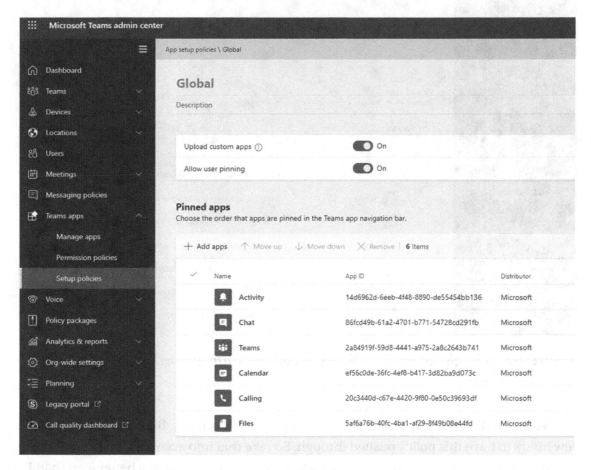

Figure 7-2. *The global app setup policy default setting*

Now let's add our company app by clicking the "add apps" button. This provides us with a search box that helps us locate our app. If we now add our application, we can even select it to be pinned to the top of the Teams client navigation, which for our company app is the best location, since we want users to go there every day. You should have a similar result as in Figure 7-3.

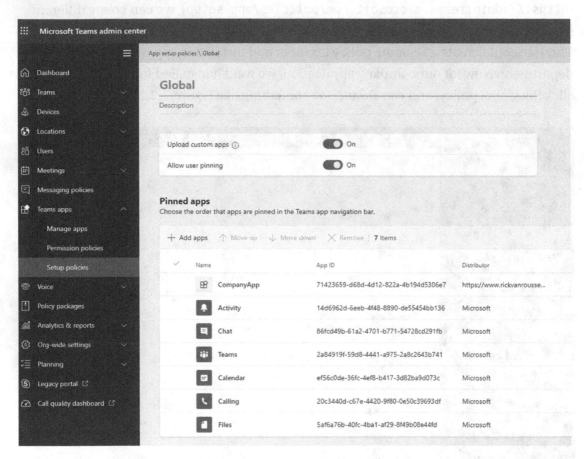

Figure 7-3. *The global policy will set our company app pinned to the top of the navigation in Teams*

Now, usually, we should see the pinned app, you might think. But it usually takes a few hours to have this policy pushed through. So take that into account when installing an app that it's not immediately visible. And make sure that you have a better icon than I have for this example, because this is just the default icon and not that pretty for users to have in their Teams client.

Deploying it again

Now that we have our app deployed in Teams, we would also like to have it shown in SharePoint on a page. Well, for this, we need to install it a second time. The Teams Tenant app catalog is not the same as the SharePoint app catalog. They have no communication between them. Let's navigate to your SharePoint app catalog. For installing apps in SharePoint, you should also be a global admin, SharePoint admin, or an admin on the app catalog site collection. Because, in SharePoint, the app catalog has to be created manually, this location can be different per tenant. The easiest way to find your app catalog is to navigate to the SharePoint admin page (`https://<yourTenantName-admin.sharepoint.com/_layouts/15/online/AdminHome.aspx#/classicFeatures`) and click the apps button. This navigates you to an old SharePoint page where you can navigate further to the app catalog. Now the app catalog in SharePoint is just a site where you can upload your apps. Navigate to the "Apps for SharePoint" library and upload the same package as we did for Teams. When the upload completes, we get the option to deploy the app to all sites in the organization.

You can compare this with the global policy of Teams. If you check the checkbox, then users don't need to install the app from the Tenant catalog on their site. It's already there, and they can just use it. Activating this depends again on your use case. Like with the global policy, if you have built an app for the finance department, then it would not be a good decision to make it available for all the sites in the Tenant. If you click the deploy button, the app gets installed, and it could be that you still need to check in the app, which is a SharePoint-specific behavior. If there is a little green arrow in the icon next to the name, then you need to click the three dots, and under advanced, you can find the check-in functionality.

Navigate to any SharePoint site (where you have editing rights) and edit the home page. Here, you should be able to add a web part like in Figure 7-4.

Figure 7-4. *Add our company app as a web part*

We could also opt for a page-wide solution. To get this, you should add a new page by clicking the gear icon in the top-right corner and selecting "add a page." Under the Apps tab, you can choose our company app, like in Figure 7-5. Selecting this should trigger the configuration page we created, and after choosing an office location, you should see our app with the same look and feel as in Teams. I hope you agree with me that this is an excellent and useful feature because it allows the same app we created to be viewed from different locations with no additional development. The technology behind this is, as you might have guessed, an iFrame. Our Teams application is rendered within an iFrame just the same as in Teams, so bringing this method over to SharePoint was a quick win for Microsoft and us developers. Because of this, this works in both directions. You can also create a SharePoint web part and bring that over to Teams. Just be careful when using the Teams context when building your app to run inside of SharePoint because there is no Teams context anymore, meaning you cannot get a team or channel ID.

Figure 7-5. Our app under the apps-tab in SharePoint

Final thoughts

With this final step of deploying our Tabs, we have come to the end of a milestone. We now understand how Tabs, both static and configurable, work and how to use the Teams Client JavaScript SDK to get information from Teams while executing our logic. We can authenticate users and have our application installed in a production Tenant for both Teams and SharePoint. Or we can switch it around and build an SPFx app for SharePoint and use that as a Teams app. In the next part, we are going to dig deeper into Bots and chatbots and see how they integrate with Microsoft Teams.

PART 3

Bots

CHAPTER 8

Introducing bots

The next big integration that Microsoft Teams provides is Bots. Bots are a broad name, especially in Teams. The basic definition of a bot is that it's a computer program that can autonomously execute tasks. Chatbots more specifically are programmed in such a way that they can understand our language and then can act, more or less, in a human way on it. They can execute a command, but they are also used, for instance, to moderate chatrooms, where they are trained to understand profanity.

Why bots

Now, if you are new to this "bots and chatbots" story, then no worries. Bots are not new. Bots are, as with most new technologies, something that already existed and rebranded and improved. Chatbots have been around for a very long time. If you open up your command-line terminal and start typing in commands there, then that, according to the definition, is a chatbot. The only difference between modern-day chatbots and the command-line terminal is that for you to use the terminal, you had first to learn what those commands were. You can type in full sentences, but the computer will not understand you. Therefore, you learned the computer's language (or an intermediate language). These days, there are Artificial Intelligence systems created that help a chatbot understand our language. This significantly lowers the threshold for usability, even in such a way that everybody can use them, not only trained IT professionals.

Bots can be divided into several categories. The main one we will be using is chatbots, and I will also refer to them as Bots to keep it simple. But understand that there are other bots out there. In video games, the automated opponents are also a bot, because they mimic real-life players. The pieces of software that Google or Bing uses to index the Internet are also called bots, more specifically spiders, because they also autonomously execute the task of indexing the World Wide Web.

© Rick Van Rousselt 2021
R. Van Rousselt, *Pro Microsoft Teams Development*, https://doi.org/10.1007/978-1-4842-6364-8_8

A once-in-a-decade opportunity

The emerging bot technology also gives us developers a once-in-a-decade opportunity. First off, they are all the hype these days. Chatbots are in high demand with companies because they help automate the workload. Robots have been around in factories for quite some time now, and recently chatbots made their entry into the information worker area. Given the enormous boost in the production rate that robots had inside factories, it's only reasonable for companies to assume that chatbots will have the same impact.

They also allow for a more natural experience. It's way easier for an end user to type or say a complex command than to follow an application's flow that does the same thing. An example of this could be an office where, if you have a visitor from another company, you need to register them so that when they show up at the reception, there is a badge waiting for them. If you create an application for this, then the person who wants to register that visitor should do the following steps:

1. Open the application.

2. (Optionally) use the navigation in the app to go to the correct screen.

3. Enter the first name and last name of the visitor.

4. Add the date and time when the visitor is expected.

5. Press the submit button.

If you convert these actions into a chatbot that would be easily accessible by the user, let's say a chatbot inside of Microsoft Teams. To start with, the user would probably already have Teams open because they were interacting with other colleagues, and the user would then just say to the bot "Rick Van Rousselt will be visiting me today at 2 PM." As you can see, this one short sentence contains already the data of steps 3 and 4 earlier. The chatbot then needs to comprehend the sentence and can convert that into the same information that generally was entered in steps 3 and 4. As for the navigation component to view the correct screen. One of the main benefits of a bot, in my opinion, is that it can hold more features than a regular web page or application. In an application, you only have x-amount of screen space. But a chatbot can understand sentences about a wide variety of topics, and then you could have it execute way more functionality.

One more reason could be that more and more people are spending time inside of messaging apps. Messenger, WhatsApp, WeChat, Telegram, and so on—you name the messaging app, and it probably has more than a few million users. Bots are platform independent; OK, there are some differences in the functionalities that are possible with bots in each of those platforms, but there is no reason that if you create a bot, you can't deploy it on multiple platforms. In an enterprise context, we tend to think more in the direction of Teams, but you could also use that same bot on a web page or Slack. All these different platforms where you make your bot available are called channels. The reason for this is, is that a chatbot is in its most basic form, is just an API. The platform or channel of your choice calls your API; this executes the logic you programmed it to do, and you return an answer back to the channel.

Breakdown of language

Before we start building bots, let's first examine what it takes for a bot to understand human languages. We could just start building a bot that takes simple commands, but once you begin with bots, the transition to language-understanding bots is, from a technology standpoint, quite small, or at least it is these days. You should take into consideration the way languages are built up when starting to build bots; this will make it easier to understand.

First off, you have the basic foundation of every language. And those are the words we use. It's also referred to as a shared reference. When we were children, our parents started by teaching us the basic words first. My parents saw that at a given moment in time, I was looking at a rabbit. At that moment, they explained to me that the thing I was looking at was called a rabbit. Your parents did the same when they noticed you were looking at a rabbit. We can say all over the world when children look at a rabbit, there is somebody around who explains to them that that thing is called a rabbit. This concept, where we link an object to a specific word, is a shared concept. Hence, it's called a shared reference. Shared references are the foundation of a language. We all use the same words (not considering dialects, of course) for the same objects. We can say: language begins with the naming of items in the world.

But this is not enough. Language is, of course, more than words. Even when we are having a conversation, we negotiate about our language without even knowing it. Human conversations are viewed as flexible. What I mean by this is when we are having a conversation, and I use a word that you are not familiar with, then, unknowingly, we can derive the meaning of that word from the conversation, either from the topic we are discussing or by asking different questions about it. In Figure 8-1, you can see this with an example. Let's assume you have no idea what a fish is, and I would ask you to get some fish. Then you would ask an additional question about a fish. I would then say, "yea, but a fish, well, you can catch that with a fishing rod." You now already have a concept forming that explains what a fish is. If we then assume that you would have no idea what a fishing rod is, then you would ask a follow-up question again. I again would answer: "well, a fishing rod is a stick with a string and a hook." This again explains the concept of a fishing rod. If you break down the conversations that we have day to day, then you wouldn't notice that people do this during conversations, but once you start to pay attention to it, then you would.

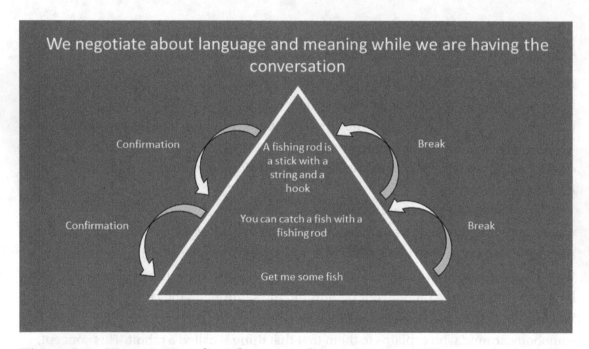

Figure 8-1. *We negotiate about language during a conversation*

Even the ability of naming objects and having a way so that if another person doesn't know the object to explain it to them is not enough to have a decent conversation. A conversation also must follow specific rules. Paul Grice (https://en.wikipedia.org/wiki/Paul_Grice) was a British philosopher of language, and he broke down the rules of a conversation into four maxims. They are called Gricean maxims and describe how effective communication takes place (cooperative principal, `https://en.wikipedia.org/wiki/Cooperative_principle`).

Maxim of Quality: Say only things that are true

We always say: "I hate carrying blocks."

We don't say: "I love carrying blocks, especially when they are covered in fire ants."

This maxim implies that during a conversation, we only say things that are true. You might think of an immediate exception on this, which is called sarcasm, but, as you know, every rule in the world has exceptions.

Maxim of Relevance: Say only things that matter.

We always say: "Bring me the block."

We don't say: "Bring me the block and birds sing."

This maxim is quite straightforward, and indeed, if we would have a conversation like in the example, then that would be one weird conversation.

Maxim of Quantity: Say only what is not implied.

We always say: "Bring me the block."

We don't say: "Bring me the block by transporting it to my location."

This maxim is straightforward. To make a conversation understandable, we give the information that is needed, and we don't add additional information that is not required.

Maxim of Manner: Speak in a way that can be easily understood.

We always say: "Bring me the block."

We don't say: "Use personal physical force to levitate the block and transport it to me."

The last maxim is something we take for granted and can also be referred to just keep it simple.

As you can see, there are many rules we follow, without even thinking about it, while having conversations. And to make it even more difficult, it's also the way we pronounce things that has an impact on our meaning. Take this sentence, for instance:

- You know. *I* don't. [So don't ask me.]

- You *know* I don't. [You know that I don't.]

Because we put the *emphasis* on a different part of the sentence, we mean something totally different.

So, why am I explaining all of this to you? Well, if you are starting with bots, then don't underestimate that building a good chatbot is that simple. If you start looking into the examples you find online or websites that help you build a bot in a day, then they are mainly focused around the technology side of it. And that is true. Building a bot is something that can be accomplished in half an hour. But building a good bot takes time, not creating it, but thinking about it. I have spent some time building bots myself, and I would like to share some lessons learned with you before we start with the technology. And if you ever have a conversation with somebody who tells you that you need to build a bot and deploy it into production next week, then you can explain all the different parts of a conversation, and you can give valid reasons why bots should not be built in a week.

Lessons learned

It's not should I build a bot, but what is the outcome I want for the users of my product or service.

I've personally seen this a few times in enterprises. The CEO or CTO sees a keynote about bots and decides that their company should also have a bot. But there is no real business case that supports this. I recently was at a customer where the CTO said that the first department that had a bot in production could decide on the architecture, setup, technology, and so on. This had the impact that every department started experimenting with bots. Now, for the HR department or the IT department, there are plenty of business cases where a bot is a good idea. For HR, for instance, you could create a bot where people can ask questions about HR-related items instead of having somebody from the HR team be constantly spammed with questions in emails. But this also meant that the finance department started experimenting with bots. Now, if you ever find a good business case why a finance department that creates invoices should get a bot, then you can let me know because I do not see it.

What is the business outcome you want to drive?

This one is similar to the one earlier but more specific to the added value for the business. One of the most used examples is the helpdesk bot. And in my opinion, this is a very valid business case. A helpdesk agent always has to ask the same questions at the beginning of every call. Depending on how good the system is but they usually are something in the lines of: What's your name or userid? What's your type of PC? What application are you having an issue with? These similar questions are repetitive and can easily be automated by a bot. Even if the bot doesn't know the answer to the caller's problem, it still can collect the necessary data and hand over the conversation to a live person.

Is a conversational chatbot the best medium for your outcome?

If you have a site like Booking.com or Airbnb.com and a chatbot that explains to people that there are a certain amount of locations available and they have this feature, like two swimming pools and three bathrooms, then is that really what people want? If I want to go on a vacation, then I want to look at photos and search between options, not have a conversation with a bot that tells me what it sees in the picture. I want to see the photo myself.

Does your idea try to replace tasks that people love doing?

Every year, my wife plans a family trip with her entire family. All her cousins, nieces, uncles, and aunts join. She starts the preparation of this trip months in advance. On Friday, we leave at 6 o'clock. We arrive at 8. Then we are going to eat this as a meal. On Saturday, we are going to do this excursion. And so on. She loves doing it, not only the trip but also the planning of it. You can imagine that when I would build a bot that would plan the trip for her, she would not like the bot at all because it replaces a task that she loves doing.

Is the cost for using your chatbot-powered product or service less than the perceived value?

Remember that building bots take time. You must design, build, and test it, which means that for some applications, it would be useless to build a chatbot. Open your phone and go to the app store. There are hundreds of shopping list apps out there. Building a chatbot that would replace a shopping list app would, therefore, be a bad idea. The cost of building it would not be in reference to the value it would have afterward. Not to mention that building a chatbot for a shopping list is a hard task, as you can see from the example in Figure 8-2 that Scott Hanselman tweeted about.

With great power comes great responsibility.

Figure 8-2. *A shopping list bot that's not too smart*

Building an application or a website has a different impact on people than building a bot. It has to do with human nature. When talking to chatbots, we tend to view them as persons. We know they are not real, but we treat them differently than an application. If you build an app and it's terrible, then you go back, rebuild it, and ask the user to test it again after some time. With bots, it's not that simple. It's like with people, first impressions matter, and they don't go away over time. Therefore, this tip is all about test, test, and test again. But I don't mean the functionality of the bot. Of course, you need to test if it does what it needed to do. But also test the personality of the bot. There have been studies done where they let people have conversations with bots, and afterward, they would ask: so, how did you perceive the bot?

One constant thing was that we tend to give a bot a gender. People would not say: "Oh, I think it was amicable." No, they would say: "He/she was amicable." So, keep this in mind. If you give your bot a female name, then make sure that it at least talks as a female. I once created a bot that had a female name, and we were with seven men building it. Of course, when we let people test out the bot, they said: "It works... but still, there is something not quite right, but I cannot put my finger on it." Well, it turned out that it was the style of speech that the bot responded in. It was talking in a male form and not a female manner. So, with bots, sometimes the most subtle differences are the most important ones.

I hope these lessons I've learned over the years can help you along with your bot development. But there is even more, and we should also understand our users. Let's discuss some facts about them.

Facts

Fact 1: Users love buttons

Studies have been done that asked people what they used first if there was an option of rich controls, text, and voice, and this was the result:

- UI controls first: A button that says "Submit" is so much easier than a user typing "Submit".

- Text second: If a button is not possible, then typing is a valid alternative.

- Voice third: If the preceding options are not available, then people will resort to voice. An excellent example of this is driving a car. Then the preceding options are out of the equation, and people will not mind using their voice. That's the reason why Alexa, Siri, Cortana, and so on are not used heavily on desktops and laptops.

Fact 2: Users never say things the way you expect

If you start with natural language enhancement of your bot, it's quite easy to expect that a user asks the following question when you are building a bot for a real estate agency.

I want to find a house for sale that has 3 or 4 bedrooms, priced between $300 and $350 with a large garden, about 2000 square feet, preferably green, within 10 miles from my work which is in the city center, with a large garage and a backyard with a pool.

This question… said nobody ever. This is a query you would launch to your database because this is the data you need. When building out a language-understanding model, you would assume this is the data I need, so people will ask this question. But the opposite is true, and people will be more likely to ask this question:

I want to find a house.

Now it's up to your bot logic to ask additional questions to get the data you need—to see what is missing and to guide the user into telling you all the information you need.

Fact 3: Search can do wonders for bots

Search engines have come a long way since they first were born during the start period of the Internet. The bot doesn't specifically need to understand what the end user means. Their question can sometimes easily be solved by performing a search query. In later chapters, we will dig deeper into what I mean by this with a real-life example.

Fact 4: Not all bots need to have conversations

We don't need to make every bot complex with language understanding, different capabilities, and features. It can also be that a simple bot solves the business case. You can build a bot that only shows some buttons. And these buttons are all that's needed. It will never be a business requirement that your bot passes the Turing Test (`https://en.wikipedia.org/wiki/Turing_test`), and we should always be aware of the engineer's urge to overcomplicate things.

Fact 5: People get bored

One of the most challenging problems with software development is that the people using that software will get bored with it. In an enterprise context, this is less relevant than in a commercial setting, but it still is something to keep in mind. Facebook, for instance, has unique algorithms that make sure that your feed is always different. If you open Facebook, then your feed will always look different. This is done to avoid boredom of the product.

Take this into consideration when building bots. Give them some variation. It's not that much work to incorporate some variety on specific answers. Instead of letting the bot always say "Can I help you with something," incorporate different styles of the same question and randomize it. Utilizing this is called "the hook model" (Figure 8-3), and if you want to learn more about it, I can recommend you look deeper into it. It's invented by Nir Eyal (`https://en.wikipedia.org/wiki/Nir_Eyal`), and it goes pretty deep into how to engage people with your product.

Figure 8-3. *The hook model*

The technical side

Now that we know what things to take into consideration when building a bot, let's see how the architecture of a bot works. Microsoft has provided us with the Bot Framework for building bots. Your bot is just a web service. Like any other website out there, it lives on the Internet and uses APIs to send and receive information. The Bot Framework is a stack of tools and technology that is provided so that our life as a developer is made easier. Like any application, a bot can do the same things, read and write files, use a database, log errors, and so on. The only difference is that they communicate in a human-to-human conversational way.

157

Specific to Microsoft Teams, the Bot Framework will make sure that Teams forwards the messages of end users to your bot. When creating a bot, we need to specify that we are going to use Teams as a channel, and the communication between Teams and the Bot Framework will be taken care of for you. The thing we need to build is our bot, and we need to make sure that the Bot Framework can communicate with our bot. If you look at Figure 8-4, then you can see that the channel here would be Teams and that the Bot Framework will translate all that happens inside of Teams between your user and your bot into something that your application can understand.

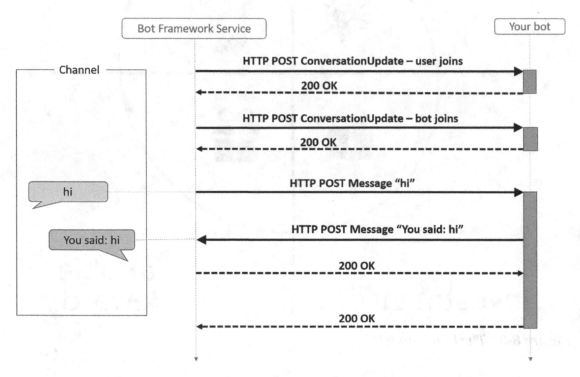

Figure 8-4. *Communication between the Bot Framework and your bot (source: Microsoft Documentation, https://docs.microsoft.com/en-us/azure/bot-service/bot-builder-basics?view=azure-bot-service-4.0&tabs=csharp)*

As you can easily see from the image, Bots are not using a new technology. They rely on HTTP messages being sent back and forth, and they contain JSON. The JSON sent over is quite big sometimes because it holds all the information needed, like information about the user and the bot, the channel, the text the user typed, and much more. Now don't confuse a channel in the Bot Framework with a channel in Teams. A channel in the Bot Framework is the application where you allow users to have conversations with your bot. This can be in Teams, but can also be a web page or even SMS or email. As you can see, there is a lot of communication between the Bot Framework and your bot for just two short sentences. Luckily, the framework takes care of most of this so that we don't need to.

Conclusion

In this topic, we learned that language and conversations have a lot of rules, and when you think about building bots, you should always keep these rules in the back of your head. The tips provided are lessons I learned from building bots; when you start building your first bot, then you will learn even more, and that's the only golden piece of information I can give you as the last tip. Just start building and playing around with bots. Set up a separate environment and learn and play with them. That's the best way to find out how you react to them. Show it to your colleagues and see what they think of it. The point I'm trying to make is don't be afraid. All the information in this chapter can be quite overwhelming. Still, once you get started, you will see that the pieces of the puzzle will fit together. Now enough with the theory of bots and chatbots, in the next chapter, we are going to dive straight into bot creation.

CHAPTER 9

Natural language processing bots

Now that we know all the different aspects of language that we must take into consideration, we can start with building our Teams-integrated bots. Bot features are used very extensively in Teams, and the Bot Framework is heavily used for Teams development, not only to build chatbots but also for other functionalities. This is because the Bot Framework works with authenticated HTTP Post calls between your code, Azure, and Teams. This secure way of communication allowed the Teams team to reuse the technology to get other features working as well. One might say that bots are used even more inside of Teams than Tabs. In this chapter, we will go deeper into building NLP (natural language processing) bots and how they work.

Proof of concept

One item on my list that I want to share with you is how you can easily set up a bot in Teams when you are doing a proof of concept of a bot. I regularly do this during meetings with customers so that they can have a feel for how the bot will act and respond. This allows for the conversation to be on another level and makes the discussion about the features that a bot should have much easier. For this, we are going to create a QnA bot. QnA stands for Question and Answer and is the quickest way to get started with Bots in general. QnA maker is based on already proven language understanding models. Once we get deeper into language understanding, we can start making use of LUIS to build our own models. LUIS stands for Language Understanding Intelligence Service and is part of the cognitive services that Microsoft provides. But more on that later. To get started, navigate to `www.qnamaker.ai/` and sign in. QnA maker allows for a no-code experience to get started with bots. Once signed in, you should see an almost empty screen. This is because we haven't created any knowledge bases yet. The goal of QnA maker is to allow

© Rick Van Rousselt 2021
R. Van Rousselt, *Pro Microsoft Teams Development*, https://doi.org/10.1007/978-1-4842-6364-8_9

you to have something that is called a knowledge base. This knowledge base will hold questions and answers. When the users ask one of these questions to your bot, then your bot, in turn, will call the QnA maker API. This API will then search the knowledge base for the question, and it will respond with the correct answer. Now don't think that this is just a table where you have a question column and an answer column next to it. The natural language model in place will also provide an answer if the question is asked similarly but not the same. An example of this is that while I entered the question "How do I set my Outlook signature" and a user asks the question "What would be in my signature," then the AI model behind QnA maker is smart enough to match those two questions together and will provide the same answer.

Let's start by creating our first knowledge base. Click "Create a knowledge base." The first thing we are required to do is have a QnA service in Azure. This QnA service is just a key that Azure provides and is used for billing when you heavily use the QnA service. There is a free QnA service pricing tier that will get you along for a long way. But you do need an Azure subscription for it, even when it's free. It used to be different, but I guess that Microsoft needs to know who is using their services, and for this reason, you need an Azure subscription that identifies you with a phone number and a credit card, even when it is a free one. If you don't have an Azure subscription, you can create a free one; this comes with a $200 free credit to test things, but more importantly, there are also a lot of services that provide a free option so that you can test them, like the QnA service we are going to use. If you click the create service, you will be navigated to the Azure Portal, where we can start filling in the required fields to create our service. Fill in the fields with the following information:

- Name: ProTeamsDevQnA (or choose another unique name).

- Subscription: Select your subscription here.

- Pricing tier: Choose the F0 tier which is the free one.

- Resource Group: Create a new resource group and name it ProTeamsDev.

- Resource Group Location: Choose the location that you prefer. For a QnA service, this is not important, but when we start with LUIS, then the location is important because there you use different URLs for different regions. More info can be found here: `https://westus.dev.cognitive.microsoft.com/docs/services`.

- Azure Search pricing tier: QnA maker uses Azure search to store its data; again, choose the free tier.

- Azure search location: For optimal performance, you should select the same region as the resource group. For development purposes, you are not going to notice that one service resides in another region than another service, but in production, this might be the case. Or if you have data constraints like all the data must reside in Europe or the United States like some enterprises do, then this becomes important.

- App name: QnA maker is an API, and that API should have a URL, so this is what you select here. Your users are never going to see this URL, so pick something unique.

- Website location: Again, pick the same region as for the other services.

- App insights: Enable and choose the same location as the other services.

When you are done filling out the information, click the create button. The QnA service and all required resources like Azure Search and the website are going to be created. Microsoft has made it very easy to select it, so, once completed, we can close the Azure Portal and go back to the QnA Maker page. Refresh the QnA maker page so that it can find your subscription and key and select those in the QnA creation page. For the language, we are going to stick with English. If you open the drop-down, you will see which languages are currently supported, and there are already quite a few supported. Some also support the chit-chat and extraction features. Now, these chit-chat and extraction features are going to make our lives a whole lot easier. Chit-chat is an already created question and answer set by Microsoft that allows your bot to respond to basic small talk conversational questions like "When is your birthday?". These already populated questions are one of the items that make our proof of concept set up so fast. It would already take you a few hours to create these basic questions that any user testing out your bot is undoubtedly going to ask.

As you can see, you can select different personalities. This is, as we discussed in the previous chapter, vital because it allows you to give your bot a personality. When working in a professional environment, I usually take the "Professional" or the "Friendly" personality. Still, you are free to experiment with the different styles of answering that match the different personalities.

Don't forget to name your knowledge base, and as the last part, we are going to automatically have premade questions and answers added to the QnA service. We could manually add questions and answers after creation, but we can also have the service automatically extract them from several sources if they are in the form of Frequently Asked Questions. This can be a web page or an Excel or a Word document. In this case, I already prepared a web page available for you to extract so that you don't need to add questions and answers manually. In the "populate your KB" field fill in the following URL: https://aibotworkshop.z6.web.core.windows.net/. This functionality will, when you click create, scan the web page and extract the questions and answers. Now, if you visit this website, you can already see that there are nine questions and answers in there. Yet in the QnA maker, there will be ten questions and answers. This is because the QnA service downloads the page, and it just scans the HTML of the page for headers. There are ten headers on the page, but one is hidden with CSS. A simple "display:none" hides the last question. Take this into account when you are using this service. If you have an existing FAQ, but some questions are hidden because they aren't relevant anymore, then those will still get picked up by the QnA service and added to your knowledge base. When everything is filled in, then click the create button, and your knowledge base is going to get generated, and you should have a similar outcome like in Figure 9-1.

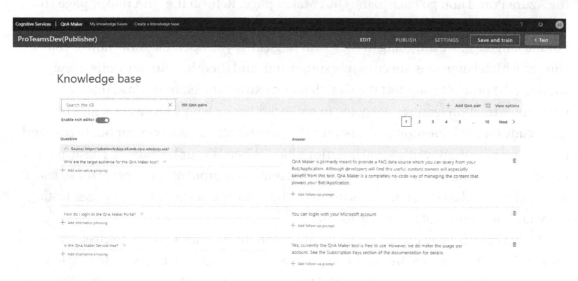

Figure 9-1. *QnA maker knowledge base with populated information*

When our knowledge is generated, we see that we have two sources defined. One is coming from the website with the FAQ on, and another is coming from selecting the chit-chat personality. Let's first test what we have now. If you click the big blue test button in the top-right corner, a chat box opens up, and you can test out the QnA bot we just created. We can test both sources. If you type "How do I log in to the QnA Maker Portal?" which is an exact copy from the website, you should get the answer "You can login with your Microsoft account." But let's face it, this is probably not what the user is going to ask. So let's type in something similar, yet different. "Can I log in to the QnA portal?" As you can see, we get the same result back. This is the language model that accomplishes this. It detects what we mean and tries to match that into a question that it knows. If you click the inspect link right under the answer, then we can find out why it thought that this was the correct answer. You should see a screen like Figure 9-2, where you can see the confidence score. This score tells us how certain the QnA service was that the answer was correct.

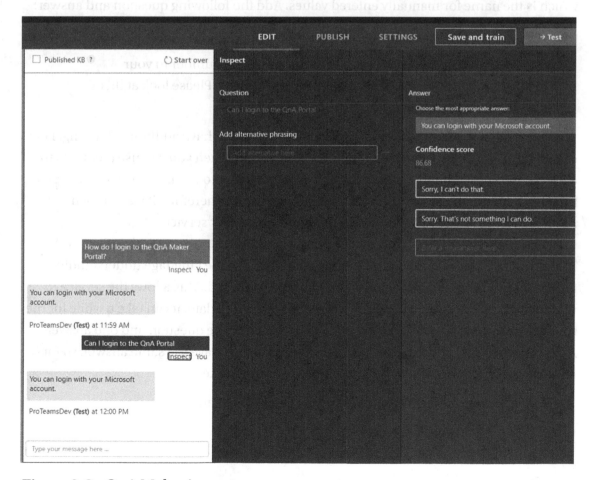

Figure 9-2. *QnA Maker inspects answers*

If you look at the first question we asked, which was an exact copy, we get a score back of 100, meaning it was 100% sure that this was the answer. The second question we asked was 86% sure that the correct answer was sent back. Now, why is this important? Well, later on, when we start implementing our own logic into our bot, we can take the confidence score to apply logic to our bot. If we get an 80% confident result back, we can provide the user with the answer. But let's say the service is only 40% sure or less, well, then we can take an alternate path in our bot logic and ask additional questions to the user before providing them with an answer. You can test out some of the chit-chat questions as well. I am confident that with these few steps you are already positive with the outcome and that this is already something that you can use during a meeting to demonstrate the power of chatbots. Now let's take this one step further.

Add an additional question and answer manually. You can do this by closing the Test blade and by clicking the "Add QnA pair" button. This will create a third source, editorial, which is the name for manually entered values. Add the following question and answer:

- Q: How do I set my Outlook signature?

- A: At our company it's policy to add your phone number to your
  Outlook signature as well as a link to our website. Please look at this
  link for an example.

We could also add metadata. This is to allow our bot to have additional filtering. Let's say we have two different answers to the same question. Then you can use metadata to allow for additional filtering. In this case, we are not going to use it, but you can imagine that there are lots of use cases where this could be useful; therefore, it was a much-requested feature that was later added onto the QnA maker service.

Now after entering this Question and Answer pair, be sure to press the "Save and Train" button. This not only saves your data, but it trains the language understanding algorithm model with the new information you just entered. This allows the service to understand the question. Therefore, when entering lots of data, it can take a while for the training to be complete. As you can see, we just entered one question and one answer. A best practice is to add multiple alternate questions that have the same answer, so for completeness, we should also have additional questions like

- Is there a company policy regarding Outlook signatures?

- What must be in my signature?

As you can see, generally, it's the same question just asked differently; you should end up with something like in Figure 9-3.

Figure 9-3. *QnA maker service with additional questions and an answer*

You should also be aware that the QnA maker service has the option now to add follow-up questions. This is something we had to program ourselves in the back-end code, but now it's made available right from the portal. This feature can come in handy sometimes if you need to ask the user for something before you can provide the correct answer. We won't be using it in this example, but you should know that it's possible. Another item that you should be aware of is the existence of an API for this portal. We are doing everything manually now in the UI, but we could also call an API that does this for us. We can create Question and Answer pairs, create new knowledge bases, and update knowledge bases, all from code. The documentation for this is well hidden. It's not where you would generally suspect it to be on www.docs.microsoft.com, but on a separate website: https://westus.dev.cognitive.microsoft.com/docs/services/5a93fcf85b 4ccd136866eb37/operations/5ac266295b4ccd1554da75ff. The documentation is quite extensive, and you even get a console to test your API calls. The reason why you would need the API is the same as with any other service you use, automation. Let's say, for instance, you don't want to give another person maintaining this knowledge base access to Azure or this portal. Then, you could create your own application to maintain this knowledge base. Or if the questions and answers are managed in another system, like a public website or SharePoint, then you could keep them in sync by writing a sync job. I can recommend using Postman and the Postman collection to see how the QnA maker back-end API service works: https://github.com/selectedtech/Samples.

Now back to our proof of concept. Showing this during a meeting where you have a working bot in five minutes is, of course, cool. But we cannot expect everyone to get access to the QnA maker portal and test out our bot. Therefore, we can easily surface it in Teams. First, we must publish our bot. We have trained our bot, and it knows the new questions and answer we added, but it also must be published. If you click the big publish button in the top-right corner, you will get the opportunity to publish this version. QnA maker works with a test version and a published version. This allows us to add additional questions and answers and test them out while not impacting the current version that is going to be used by our bot. Once publishing is completed, you will get a "Create bot" button. It will also already reveal what the endpoint is to the QnA maker service we have just created and how we can request an answer from it with a question. If you select the curl option, you can test this out immediately. Curl is a small little program for executing web requests, and if you have the Windows 10 1706 build or newer, it's automatically installed in Windows. Open up a command line and copy-paste the request; don't forget to change the question and execute the request. This will call the QnA maker service you just published and will return the answer and some additional data like the score in Figure 9-4.

```
C:\Users\RickVanRousselt>curl -X POST https://proteamsdevqna.azurewebsites.net/qnamaker/knowledgebases/1b7521c0-4914-448
3-833e-3d474f4fc84a/generateAnswer -H "Authorization: EndpointKey e8c4e1a2-ecc4-4d68-bd2c-25d2b44f6300" -H "Content-type
: application/json" -d "{'question':'how do i set my outlook signature'}"
{"answers":[{"questions":["How do I set my Outlook signature","Is there a company policy regarding outlook signatures?",
"What must be in my signature"],"answer":"At our company it's policy to add your phone number to your Outlook signature
as well as a link to our website. Please look at this link for an example.","score":100.0,"id":101,"source":"Editorial",
"metadata":[],"context":{"isContextOnly":false,"prompts":[]}}],"debugInfo":null,"activeLearningEnabled":false}
C:\Users\RickVanRousselt>
```

Figure 9-4. *Using curl in the Windows command line asking a question to QnA maker and getting an answer back*

Now there are plenty of options to test a request; you could also use Postman or Fiddler or any other tool capable of executing HTTP post requests. It's only on rare occasions that you are going to need to test the endpoint this way. Usually, you can detect if something is wrong from how your bot using this service reacts. I've needed it a few times because using the free version, you are limited to a maximum number of requests, and it has happened that I reached this limit. This, executing the request manually, helps out because you get an error message back that you have reached the limit of the service you are using. Once you tested out the API with curl, it's time to click the "Create bot" button. This will take you back to the Azure Portal and send you to the create bot blade. Fill in the required information, make sure you take the free tier, and click create. You can choose between C# and Node.js as a base for your bot. What will happen in the background is that Azure will use a code template, configure that with your settings, and will deploy the code into an app instance, which we can download later as a starting point like described in Chapter 3. Only this time, instead of a bot that echos back what we type, we are getting a bot that can actually answer questions and will be able to do some small talk.

As you might have noticed, the app service plan that is already created is the one created for the QnA service endpoint. If you don't want your subscription to cost a lot of money, then after you click create, I would recommend that you navigate to this app service and lower its pricing tier. It defaults to an S1 instance, but you can easily go to a B instance. Changing the pricing tier can be located under the "Scale Up" blade when selecting the app service plan, like in Figure 9-5. If you are using the free trial of Azure or if you have an MSDN license, then you have nothing to worry about. The S1 instance is cheap enough to keep you under your spending limit.

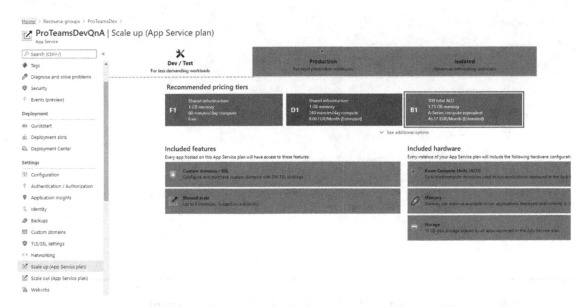

Figure 9-5. *Change the pricing tier of the app service plan*

Once our bot is created, open it up in the Azure Portal. Let's first test if the bot still works here. Click the "Test in Web Chat" blade and type in our test question again. As a reminder, our test question is, "How do I set my outlook signature?". We should get the answer back the same as in the test blade in QnA maker or as in the curl request (Figure 9-6).

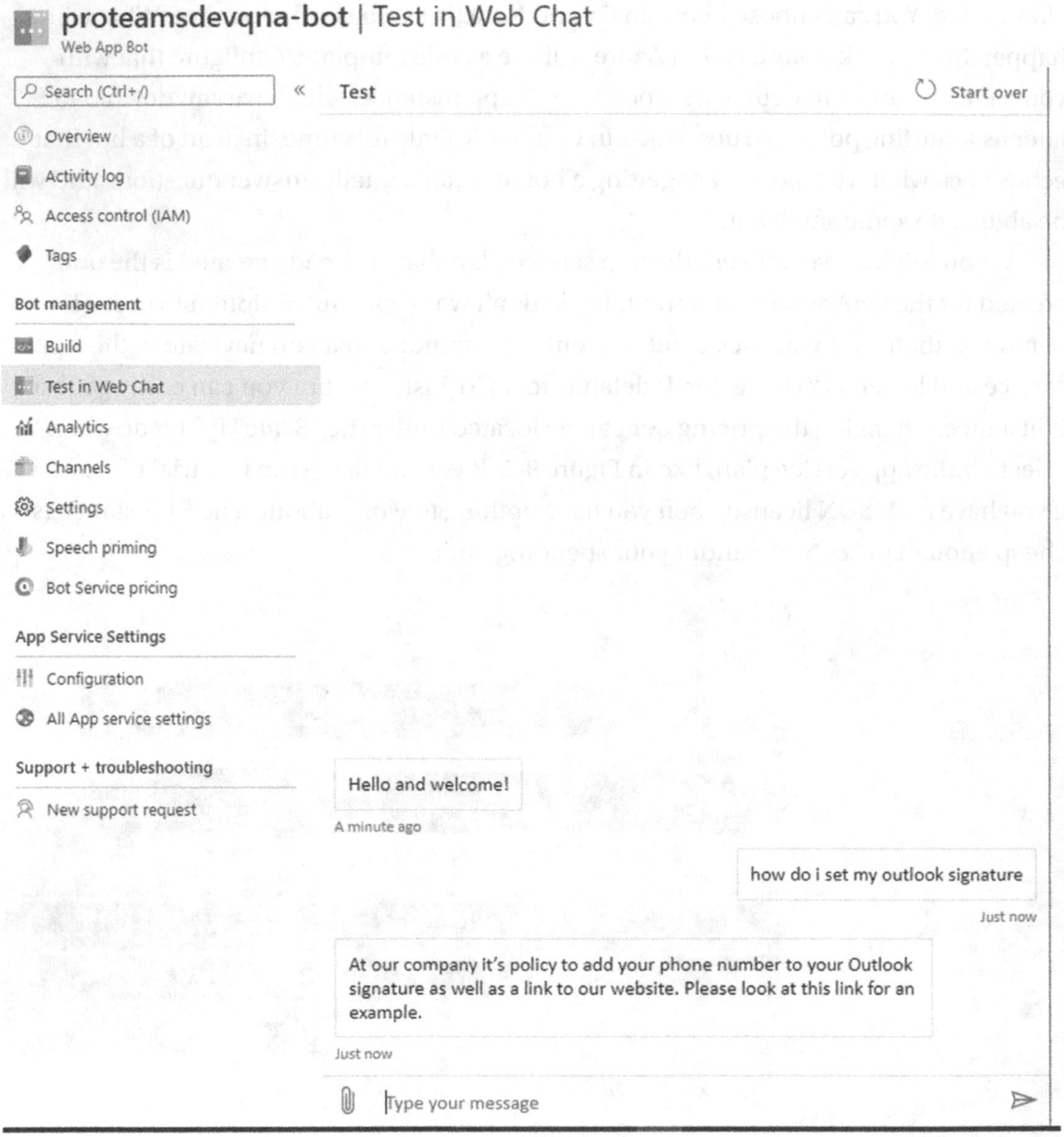

proteamsdevqna-bot | Test in Web Chat
Web App Bot

Search (Ctrl+/)	« Test
Overview	
Activity log	
Access control (IAM)	
Tags	
Bot management	
Build	
Test in Web Chat	
Analytics	
Channels	
Settings	
Speech priming	
Bot Service pricing	
App Service Settings	
Configuration	
All App service settings	
Support + troubleshooting	
New support request	

Start over

Hello and welcome!

A minute ago

how do i set my outlook signature

Just now

At our company it's policy to add your phone number to your Outlook signature as well as a link to our website. Please look at this link for an example.

Just now

Type your message

Figure 9-6. Testing our bot in the Test blade in the Azure Portal

Once we are satisfied that our bot still works, then it's time to activate it inside of Microsoft Teams. Click the Channels blade and under "Add a featured channel," you can select Microsoft Teams. Default-only webchat is turned on. You can see this as a security setting. Unless you configure a channel, your bot is not capable of communication through this channel, because it could be that your bot doesn't have specific code to work with a specific channel. In the case of Teams, there is no specific code required, at least not for the limited capability that the bot has now. So select the Teams channel, agree to the terms, and click save. You have now activated your QnA bot for usage in Teams. The other tabs like "Calling" which is used for media bots that we are going to tackle in one of the next chapters and the "Publish" tab, which, besides linking to the docs, has no additional value we don't need. Now the trick here is to click the cancel button, which navigates us back to the Channels blade default view, or you can navigate to another blade and back again. If you now click the link behind Microsoft Teams, a new tab will open asking you to open the Teams client. This is a deep link that navigates immediately to a chat with a user, and that user is the bot you just created. In the Teams client, test the bot with our test question, and you should get a response back like in Figure 9-7.

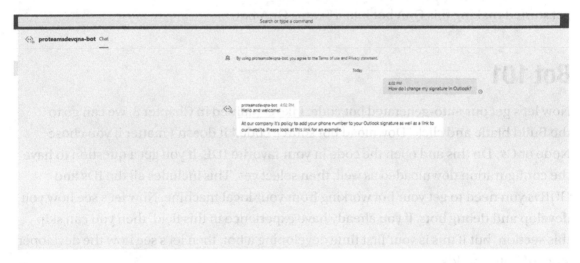

Figure 9-7. *Testing our FAQ bot in Teams*

Congratulations, you have just created your first Teams bot, and it's capable of answering the questions from a website and having some small talk conversation, and it responds to additional questions you manually entered. A small tip I can give you is if another user wants to chat with the bot, then they must search for it to start a conversation. If you type the name, the user will not find it. The trick is to use the Microsoft App ID used by the bot. You can find this in Azure under the settings blade of your bot. Then people can use that ID in the search bar of Teams, and then if they filter on people, they can see the bot. You can see an example of this in Figure 9-8.

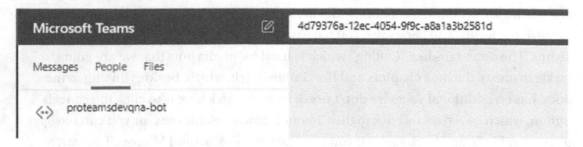

Figure 9-8. *Search for a Teams bot with the ID, not with the name*

The reason for this is that we have activated the bot in our Tenant and we activated the Teams channel. But we haven't created a Teams app package for it. So for a proof of concept or a quick test, this is perfect, but not if you want to roll it out to your users. Let's get started making this QnA bot into a Teams QnA bot.

Bot 101

Now let's get our auto-generated bot code. Like explained in Chapter 3, we can go to the Build blade and click "Download bot source code." It doesn't matter if you chose Node or C#. Do this and open the code in your favorite IDE. If you get a question to have the configuration downloaded as well, then select yes. This includes all the IDs and GUIDs you need to get your bot working from your local machine. Now let's see how you develop and debug bots. If you already have experience in this field, then you can skip this section, but if this is your first time developing a bot, then let's see how the developer story of bots unfolds.

C#

After downloading the code, take your time to explore the solution provided. As you can see, this is a .NET Core app that has only a single controller. This controller is our API that is called by the Bot Framework. All traffic that your bot generates goes through this controller. With all the different types of traffic like a chat, a user typing, a user entering a channel, and so on, this would get one big messy pile of code. But as you can see, it's clean code. The Bot Framework together with dependency injection takes care of that for us. In the startup.cs class, we can see that it's using dependency injection to load the correct bot when our application starts. Now, with this example, you only have one bot. But it can easily be that you have multiple bots in the same code base. Dependency injection helps with keeping your code loosely coupled which in turn increases code reusability and maintainability. That's why our controller has such clean code. It expects a class that implements an IBot interface, but it's not hard coded in the controller which one. This will be injected at runtime by our code in the startup class. If you want to know more about how the Bot Framework works with C#, I can recommend reading the Microsoft documentation on it (`https://docs.microsoft.com/en-us/azure/bot-service/bot-builder-basics`).

The main thing you should remember is the flow that the bot follows. A request is made to your bot. This goes through the controller class, which in turn calls the QnABot class in this case (configured in the startup class). You can see the flow through the different classes in Figure 9-9.

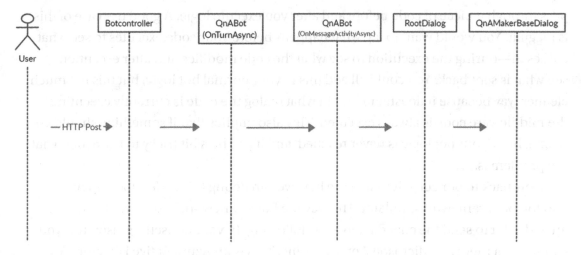

Figure 9-9. *The flow that the bot follows when a user asks a question*

In the QnABot class, here, the framework is nice enough to already split up what is happening for us. You can see that different actions, like members added or message received, call different pieces of code. In this example, there are only three activities configured with the overrides, but there are around 14 available should you need others. The last part is dialogs. We can initiate different dialogs according to different needs. If you check out this example, only when a message is received is the RootDialog executed. As you can see, when a user has been added, we just send back some text, but we could easily change this to also kick off a new dialog. Dialogs in the Bot Framework are where we are going to add our bot logic. You should view dialogs as a way to manage your conversational flow. They are like specific functions of a conversation and can be stacked on top of each other. In this example, the conversation starts in the rootdialog, and this is placed on top of the stack as the active dialog. Now this doesn't do much except call another dialog, the QnAMakerBaseDialog when it gets called. The QnAMakerBaseDialog is then placed on top of the rootdialog as the active dialog. This calls the QnA maker service we created; now this class looks very simple, but the actual logic is already built for us and provided in the Bot Framework. If you look at the QnAMakerDialog that is a base for the QnAMakerBaseDialog, then you will find that there are several steps that this dialog does before returning the answer to the user. Once completed, the base dialog will call the EndDialogAsync method which closes the dialog and pops it off the stack.

To make things even more complex, especially when you start with bots, there is also something called middleware. This code is executed between the adapter, in this case our controller, and the QnABot class. Middleware is a way to have the conversation pass through a piece of code before and after you execute logic. A good use case of this is logging. You would want to log what happens before your code executes to see what comes in—during the execution to see what the code modifies and after execution to see what is sent back. You could all add this to your normal bot logic, but this is a much cleaner way because it doesn't matter in what dialog the code is currently executing; the middleware code is always executed. This also implies that if something should go wrong, here, your bot logic is never reached, and it can be a bit tricky to figure out what the problem is.

Now back to our code, let's first see how we can debug this code. Open up ngrok and the Bot Framework emulator. The way the Bot Framework knows what to use as an endpoint to send the chat data to is the following. In your appsettings.json file, you can see that there is a Microsoft App ID setting. This is an Azure Active Directory App registration that was created for us when we created the bot. By using this ID, the Bot Framework goes to Azure, authenticates, and checks the configuration in the Azure Portal of your bot. If you go to the settings blade of your bot, you can see that there is a messaging endpoint configured. This is what the Bot Framework uses to send out the JSON it gets from its channels. This endpoint should be pointing toward the web app you created. Now there are two ways of testing your bot with the emulator. We can either change the configuration in Azure to have it point to another URL we get from ngrok or we can connect with it locally. I usually go through the Bot Framework and almost never locally, but they both have their positive and negative points. If you want to connect locally, just remove the App ID and App password from the configuration file, fire up a debug session, and connect the Bot Framework emulator by entering the localhost URL, port, and /api/messages because that's our controller we need to hit. If you want to change the configuration in Azure, then fire up ngrok, get a URL with the command `ngrok http 3978 -host-header="localhost:3978"` which will provide you with an endpoint, and replace the messaging endpoint with this URL. Again, don't forget to add the route to your controller. A little tip, save the original URL somewhere because you are going to need it when you want to point back to your web app. Now, connect in either way the Bot Framework emulator with your bot and see if we can ask our test question again. Normally, you should see a response like in Figures 9-10 and 9-11. If you put breakpoints in your code, you should also be able to hit those breakpoints.

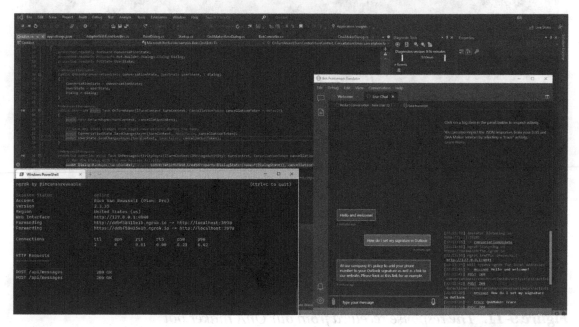

Figure 9-10. *Running ngrok, the emulator, and Visual Studio to debug the QnA maker bot*

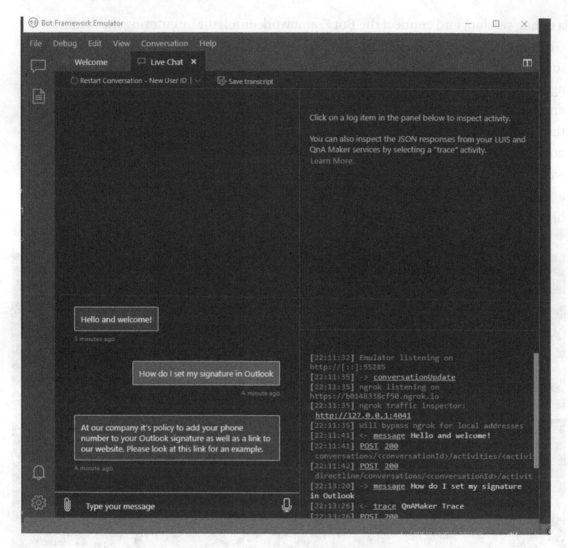

Figure 9-11. *The response received from our QnA maker bot*

These are the basics of Bots in C# and should give you a basic understanding on how the Bot Framework works. There is enough to Bots to fill an entire other book so if you want to go further with developing bots and chatbots, I can recommend you start with the AI school from Microsoft to get started: https://aischool.microsoft.com/en-us/conversational/learning-paths/getting-started-with-azure-bot-framework.

Node

After downloading the code, take your time to explore the solution provided. As you can see, this uses some packages from Microsoft like the botbuilder framework. This will do all the heavy lifting for us. Since we now know that bots are just APIs, we need something to manage the requests going back and forward. This is where the restify package comes into play. One thing I learned with developing with Node is that whatever you want to accomplish, there is always a package that does it for you. So, next time you need to do something, make sure that you check first if somebody didn't create a package for it already. The structure of the solution is following almost the same logic as with a C# application. When you chat with the bot, the Bot Framework sends that information to your code. This enters in the index.js file where you see the adapter get created. So whenever your bot code is called, this will route the information to the correct bot depending on the endpoint. Now we only have one bot in this solution which is the QnABot. The QnABot is where the framework helps us make the differentiation between the different actions that can take place, like a new message or a new member added to the conversation. The QnABot extends the ActivityHandler which is provided by the Bot Framework and provides us with lots of different methods to override that can differentiate in the communication that comes into our bot. This in turn calls the rootDialog and which in turn calls the qnamakerBase dialog. It all looks very similar to C#, and the Bot Framework Team has made a good job of keeping both methods of development aligned. This helps with understanding how the flow and the Bot Framework work. If you are a Node developer and you have a conversation with a C# developer about the Bot Framework, then you both use the same concepts and flows. Using the same concepts and flows as other language developers, also helps if you are having an issue and you are looking for a solution online, then don't just dismiss code that is not written in the same language. It could just be the same problem you are having that somebody who writes code in a different language is having.

To get started with the debugging of this code, you first need to install the missing packages; this can be done with `npm install`. Next up is starting a debug session. Now don't use npm start like the readme file says, but just press F5 and select Node.js as an engine. This will allow you to set a breakpoint later. Let's fire up ngrok with the following command: `ngrok http 3978 -host-header="localhost:3978"`. In the Azure Portal, go to the settings blade of your bot and change the URL here to point to the URL you received from ngrok. Open the bot emulator and connect with your bot. The endpoint URL is the same as you entered in the Azure configuration, and don't forget to add your

Client ID and secret. This can be found in the .env file in the solution. After connecting to our bot, test out the bot with the same test question as before, and you should get the answer from our QnA maker service back like in Figure 9-10. If you set a breakpoint in the rootdialog, you should also be hitting that breakpoint (Figure 9-12).

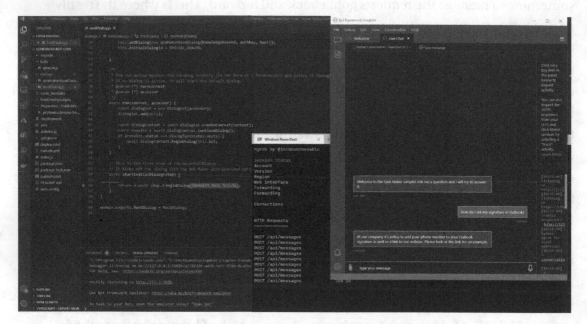

Figure 9-12. *Running ngrok, the Bot Framework emulator, and Visual Studio Code to debug the QnA maker bot*

Recap

With this small intro into how the Bot Framework works, we have covered enough to get started with Bots. We have seen how to test our bot and debug our code—both for C# and for Node.js. But we haven't touched Teams yet. Let's see how to Teamify our bot.

Teamify our bot

We have our QnA bot ready which calls our QnA maker service. But how do we get that into Teams? The simplest way is to use App Studio, because we are missing a Teams package that we can upload containing a manifest that will give Teams the information it needs to add this bot to our tenant.

Open App Studio in Teams and create a new package. Fill in all the required information on the first tab, and in the bot tab, select set up an existing bot. This is because we already build our bot; we just want it to be visible in a nice way in Teams now. The way Teams identifies your bot is with the Client ID—the one we also used to connect the Bot Framework emulator to test our bot. There are a lot of options we can choose that our bot is capable of. We don't need any of them. The only thing specific to this bot is that we can use it in a certain scope. Same as with Tabs, you can have a bot surface in a personal scope, a group scope, or a Team scope. Let's take the Team scope because we would like to ask the questions inside of the channel. I have added an example of the Teams package, so if you want to see how the manifest looks like, or what I filled in, then you can always unzip the package and check it out. If you are wondering why I created two, that's because I have a C# version and a Node version of the QnA bot. But they both connect to the same back-end service and perform the same tasks, so if you have just one, that's perfect. If you do want to have the two bots running in your environment, then make sure they have different IDs. You can't have different Teams apps installed in your tenant with the same ID. After creating the Teams app package or adjusting the one provided to your bot, install it in the environment.

Now that we created and installed our QnA bot into Teams, we can chat with our QnA bot in Teams. If you still have your debug session running, you can test it out. If not, then don't forget to update the URL in Azure again if you have restarted ngrok. When we add the bot to a Team, we can at-mention it and ask it our test question. You should see the same result as in Figure 9-13. Now this is already a perfectly working bot we can use in Teams. If we should point our Azure bot configuration back to the original URL of our web app, we have a working bot in Teams. If the bot needs to know more information, we can update the QnA maker service with new questions and answers, publish that, and our bot is automatically updated. Be aware that not all questions are going to get answered correctly. It could be that the QnA maker service cannot find a correct answer. This is because when you ask a bot a question in a channel, you have to at-mention it. This means that the name of the bot also gets sent over as a part of the question. If your question is long enough like in Figure 9-13, then the model of the QnA maker service can figure out the correct answer. But if you would just send "Hi," then it will not find the correct answer. We will discuss how to remove the at-mention out of the question in the next chapter.

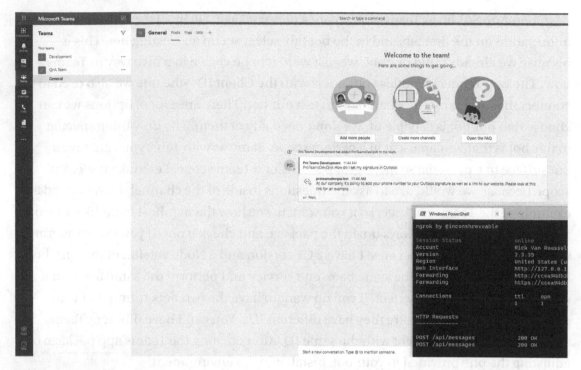

Figure 9-13. *Our QnA bot running in Teams and answering to the questions asked*

Now before we do that, first, let's add some Teams-specific code to our bot. The Teams integration with the Bot Framework has been around for some time, but it used to be separate packages, which were always difficult to add and maintain. Now not anymore. Teams has become a first-class citizen of the Bot Framework, and interacting with Teams, if our bot is deployed into Teams, is built into the framework.

Let's open up our QnABot class; as I already mentioned, the differences between C# and Node are not that big when working with the Bot Framework. Both have an implementation of the ActivityHandler. This turn handler is responsible for handling all the different activities that can come into our code from a bot. For Teams, we have access to a greater set of activities that can come into our code, for instance, when a Team is renamed or when a channel is created. We would like the option for our bot to know such things. Let's change the ActivityHandler to the TeamsActivityHandler and add an additional method that will handle the event when a channel is renamed.

C#

```
    protected override Task OnTeamsChannelRenamedAsync(ChannelIn
    fo channelInfo, TeamInfo teamInfo, ITurnContext<IConversation
    UpdateActivity> turnContext,
CancellationToken cancellationToken)
{
    turnContext.SendActivityAsync(MessageFactory.Text($"You
    have renamed this channel to {channelInfo.Name}"),
    cancellationToken).GetAwaiter().GetResult();
    return base.OnTeamsChannelRenamedAsync(channelInfo, teamInfo,
     turnContext, cancellationToken);
}
```

Node

```
this.onTeamsChannelRenamedEvent(async (channelInfo, teamInfo,
turnContext, next) => {
    await turnContext.sendActivity('You have renamed this channel!
    to.' + channelInfo.name);
});
```

When you add a channel to your team and rename it, your bot should update you with the correct information like in Figure 9-14.

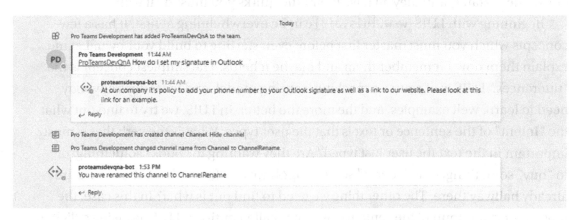

Figure 9-14. *Our QnA bot is aware that a channel is renamed in Teams*

As you can see, with this small adjustment, we can access Teams-specific data in our bot. This can come in very handy. But remember, if you want your bot to surface in different channels, then you are going to take this into account, because like in this example, a channel rename is not possible in a chat box on a website. If you plan to make a specific Teams bot, then I recommend you take advantage of these additional handlers provided. But if you want to surface your bot in lots of places, then try to keep it as generic as possible.

Next steps

We are not going to go deeper into natural language processing bots because this would sidetrack us for too long. But I do want to give you some additional tips and tricks and some general guidance on where you can go next from here.

One of the natural flows of a bot life cycle is that one day, when your QnA bot is becoming more and more heavily used, it is just not manageable anymore. You have too many questions and answers which are bringing you closer to the limits of the service. Or your questions are too similar and are having a bad influence on your model which in turn returns the wrong answers. When this happens, it is time to move from QnA maker to LUIS. As mentioned, LUIS (Language Understanding Intelligence Service) allows you to create more complex models. It still follows the machine learning models that Microsoft has programmed into this. When you find that this doesn't even suit your needs anymore, then it will be time to create your own machine learning models that can do natural language processing. I have been in different projects that were in either one of these states, and they all have their little quirks you must deal with.

Beginning with LUIS (`www.luis.ai/`) can be overwhelming at first. It has a few concepts which you must master first before even starting to build your own. Let me explain them how I remember them and maybe it helps. The simplest concept is the "utterances." LUIS is of course a machine learning model, and what does anybody need to learn, well examples, and the more the better. In LUIS, we try to find out what the "Intent" of the sentence or text is that the user types. What is the verb that is most important in the text the user just typed? Are they wanting to "book" something, or to "buy" something, or to "report" something? If we can figure this out, then we are already halfway there. The other thing we need to find out is what? In this case, the most important noun of the sentence, which is called entity in LUIS. Booking a flight or booking a hotel? It's the same verb but different noun, which is equally important to find out what the user really wants. All of these things we need to define in LUIS and we do that by giving it example sentences. So let's say we want to "Schedule a meeting," then we would have an intent of scheduling and an entity of meeting. Once we add those, we need to give as many example sentences of scheduling a meeting but phrased in a different way, like "plan a Teams call." The user wants the same but said it in a different manner. Figuring this out is a process that can take a while. It is also best that you start small. Remember the previous chapter, there is no need to pass the Turing test. Start off with one intent, or even two, and work your way up from there. So to sum up the differences, we can say that

- Utterances are what a user says.

- Intents are what a user means.

- Entities are what to extract.

On a technical level, LUIS is again a web service which we call from our code like the QnA maker service. There are packages available for C# and Node like for the QnA that will do the heavily lifting for us, call the service with the text of the user, and return an answer. But in the case of LUIS, you will not configure answers in the service. You will get the entity and intent discovered by LUIS back. From this point, it's all up to you. That's why my advice is to keep it simple. You must program responses or actions depending on the business case for your bot for all the intents and entities that you put in. Otherwise, what would be the point of adding them? And that takes time. Once you have played around with LUIS, I can highly recommend using something that is called dispatch (`https://docs.microsoft.com/en-us/azure/bot-service/bot-builder-tutorial-dispatch`). Dispatch is a little node package that the Bot Framework Team created to have multiple QnA models and LUIS models linked together in one bot. It scans your LUIS model and your QnA model and creates a LUIS model on top of that. This LUIS model that sits above your models is the one you call with the chat message of the user. This model then knows what is in which of your two models and redirects the code to the correct one to handle the incoming message. This is especially useful when you start to have multiple bots. It's very annoying for users to go to different bots for different purposes. They already have a different app on their phone for every different thing; bots should be better at this. Dispatch can help you create the idea of one bot that you surface in different channels, but in the back end, it can be that there are two, three, or more bots linked together.

When your bot outgrows all these technologies or the use case you have cannot be covered with these prepackaged services, then it will be time to turn into a data scientist and start building your own machine learning and Artificial Intelligence models. If you want to know when it's time to make the switch, this article from Microsoft explains it very extensively: https://docs.microsoft.com/en-us/azure/architecture/data-guide/technology-choices/natural-language-processing. The one thing I can say is that these projects are not as simple and fast as our proof of concept that we started out with. There are so many factors to take into consideration when building your own NLP models that sometimes a word can trigger a crash of the entire application. I once was part of a project where they created their own NLP model which we hooked up to Outlook. The emails of a specific insurance department were then fed into the NLP model and all the documentation they had gathered through the years about insurance. When they got a mail, the goal was to have the model be smart enough to propose an answer to the incoming mail which would help the person in the insurance department spend less time searching for answers in their old mails or in their documentation. The model worked quite well, until one day somebody got a mail that had the word "Snow chains" in it. This caused a memory overflow in the Apache Spark cluster where the model ran, and it took a whole day to get it back online. Until this day, the error is still in the model, and they cannot find the reason why a simple word like this triggers an error in the NLP model that crashes the system. I would like to end this chapter with a piece of advice. Start small and check out the chatbot conversation framework (Figure 9-15). The chatbot conversation framework states that if you build your bot for a closed domain, meaning for a small portion of information, and you can get your data out of a repository instead of generating an answer from scratch, then this is the simplest bot to build.

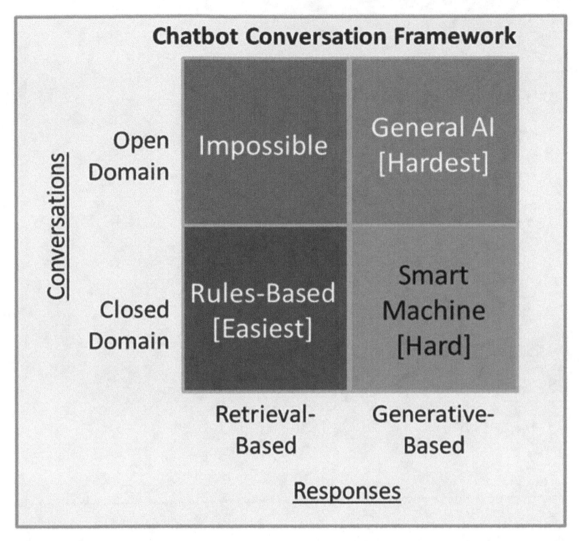

Figure 9-15. *The chatbot conversation framework (https://chatbotslife.com/ ultimate-guide-to-leveraging-nlp-machine-learning-for-you-chatbot-531ff2dd870c)*

Summary

In this chapter, we started by creating our bot with the QnA maker service, and within a few minutes, we achieved to have a working bot inside of Microsoft Teams ready for production. We have used the Teams-specific handlers available in the Bot Framework to get Teams activities reported to our bot. This chapter was a bit of a sidetrack, so join me in the next chapter, where we pick up again on our company app. I especially created this chapter as a sidetrack because this way you can easily create your own QnA maker bot without the need to reverse engineer the code out of our company app.

CHAPTER 10

Activity feed bots

In this chapter, we will start building a specific bot for Teams and integrate that in our company app. We are going to start small with a bot that does nothing more than notifying the user in their activity feed, but we will quickly surpass that and build a bot that has the power to help our users on a day-to-day basis.

Botify

Our app is still just a web application. We need to make sure that we turn it into an API that can communicate with the Bot Framework. Let's walk through the steps our app needs to become a bot in Teams. From here on, we will go further as an example with the C# application due to the easy integration with bot packages. We have seen that the difference in using the SDK is minimal. The difference is more language specific than there is in the Bot Framework, and therefore most items will just be duplicates.

Add the Bot Framework–specific packages. You can simply right-click your project or solution and select "Manage NuGet packages." This will present you with a selection screen and search box. Just copy the names of the packages in the search box and add the following packages. The first two are to get everything working, and the third one is already there because we want to take advantage of our QnA service we created earlier.

- Microsoft.Bot.Builder.Integration.AspNet.Core

- Microsoft.Bot.Builder.Dialogs

- Microsoft.Bot.Builder.AI.QnA

Next up is to add the different classes we need. We are going to need a controller, of course, and our bot. Later, we will add dialogs, but this is the basic bot you can build. You could as quickly get started with the example from Chapter 3, but I wanted you

© Rick Van Rousselt 2021
R. Van Rousselt, *Pro Microsoft Teams Development*, https://doi.org/10.1007/978-1-4842-6364-8_10

to see how easily you can extend your Tabs app to a bot. Add a new controller called BotController and add this code:

```
[Route("api/messages")]
    [ApiController]
    public class BotController : ControllerBase
    {

        private readonly IBotFrameworkHttpAdapter _adapter;
        private readonly IBot Bot;

        public BotController(IBotFrameworkHttpAdapter adapter, IBot bot)
        {
            _adapter = adapter;
            Bot = bot;
        }

        [HttpPost]
        public async Task PostAsync()
        {
            await _adapter.ProcessAsync(Request, Response, Bot);
        }
    }
```

We already know what this code does from the previous chapter. The Bot Framework adapter handles our request and sends it off to our bot. Next, create a folder called Bots and add a class called QABot. The code is rather simple now.

```
    public class QABot : ActivityHandler
    {

        public QABot()
        {
        }

        protected override async Task OnMessageActivityAsync(ITurnContext<I
        MessageActivity> turnContext,
            CancellationToken cancellationToken)
        {
```

```
    await turnContext.SendActivityAsync(MessageFactory.Text($"Hi"),
    cancellationToken);

    }
}
```

As you can see, we inherit from ActivityHandler, and when a message is entered, we just respond with "Hi." For the final piece, we need to implement the adapter, so create a folder called Adapters and add the "AdapterWithErrorHandler" class. This is the code for it:

```
public class AdapterWithErrorHandler: BotFrameworkHttpAdapter
{
    public AdapterWithErrorHandler(IConfiguration configuration, ILogge
    r<BotFrameworkHttpAdapter> logger)
        : base(configuration, logger)
    {
        OnTurnError = async (turnContext, exception) =>
        {
            // Log any leaked exception from the application.
            logger.LogError($"Exception caught : {exception.Message}");

            // Send a catch-all apology to the user.
            await turnContext.SendActivityAsync("Sorry, it looks like
            something went wrong.");

            // Send a trace activity, which will be displayed in the
            Bot Framework Emulator
            await turnContext.TraceActivityAsync("OnTurnError Trace",
            exception.Message, "https://www.botframework.com/schemas/
            error", "TurnError");
        };
    }
}
```

I didn't write the adapter code myself. You can find a lot of examples online, and this is one of the simplest implementations. We can create a very complex adapter that logs the errors to application insights and nicely handles errors, but this is a pretty basic implementation. The next thing we must do is connect all these pieces, because the

Bot Framework still has no idea how we are linking these classes to create our bot. In the startup.cs file, we are going to define this. In the ConfigureServices method, add the following two lines of code:

```
// Create the Bot Framework Adapter with error handling enabled.
services.AddSingleton<IBotFrameworkHttpAdapter,
AdapterWithErrorHandler>();

// Create the bot as a transient. In this case the ASP
Controller is expecting an IBot.
services.AddTransient<IBot, QABot>();
```

I hope you agree with me that there isn't much to it to update our company app to also have bot capabilities. It's time to test it out. Open the Bot Framework emulator, fire up your debug session, and connect to your bot. We didn't create an entry in Azure for this bot yet, so the only option we have is to go through our localhost. Connect to the correct port (in my case, 56797) and the /api/messages endpoint. This should give you a connection, and whatever you say to your bot, it will always respond with Hi like in Figure 10-1.

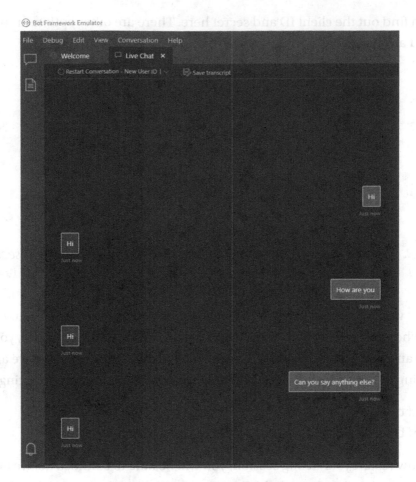

Figure 10-1. *We added bot capabilities to our tabbed app*

As you can see, in a few simple steps, we already have a bot, not a very smart bot, but still a bot. There is, however, a big thing missing. We can't talk to it in Teams. First, we need to create a bot channel registration in Azure. We can also create a web app bot if needed. The difference is that in a bot channel registration, you just register the bot, and that's it. With a web app bot, you get the web app as well, and you can select some default code to be deployed automatically. It doesn't matter what you take; if you want to deploy it later to Azure, you can select the web app bot. The essential item we must not forget is to capture the Client ID and the secret that gets created for us. You can create one yourself, but I always let the portal create one for me. If you then need to figure out what they are, you can click the deployment parameters, the top link you see in Figure 10-2, and go to the inputs tab. These are all the inputs used in the deployment, and you can find out the client ID and secret here. There are other options as well, but this is what I always do.

Figure 10-2. *Get the deployment input to find out your Client ID and secret after deployment*

Now that we have our bot registration, change the endpoint setting to your ngrok endpoint. When you want to connect with the bot now through the emulator, you are going to get an error. This is because you are using the Bot Framework, but we are not authenticating our bot code yet. Add the following two settings to the appsettings.json file:

```
"MicrosoftAppId": "<the client id from the azure portal",
"MicrosoftAppPassword": "<the secret from the azure portal"
```

If you now restart your debug session, you will be able to connect. So, we are currently running our bot through the Bot Framework—another great win. The only thing left to do is to add our bot to our Teams application. This calls for some changes to the manifest. Remember, if you are ever stuck with the manifest, then you can always fall back to App Studio, configure it there, and see how the JSON should look like. But since we already know how the manifest works, let's add it manually.

```
"bots": [
   {
      "botId": "6ae6e155-6dce-4133-ab9a-ece0416e451d",
      "needsChannelSelector": false,
      "isNotificationOnly": true,
      "scopes": [
        "team",
        "personal",
```

```
      "groupchat"
    ],
    "supportsFiles": false,
    "commandLists": [
      {
        "scopes": [
          "team",
          "personal",
          "groupchat"
        ],
        "commands": [
          {
            "title": "Help",
            "description": "Shows help information"
          }
        ]
      }
    ]
  }
],
```

The most important item is that we enter our bot ID, of course. Otherwise, Teams would not have a clue which bot to talk to. The other entries all have their purpose, some you don't need to add, but I like to add all options, even when I'm just confirming the default value. This is so that should I share my bot's code with somebody else, then they can see in a glimpse what's possible and what's not, instead of having to look it up online. Let's go over the other settings.

- needChannelSelector: If set to true, then when adding the bot, this helps the user, adding the bot to a channel.

- isNotificationOnly: If you set this to true, then nobody can at-mention your bot or talk to your bot. No conversations can take place. This is then like the title of the chapter which says an activity feed bot. The only thing the bot can do is send messages to the activity feed. This can be useful in very specific cases. But I've never come across it. According to Microsoft, this should be accompanied with a proactive messaging bot. This is a bot that initiates the conversation instead of the user initiating the conversation. But in all the scenarios that I've come across where a bot initiates the conversation, we usually want the user to interact back with it. And let's be honest, most people already have a lot of notifications in Teams. Adding to this list would usually not be a good idea. Let us agree that an activity feed bot alone doesn't have a high level of added value.

– Scopes: This is where we define where users can add the bot. Similar to tabs, we can have a bot designed for one-on-one conversations or they can be added to a groupchat or to a Team.

– supportsFiles: If we want people to share files with our bot, we can set this to true, then Teams will provide the button to share files. Make sure that you never set this to true if your bot doesn't support files because that would only confuse the user.

– CommandLists: This is the strongest feature you can have for your bot in Teams. Once you have built a bot and release it to your users, how would they know what a bot can do? Do they just chat with it? Why was it build? These are a set of preconfigured questions that will pop up if users start interacting with the bot—perfect for adding, for instance, the "Help" command like in this example. But you should always define an example of the use case why you have built the bot in here (Figure 10-3).

Once our manifest is added, we can rebuild our solution, which will trigger the Teams app package to be rebuilt. Don't forget to update the version number in the manifest as well. If you have already added your company app to a Teams, then go to the settings of that Teams, and under Apps you also have to upgrade your app package. Now, if the update went well, we should be able to talk to our bot in Teams as in Figure 10-3. Well, talk is a little bit of an overstatement as it only says "Hi."

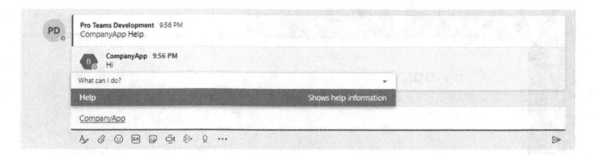

Figure 10-3. *Our bot responds in Teams and we get our command shown that helps the end users, the reason the bot was created*

I can recommend at this time that you play around with the different settings like the supportsFiles, needsChannelSelector, and the isNotificationOnly. This way, you can see for yourself what the different settings change in the Teams client for a user. Since we now mastered the skill of adding bots to Teams, we can start implementing logic.

365-QA

I've already pushed an app into the Microsoft Store for you to download and play with as an example. Getting an app into the store is not an easy task because there are a lot of checklists that you must sign off on. If you go to the store and look for the 365-QA bot, that's the one I built and added to the store (Figure 10-4). As you can see, it's under my company name because the store is only for Microsoft Partners, which is not a good decision of Microsoft. It could be that you have the best idea for a Teams app, but you can't push it to the store because the company you work for is not a partner or just doesn't want to do it. I understand the decision because they must be sure about the quality, but I do hope that they reconsider their decision one day.

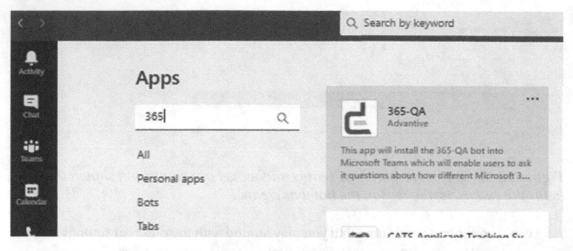

Figure 10-4. *The 365-QA Teams app in the Teams app store*

The reason I built this bot is because of the same experience I had when visiting different customers, and the vision behind it is simple. Most companies have a helpdesk or even a database somewhere with help articles. This database, wherever it resides, has to be maintained by people. But for everything Microsoft related, there is already a big, well-maintained repository of help articles, all stored at `https://support.microsoft.com/`. So why not have a bot that searches this repository for answers? Users can ask it any Microsoft-related question, and it will find an answer. And as an upside, `www.support.office.com` is multilingual, so even though the bot's main language is English, if you ask a question in a different language, it will find an answer in that language. As we discussed in the previous chapter, this bot is retrieval based. We get our data from a single website. Actually two websites, I also added `www.docs.microsoft.com` for completeness. Now, how did I pull this off? It's not like I have the Azure credit line that would allow me to scrape these websites and store all the information in my own database. I used the Bing Web Search API. (`https://azure.microsoft.com/en-us/services/cognitive-services/bing-web-search-api/`). This allows me to execute search queries toward the Web but to limit the results. And because the data is always structured in the same way, I can even have the results look nice and uniform. The results will always contain a link to the article, because let's be honest, you would rather scan an article for the information than have a bot guide you through all the steps one by one. It could easily be that you only need the information in the final step. Then it would take you way too long to have a bot ask for confirmation after every step if it can show you the next step. In our Tenant configuration, we even pinned it to the navigation of Teams (Figure 10-5) so that users can find the app quicker. Because we are searching in a range of answers, it could be that we are getting multiple answers back. This can be solved by showing a carousel of answers in the form of cards.

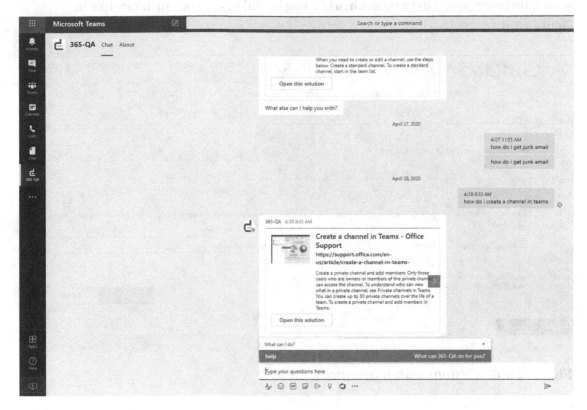

Figure 10-5. 365-QA pinned to the navigation and returned answers

Now, in this next section, we are going to build this bot ourselves. But not just re-create it, because that would be pointless, but we are going to make it even better. Let's assume a user talks to our bot and enters our example sentence in the chat: "How do I set my Outlook signature." Until now, we had that information in our QnA service. This is perfect, but what does the user actually mean when asking this? Do they mean, like we have assumed until now, that they want to know the company policy regarding Outlook signatures? Or is it just that they cannot find the button in Outlook that allows them to set their signature? This simple question can have two entirely different answers. We already covered this a little bit, but we don't need the bot to only return a single response. We can have the bot find both answers, return those, and have the user pick the one they want.

Getting started

First, we need to have our Bing Web Search API configured. Let's configure a custom search instance (`www.customsearch.ai/`). Log in and name your instance like in Figure 10-6.

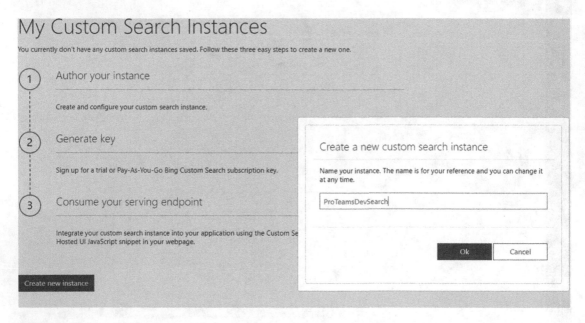

Figure 10-6. *Custom search instance*

After this, we can configure active URL lists. Add `https://support.microsoft.com/` to the list and test it with a query. You can use the same test sentence we have used before. Pretty simple configuration, right? Time to publish. Like with the QnA service, we have a published version that provides us with the API and an authoring version where we can do changes and test. Once you published this configuration, you get another page to test. You will need a key to use this service, but you can request a free one that will last for seven days. Now that you have your custom search API prepared (see Figure 10-7), write down all the necessary information like the subscription key and the URL.

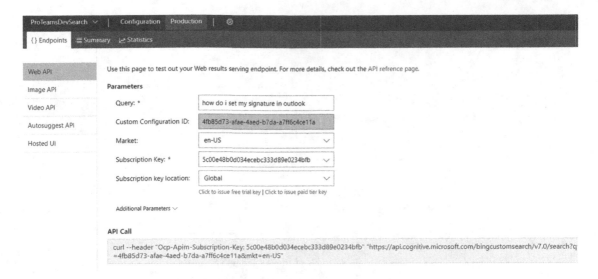

Figure 10-7. *The custom search API published and ready to use*

Now let's make our bot a bit smarter. Start with adding the Microsoft.Azure.Search NuGet package so that we can use this API as an SDK. We could also just do an HTTP client call, but the SDK makes it a lot easier to work with.

Dialogs and steps

First up, we need to make sure that we can use dialogs. Add the RootDialog class in the Dialogs folder. This is going to hold most of the logic of our bot. We are going to use something called a waterfall dialog in this bot. Waterfall dialogs are the easiest to start with and do exactly what the name says. They cascade from one step into the next. This is perfect for capturing information from the user. Every step you can ask a new question and the user responds. Now, although you can have a lot of steps, this is not such a good idea. Remember when we said that the user almost never does what we want. And when you are programming steps that follow each other, users are certainly going to want to exit your preprogrammed conversational flow. For this scenario, though, this is perfect. We are going to have three steps. The first step is going to ask the user, "What can I help you with?" The user is going to respond with their question, so in the second step, we can search both our QnA service and our Bing Custom Search API and return that result. Finally, our third step is going to ask the user, "What else can I help you with?" As you might have guessed, between steps 2 and 3, we don't need an answer; well, it turns out we can skip the user answering part, by stepping into the next step immediately, which is very handy. You can see a visual representation of the flow in Figure 10-8.

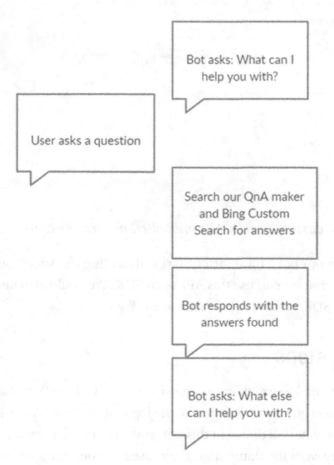

Figure 10-8. *Visual representation of our conversational flow*

But first things first. We are going to need to configure a lot of services, so let's take a look at the controller of the RootDialog class.

```
public RootDialog(IConfiguration configuration, ILogger<RootDialog>
logger, IHttpClientFactory httpClientFactory)
{
    Logger = logger;
    var httpClient = httpClientFactory.CreateClient();
    _searchClient = new CustomSearchClient(new ApiKeyService
    ClientCredentials(configuration["SearchSubscriptionKey"]));
```

```
_customConfigId = configuration["SearchConfigurationId"];

QnAMakerOptions qnaMakerOptions = new QnAMakerOptions
{
    ScoreThreshold = float.Parse(configuration["QnAScoreThresho
    ld"], CultureInfo.InvariantCulture.NumberFormat)
};

qnaMaker = new QnAMaker(new QnAMakerEndpoint
{
    KnowledgeBaseId = configuration["QnAKnowledgebaseId"],
    EndpointKey = configuration["QnAEndpointKey"],
    Host = configuration["QnAEndpointHostName"]
}, qnaMakerOptions, httpClient);
AddDialog(new TextPrompt(nameof(TextPrompt)));
AddDialog(new WaterfallDialog(nameof(WaterfallDialog), new
WaterfallStep[]
{
    InitialStepAsync,
    ActStepAsync,
    FinalStepAsync,
}));

// The initial child Dialog to run.
InitialDialogId = nameof(WaterfallDialog);
}
```

We are initializing the class with dependency injection, so our configuration, logger, and httpClientFactory will get injected into our class. The only thing left to do is use them. The configuration will automatically read our appsettings.json file so we can store the keys we need for our QnA service and our Bing Custom Search. We initialize them inside of the controller, and we also create the base layout of our waterfall dialog. We are going to use a textprompt for our first question, and we are defining our three steps, InitialStep, ActStep, and FinalStep.

Next up is defining what is going to happen in our first step.

```
var messageText = stepContext.Options?.ToString() ?? "What
can I help you with today?\nSay something like \"How do I
set my Outlook signature\"";
var promptMessage = MessageFactory.Text(messageText,
messageText, InputHints.ExpectingInput);
return await stepContext.PromptAsync(nameof(TextPrompt),
new PromptOptions { Prompt = promptMessage },
cancellationToken);
```

In this step, we are going to define a message that will get sent the first time. By doing this, we are assuming that the user always says something like "Hi" or "Hello," because as you can remember, the user has to initiate the conversation. To send the message we constructed back to the user, we are taking the stepcontext, which is a parameter we get on every step, and tell it to prompt the message back to the user. Because we just let the step end, the waterfall dialog structure is going to wait for the user to answer, and then it will automatically step us into the next step. We did the configuration of the steps in the constructor, and this will just follow along.

Now wouldn't it be nice if this was all we had to do? Well, as you can imagine, in a Teams channel, nobody is going to at-mention our bot and then say "Hi," wait for the bot to respond, and then on that thread, ask the question they have. If you look at Figure 10-9, this is not a good and user-friendly flow. We need to make a difference between a personal chat and when the conversation is happening inside a channel. Let's use the Teams integration into the Bot Framework for this.

```
var teamInfo = stepContext.Context.Activity.TeamsGetTeamInfo();

        if (teamInfo?.Id != null && stepContext.Options != null)
        // inside team
        {
            Logger.LogInformation("We are inside a Team. No need to be
            nice to the user and just respond with the answer. Skipping
            this step.");
            var message = stepContext.Context.Activity.
            RemoveRecipientMention();
            return await stepContext.NextAsync(message,
            cancellationToken);
        }
```

```
else //inside private or group chat
{
    // Use the text provided in FinalStepAsync or the default
    if it is the first time.
    var messageText = stepContext.Options?.ToString() ?? "What
    can I help you with today?\nSay something like \"How do I
    set my Outlook signature\"";
    var promptMessage = MessageFactory.Text(messageText,
    messageText, InputHints.ExpectingInput);
    return await stepContext.PromptAsync(nameof(TextPrompt),
    new PromptOptions { Prompt = promptMessage },
    cancellationToken);
}
```

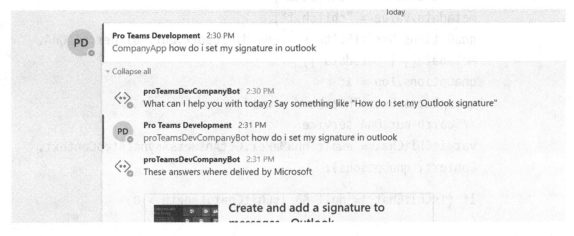

Figure 10-9. *Example of a very annoying conversational flow*

We are getting the Teamsinfo object, and from this Teamsinfo object, we can get the Team ID. When the ID is not empty, we know that we are in a Team and that a user will ask the question directly. The next problem is that in a channel, users have to at-mention our bot, meaning if we would use that as a search query, we would always add the bot name to the search query. For instance, if the user would ask "How do I set my outlook signature," the question we would receive in our bot code is going to be "<at>CompanyApp<at> How do I set my outlook signature." This would have a bad impact on the confidence of our search results. Therefore, we also remove the at-mention with the RemoveRecipientMention. This will remove the "<at>Botname<at>".

It used to be that we needed to write this code ourselves, which is not that difficult, but it's a nice add-on to one of the latest versions of the Bot Framework and makes our lives again a little easier.

Next up is the actual logic in the ActStepAsync.

```
private async Task<DialogTurnResult> ActStepAsync(WaterfallStepContext
stepContext,
        CancellationToken cancellationToken)
    {

        var searchTerm = (string)stepContext.Result;

        var metadata = new Microsoft.Bot.Builder.AI.QnA.Metadata();
        var qnaOptions = new QnAMakerOptions();
        metadata.Name = "editorial";
        metadata.Value = "chitchat";
        qnaOptions.StrictFilters = new Microsoft.Bot.Builder.AI.QnA.
        Metadata[] { metadata };
        qnaOptions.Top = 1;
        qnaOptions.ScoreThreshold = 0.9F;
        //Search our QnA service
        var isChitChat = await qnaMaker.GetAnswersAsync(stepContext.
        Context, qnaOptions);

        if (isChitChat != null && isChitChat.Length > 0)
        {

            // Restart the main dialog with a different message the
            second time around
            return await stepContext.ReplaceDialogAsync(InitialDialog
            Id, isChitChat[0].Answer, cancellationToken);

        }

        //Search Microsoft
        var results = _searchClient.CustomInstance.SearchAsync(_
        customConfigId, searchTerm).Result;

        if (results?.WebPages?.Value?.Count > 3)
        {
```

```
            var msAnswer = $"These answers where delived by Microsoft";
            await stepContext.Context.SendActivityAsync(msAnswer);
            var getFeedback = stepContext.Context.Activity.
            CreateReply();
            for (int i = 0; i < 3; i++)
            {
                var result = results.WebPages.Value[i];
                var imageUrl = HelperMethods.CheckImageUrl(result.
                Snippet);
                var heroCard = new ThumbnailCard
                {
                    Title = result.Name,
                    Subtitle = result.DisplayUrl,
                    Text = result.Snippet,
                    Images = new List<CardImage> { new
                    CardImage(imageUrl) },
                    Buttons = new List<CardAction> { new
                    CardAction(ActionTypes.OpenUrl, "Open this
                    solution", value: result.Url) },
                };
                // Add the attachment to our reply.
                getFeedback.Attachments.Add(heroCard.ToAttachment());
            }
            getFeedback.AttachmentLayout = AttachmentLayoutTypes.
            Carousel;
            await stepContext.Context.SendActivityAsync(getFeedback,
            cancellationToken);
        }
        else
        {
            var msAnswerNotFound = $"Sorry I did not find anything
            online.";
            await stepContext.Context.SendActivityAsync(msAnswerNotFound);
        }

        //Search our QnA service
```

```
        var response = await qnaMaker.GetAnswersAsync(stepContext.Context);

        if (response != null && response.Length > 0)
        {
            await stepContext.Context.SendActivityAsync(MessageFactory.
            Text(response[0].Answer), cancellationToken);
        }
        else
        {
            var msAnswerNotFound = $"Sorry I did not find anything in
             the company knowledgebase.";
            await stepContext.Context.SendActivityAsync(msAnswerNotFound);
        }
        return await stepContext.NextAsync(null, cancellationToken);
    }
```

As you can see, this is a pretty long method. I would not usually write methods this long, but it helps you to understand the flow. We could even break this up into more steps or even send it off to different dialogs. The first part is to see if a user is typing chit-chat. The chit-chat responses are in our QnA service, and they are tagged with metadata. So we do a call to QnA and tell it to use a strict filter, which is "editorial:chitchat". This only searches in questions with this metadata attached to it. If that returns nothing, note that we set the score threshold to 90% certainty, then we proceed with searching the Bing Custom Search API. If we do find a result, then notice the ReplaceDialogAsync function. This replaces our current dialog that we are in with a new one, but in this case, it's the same dialog, forcing the dialog to start over. We are adding the answer as a variable because in our initialStep we are checking if there is text in the stepContext. Options property to detect if the dialog started fresh or was triggered from step 2 or 3 in our dialog.

Calling the Bing Custom Search API with the SDK, we only need a single line of code, where we enter our config ID and our search term. The hard part here is to turn those results into something that looks nice for the user. We are going to create a carousel of hero cards. We are only going to do this if we get more than three items returned. Normally, if we do a correct search, we always get multiple answers returned. This could even be an improvement that you refactor this piece of code so that it handles a different number of results differently. A hero card takes a title, a subtitle, and a description. I've mapped those to the results returned, but for the image, it was a little trickier. We don't get images back from the custom search API, so we need something to show here. Well, if you check out the HelperMethods class, you can see that I've created a quick and dirty solution, just check for some keywords of Office applications in the description returned and use an image accordingly. If the word "Teams" or "Outlook" appears, then use an image of that product. Not a perfect solution, but it does what it needs to do—show images. A better solution would be to retrieve the OpenGraph data (`https://ogp.me/`) of that page and create a card with the information retrieved.

For the last part of this method, we are going to search our QnA service again, this time for information manually entered in the QnA service or the information we scraped from the website. If information is found, we return that as well. This is what I mean that a bot can get information from multiple data sources.

The final step is to make a clean stop. We could have added this to our second step as well, but it's to demonstrate that we don't need feedback from the user in a waterfall but that we can also force to skip to the next step.

With our dialog ready, we can hook everything up, but wait, we almost forgot one of the most important things when developing bots. Always give the user an escape and a way to ask for help. We could, of course, solve this with middleware, but I want to show you an alternate option. If you check out the QABot class, you can see that instead of calling the dialog immediately in the OnMessageActivityAsync, we build in an interrupt method.

```
if (await InterruptAsync(turnContext, cancellationToken))
        {
            return;
        }

        await Dialog.RunAsync(turnContext, ConversationState.Creat
        eProperty<DialogState>("DialogState"), cancellationToken).
        ConfigureAwait(false);
```

When a message is received, we check in the InterruptAsync method if we need to break the normal flow. Even in step 2 of our dialog, this piece will always be executed. Should the interrupt return true, then the dialog is not executed, and it's back to the user to continue the conversation again. In the InterruptAsync method, we have the following code:

```
if (innerDc.Activity.Type == ActivityTypes.Message)
            {
            innerDc.Activity.RemoveRecipientMention();
            var text = innerDc.Activity.Text.ToLowerInvariant().Trim();
            switch (text)
            {
                case "help":
                case "?":
                    var welcomeCard = CreateAdaptiveCardAttachment();
                    var response = MessageFactory.
                    Attachment(welcomeCard);
                    await innerDc.SendActivityAsync(response,
                    cancellationToken);
                    return true;
                case "cancel":
                case "quit":
                    var cancelMessage = MessageFactory.
                    Text(CancelMsgText, CancelMsgText, InputHints.
                    IgnoringInput);
                    await innerDc.SendActivityAsync(cancelMessage,
                    cancellationToken);
                    return true;
            }
        }

        return false;
```

Here, we are checking to see if it's a real message, just to be sure. We remove the at-mention; it could be that this message originates from a channel. And then, we check for specific commands. Remember that in our manifest, we specified the help command. When a user gives this command, an adaptive JSON card is returned. As you can see, we don't need to always construct our cards with code; we can also just send back the correct JSON, which is actually what our code does for us when creating cards, formatting JSON. The best practice as well is to have a quit or cancel command. Let's say you have a waterfall with five steps or even more, and the user wants to get out of that flow, then you should allow it. Now we just send back a message, but this would be a good place to clear your user state and conversation state.

We haven't discussed user and conversation state yet, but you must have seen it in the code samples. A bot is an API, and APIs are by nature stateless, which is a good thing, but not if we have a conversation that is going to be longer than only "Hi." The bot should know where it is in the conversation or steps that we programmed. To provide us with a way to preserve information about the user and about the conversation, the Bot Framework provides us with a solution. We can even add our own custom properties if needed. This way, if we need to store, for instance, the username, we can ask the user for their name and we don't need to ask it again the next time they talk to our bot. In the OnTurnAsync, we are simply saving both the user state and the conversation state. But we do need some kind of storage to store the state in. This is configured in the startup class. Here, we need to add a few more things. First, our memory, you usually should use persistent storage for saving state; of course, you don't want your bot to forget everything every time the app service where it lives is restarted. In this case, I've used a memory storage, and if you can notice that every time you start a new debug session. We also need to inject our user state and conversation state in the classes when we need them, our HTTP client, and our RootDialog into our QnABot class.

```
services.AddHttpClient();
        services.AddSingleton<IStorage, MemoryStorage>();
        services.AddSingleton<UserState>();
        services.AddSingleton<ConversationState>();

        // Create the Bot Framework Adapter with error handling
        enabled.
        services.AddSingleton<IBotFrameworkHttpAdapter,
        AdapterWithErrorHandler>();

        services.AddSingleton<RootDialog>();

        // Create the bot as a transient. In this case the ASP
        Controller is expecting an IBot.
        services.AddTransient<IBot, QABot<RootDialog>>();
```

Don't forget to add all the configuration settings to the appsettings.json file, and we can fire up our debug session to test out our bot. Be aware that this will run in Teams as well as in the emulator. Usually, I try not to add the Teams-specific things until I have most of the bot in working order. Only being able to debug in Teams is sometimes hard.

The emulator gives you usually just that little piece of information. And since we don't have that much Teams specific, we can still run this in the emulator and then move over to Teams. You should have the same results as in Figure 10-10.

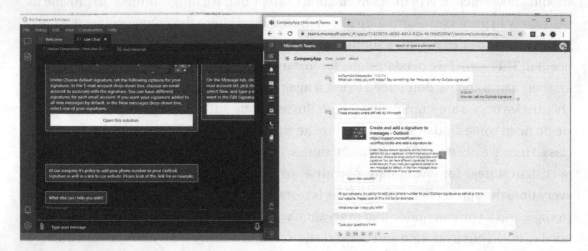

Figure 10-10. *Testing our code and seeing results being sent back from our bot in Teams and in the emulator*

Summary

In this chapter, we started from scratch to create a bot inside of Microsoft Teams for our company app. We learned how to implement the Bing Custom Search API in combination with the QnA maker service to give our bot a personality and to make it help users answer any question they might have about Microsoft products. We discussed dialogs and created our very own waterfall dialog. Now that we have a bot that has the functionality we need, let us find out in the next chapter how we can have our bot be more integrated with Teams.

CHAPTER 11

Teams-specific bot integrations

In the previous chapters, we learned how to create bots and integrate them with various cognitive services provided by Microsoft to make them smarter. This bot can run on multiple channels; it's not Teams specific yet. In this chapter, we are going to make our bot Teams aware and let it interact even more with our users in Teams. I do have to warn you; this path is very user-friendly in Teams, but we are going to decrease the usability of the bot in other channels significantly. If you start implementing this in your bots, it's always good to plan to think ahead. What channels are we going to use, and can we keep our code as generic as possible? The worst thing that you can do is have a different code base, meaning different Bots for different channels, because that is going to be a nightmare to maintain.

Teams bot

Now that we have a bot in Teams and both a static and a configurable tab, it's time for those three to come together. Until now, we could order lunch in the static tab or configure the news in a configurable tab. But what happens if our lunch order has arrived? We need a way to know that our lunch is ready. Same for the news, we need to go to the tab ourselves to check if there are new news items. Let's have our bot notify us when lunch is ready or when a new news item gets added. For this, we need proactive messaging. As already discussed, a user must always initiate the conversation with the bot. Well, that is not "always" the case. But it's tricky. Microsoft made the design decision that when in a channel, for instance, the bot doesn't know what messages get sent, until it's specifically at-mentioned. The reason for this is, when you have a bot in your channel, it doesn't have access to all the messages and cannot eavesdrop on the conversation. In Slack, for instance, this is different. If a bot is in a channel, it is notified about every message and can see the contents of it.

© Rick Van Rousselt 2021
R. Van Rousselt, *Pro Microsoft Teams Development*, https://doi.org/10.1007/978-1-4842-6364-8_11

But the Teams team left us an opening; they allow that when you have your bot installed in Teams, and you can identify the user, usually, because the user already talked to you before or the bot is in the same Team as the user. We could even preinstall our bot for all our users through an app policy in the admin center. If all this is valid, then we can initiate a conversation. This means that, first, we need to start saving the information about users that added us as a static tab or, if we are added to a Team, start saving the properties of that Team. To store data somewhere, we are going to need a database of some sort. I'm a huge fan of storage accounts in Azure (`https://docs.microsoft.com/en-us/azure/storage/common/storage-account-overview`). They can be used for blobs, files, queues, and tables. They are very versatile and easy to use. In this case, we could use any database or storage since the only thing we need to store is information about a user or about a Team, meaning strings and ids. We could even use a flat file somewhere. Create a storage account in Azure and add the NuGet package "Microsoft.Azure.Cosmos.Table" so that we can communicate easily with our storage table. This used to be another package (Azure.Storage), but the Team has split up all the different features of a storage account into separate packages. This one is more aligned with Cosmos DB. Let us create a base repository to do the CRUD operations. If you look in the completed sample, you can see not much special going on in the TableBaseRepository.

Now we are going to need some classes to hold our data. Let's create a MyTeamObject and a UserObject class. To keep it a little separate, let's create a data folder and place them in there. The MyTeamObject is not part of the SDK but something we create ourselves. The MyTeamObject will hold

- ID: Which is the channel ID.

- Name: To hold the channel name.

- ServiceUrl: This is a part of the URL of the API of the Bot Framework we will be calling to initiate the conversation. This depends on your region, so it's best that we store this for every Team.

- Location: We, of course, need to know the office location the user selected in the configuration. This way, we can filter the Teams for a specific location when sending out news.

- BotId and name: We also need to save the botId and its name. These items are required when you want the bot to initiate a conversation because, otherwise, how would Teams or the Bot Framework know which bot is trying to message?

This results in a simple class:

```
public class MyTeamObject : TableEntity
{
    public string Id { get; set; }
    public string Name { get; set; }
    public string ServiceUrl { get; set; }
    public Location Location { get; set; }
    public string BotId { get; set; }
    public string BotName { get; set; }
}
```

See how we use the TableEntity as a base class. The TableEntity is linked with our table storage. Table storage always at least needs two values: a rowkey and the partitionkey. Both combined must be unique. This is the cool thing about table storage. You inherit from this class when initiating an object from it, you set the partitionkey and the rowkey, and columns are added automatically. No fiddling around with tables, creating columns, primary keys, and all that stuff like in SQL. That's why this is a NoSQL datastore. Our UserObject will hold similar data to identify the user but in their one-on-one chat with the bot.

```
public class UserObject : TableEntity
{
    public string Name { get; set; }
    public string UserId { get; set; }
    public string ConversationId { get; set; }
    public string ServiceUrl { get; set; }
}
```

The right information

Now how are we going to find all these values we need? It's time to add our Teams-specific bot integrations. In our QABot, we are going to override three methods. When a team member gets added to get all this information, when a team member gets removed to clean up our data, and of course, we also need to have a fallback for when somebody renames the Team. The last one is not required to have our bot initiate a conversation as you will see further on, but it's always handy that we can have a quick view of what

Teams are subscribed to our service. First up is TeamMembersAdded. And keep in mind that when our bot gets added to a Team, this also triggers the TeamMembersAdded function.

```
    protected override async Task OnTeamsMembersAddedAsync(IList<T
    eamsChannelAccount> teamsMembersAdded, TeamInfo teamInfo, ITur
    nContext<IConversationUpdateActivity> turnContext,
    CancellationToken cancellationToken)
{
    var botId = turnContext.Activity.Recipient.Id;
    if (teamsMembersAdded.FirstOrDefault(p => p.Id == botId) !=
    null) //check if it's the bot that's added
    {
        if (teamInfo?.Id != null) //inside team
        {
            var team = new TeamObject()
            {
                PartitionKey = Constants.TeamDataPartition,
                RowKey = teamInfo.Id,
                Id = teamInfo.Id,
                Name = teamInfo.Name,
                ServiceUrl = turnContext.Activity.ServiceUrl,
                BotId = turnContext.Activity?.Recipient?.Id,
                BotName = turnContext.Activity?.Recipient?.Name,
            };
            await _teamrepository.CreateOrUpdateAsync(team);
        }
        else
        {
            var user = new UserObject
            {
                PartitionKey =  Constants.UserDataPartition,
                RowKey = turnContext.Activity?.From?.AadObjectId,
                UserId = turnContext.Activity?.From?.Id,
                Name = turnContext.Activity?.From?.Name,
```

```
        ConversationId = turnContext.Activity?.
        Conversation?.Id,
        ServiceUrl = turnContext.Activity?.ServiceUrl
    };

    await _userrepository.CreateOrUpdateAsync(user);
   }
  }
 }
```

The preceding code gets triggered every time a member gets added to a Team, where our app is installed, including the first time when we add our own bot to the Team. In this scenario, we don't need a notification each time the Team member roster is updated, but there is until now no BotAddedToTeam event. So, we use this one and check if the bot is the one that's added. This can happen in two cases, either to a Team or to a chat or a one-on-one conversation. In both cases, we will need different data, so we need to differentiate where the event originated from. It turns out to be quite straightforward. If there is no channel ID provided, then we know we are not added to a Team. After differentiating, we can save the data to our table storage. For the removed event, it's just a matter of cleaning up our data. But the logic is similar.

```
protected override async Task OnTeamsMembersRemovedAsync(IList<Teams
ChannelAccount> teamsMembersRemoved, TeamInfo teamInfo, ITurnContext
<IConversationUpdateActivity> turnContext,
    CancellationToken cancellationToken)
{
    var botId = turnContext.Activity.Recipient.Id;
    if (teamsMembersRemoved.FirstOrDefault(p => p.Id == botId) !=
    null) //check if it's the bot that's added
    {
        if (teamInfo?.Id != null) //inside team
        {
            var team = await _teamrepository.GetAsync(Constants.
            TeamDataPartition, teamInfo.Id);
            await _teamrepository.DeleteAsync(team);
        }
```

215

```
        else
        {
            var user = await _userrepository.GetAsync(Constants.
            UserDataPartition,
                turnContext.Activity?.From?.AadObjectId);

            await _userrepository.DeleteAsync(user);
        }
    }
}
```

The only thing left for us to implement is when a Team gets renamed—a channel we don't care about because we are storing the IDs of a channel and not the names. We could as well store the ID of the Team which is a better practice, but I wanted to show you that we can also use the Team name.

```
protected override async Task OnTeamsTeamRenamedAsync(TeamInfo
teamInfo, ITurnContext<IConversationUpdateActivity> turnContext,
CancellationToken cancellationToken)
{
    var team = new TeamObject()
    {
        PartitionKey = Constants.TeamDataPartition,
        RowKey = teamInfo.Id,
        Id = teamInfo.Id,
        Name = teamInfo.Name,
        ServiceUrl = turnContext.Activity.ServiceUrl,
    };
    await _teamrepository.CreateOrUpdateAsync(team);
}
```

Sending messages

Now that we have our events ready and we save all the channel and chat information where the bot is added, we still need a way to notify our users.

If you check out the newsconfiguration.js file, you will notice that I updated our button save event. Instead of just sending back the location, we are also sending back some much-needed information like the channelId, groupId, and teamId. With this information, we can match the information we have in our table storage with the location that Teams have picked to receive news from.

```
$(document).ready(function () {
    $('.btn').on('click', function (event) {

        var selectedLocationTypeVal = $('[name=Location]:checked').val();

        microsoftTeams.getContext(function (context) {

            var options = [{
                "location": selectedLocationTypeVal,
                "channelId": context.channelId,
                "groupId": context.groupId,
                "teamId": context.teamId
            }];

            $.ajax({
                url: '/SaveConfiguration',
                data: JSON.stringify({ NewsConfiguration: options }),
                contentType: 'application/json;  charset=utf-8',
                dataType: 'json',
                type: 'POST',
                cache: false,
                success: function (data) {
                    locationSaveButtonSuccess(selectedLocationTypeVal);
                },
                error: function (jqXHR, textStatus) {
                    alert('jqXHR.statusCode');
                }
            });

        });

    });
```

Now we don't need all this data. The channel ID would suffice to make a match with the information we have stored in our table. I just added some more information here to demonstrate that we can even get more information from the Teams context, as you already know. Now, why is this information not enough? Well, to start within the

Teams JavaScript SDK, we don't have a notion of our bot, so no bot ID and name and no service URL. I know this can be cumbersome to get little pieces of information in different places, but this is the way Teams works. You only have access to the information needed at a given point. If Teams would provide us with all the data all the time, then there would be security issues. We don't want spamming bots to start popping up in Teams. If we are building apps for our own company or for a customer, then this would not be a real problem because we know what we are doing. But in the case of third-party apps, the apps you can install from the store, this would be a problem. Now for the actual notification of our users. In our LunchController class, we are going to create additional methods to notify our users. This doesn't have to be a button in a screen. With the information we have, we would quickly build this functionality in our bot or even in a separate solution.

In our LunchController class, add the following three methods:

```
public ActionResult Admin()
{
    return View();
}

public async Task<ActionResult> NotifyLunch()
{
    return View("Admin");
}

public async Task<ActionResult> NotifyNews()
{
    return View("Admin");
}
```

First is our admin page; nothing fancy here, just two buttons that will trigger our other methods.

```
@{
    ViewData["Title"] = "Administration";
    Layout = "_LayoutForLunch";
}

<h1>Notify all users for Lunch and news</h1>
```

```
<div>
    <a href='@Url.Action("NotifyLunch", "Lunch")' class="btn btn-
    primary">Notify for Lunch</a>
</div>
<div>
    <a href='@Url.Action("NotifyNews", "Lunch")' class="btn btn-
    primary">Notify for News</a>
</div>
```

The other methods are not that easy. First is notifying users that their lunch is ready. I've not added any filtering logic because that's something you can write yourself.

```
var user = _userObjectRepository.GetAllAsync(Constants.UserDataPartition,
1).Result.ToList()[0];
```

I just get the first user in my database. Since I'm the only one developing on this Tenant, it's also the only user that has the app. Next up, we need to have something that is connected to the Bot Framework, but more importantly that is authenticated.

```
ConnectorClient _client = new ConnectorClient(new Uri(user.ServiceUrl),
        new MicrosoftAppCredentials(
            _configuration["MicrosoftAppId"],
            _configuration["MicrosoftAppPassword"],
            new HttpClient()));
```

The connectorClient is part of the Bot Framework. When we have a normal bot, then we also have a connectorClient, but the Framework does the initialization for us. We normally don't come into contact with this boilerplate class, or at least less and less. In the previous version of the Bot Framework, especially before version 4.8, you needed to create this yourself sometimes. But since we are initiating the conversation, we do need to set it up manually. This class is the one responsible for the connection between your bot and the Bot Framework. Therefore, we need to authenticate; to accomplish this, we will use the client ID and secret from our bot, the one we got when we created our bot registration. And since a bot is just an API, we also need an HTTP client to send the information back and forth. We also need to make sure that we connect to the correct region, and this is where the ServiceURL comes into play. Should we hard code this or reuse this all the time, we might get into trouble if a user is in another region. Now that we have a connection, we, of course, need to send some information. We could do something simple like send a text message. This is what you find in the documentation:

```
var message = Activity.CreateMessageActivity();
        message.Text = "Hello World";
```

Well, we don't want to just send a text message; we have the power of cards at our disposal so let's create a thumbnail card.

```
ThumbnailCard c = new ThumbnailCard()
        {
            Title = "Lunch",
            Subtitle = "Lunch has been served",
            Text = "Your lunch is ready for you",
            Images = new List<CardImage>(),
            Buttons = new List<CardAction>(),
        };
        c.Images.Add(new CardImage { Url = "https://cdn3.iconfinder.
        com/data/icons/hotel-service-gray-set-1/100/Untitled-1-09-512.
        png" });
        Attachment card = c.ToAttachment();
        var message = MessageFactory.Attachment(card);
```

I like cards and even more adaptive cards. Adaptive cards are platform-independent cards delivered in JSON. We provide the JSON and the platform renders them in such a way that it is consistent with its UI. You can find out more information about adaptive cards here: `https://adaptivecards.io/`. The only problem with adaptive cards is the support in Teams for them. They always are using either an older version or a version where something is not working correctly. So, whenever you start using cards, make sure that you not only make your card but also check out the "not-supported" items (`https://docs.microsoft.com/en-us/microsoftteams/platform/task-modules-and-cards/cards/cards-reference`). I know it can sometimes get very frustrating that the card you just need is not supported in Teams. But the Teams team is trying to keep up with all the changes going on in the cards that are possible with the Bot Framework, and I rather have lesser cards but the ones that are there working perfectly than the other way around. At Ignite 2019, they announced that they will add additional resources into aligning the Bot Framework with Teams, and the Teams team is really pushing hard on it. After we designed our card, we still need to identify the user we want to send this information to.

```
var parameters = new ConversationParameters
            {
                Members = new[] { new ChannelAccount(user.UserId) },
                ChannelData = new TeamsChannelData
                {
                    Tenant = new TenantInfo(_configuration["TenantID"]),
                },
            };
```

To send information to a direct chat, the properties in our conversationParameters are somewhat limited, just the userId and the tenantID. In this case, I did put the TenantId in our appsettings file. You could also extract this information from either the MembersAdded event in our bot or from the tab when we save information. Depending on your use case, you might want to do this. I'm confident that this bot is only used in my Tenant, but if you're going to create a Teams app for the Teams app store (aka App Source), then you have no idea in what Tenant this gets installed in, so you would need to save that as well somewhere. The next item is something we always must do when sending proactive messages.

```
AppCredentials.TrustServiceUrl(user.ServiceUrl, DateTime.MaxValue);
```

This single line of code is a showstopper. If we don't execute this code, we will not be able to initiate the conversation. This code adds our service URL to the trusted URL's list for the app credentials we are using in our bot. If the URL is not trusted, we will not get our call through. After this, it is just a matter of creating the conversation and sending out the information.

```
var conversationResource = await _client.Conversations.CreateCo
nversationAsync(parameters);
await _client.Conversations.SendToConversationAsync(conversatio
nResource.Id, (Activity)message);
```

First, we create a conversation with the given parameters, userID and tenantID. This way, Teams knows which user to contact. It will return an ID of this conversation, which we can then use to send our card to. Don't forget to cast our card as an activity, because this is what we need to send to our users. More in-depth information can be found in this blog post: https://blog.botframework.com/2019/07/02/using-adaptive-cards-with-the-microsoft-bot-framework/. Casting our card to an activity is a little bit annoying, and there are numerous issues on GitHub for this that our message, which is of type IMessageActivity needs to be cast to an Activity. This is something that the Bot Framework should take care of. I lost, on several occasions, a lot of time because I did something wrong, and the casting didn't work. It's not like you get a decent error back when this cast fails. Now when we run our code, this should do the trick.

Make sure that you remove the app. You already installed it as a personal app to test out the code a little while back. Well, to get this event triggered, we need a fresh installation. Just right-click it and click install. Make sure that your code and ngrok are running. Place a breakpoint in the OnTeamsMemberAdded and the OnTurnAsync methods in the QABot. If you then remove the app and reinstall it, the first thing that's called is our OnTurnAsync method. Remember, this is where we save our state. The next method is our OnTeamsMemberAdded. When we debug the code, we can see that the teamsMemberAdded property contains two values. One is our user, and the other one is our bot. If you check out the values, you can see that with our user, there is a lot of data, but from our bot, we only get an ID. This is normal. A bot is not a user, doesn't have a license, has no login information, and so on. One thing you should notice is that your user ID starts with a 29, and the ID of the bot starts with 28. Until now, I haven't seen anything different. The reason for this design decision by the Teams team is unknown. But we can make an educated guess. The Teams team probably needed a way to differentiate between bots and users in their own back-end code. It's also pretty handy for us. If we ever need to store all the members of a Team like the method `TeamsInfo.GetPagedMembersAsync` provides us, then we can easily separate the real users from the bot.

Since our bot is part of the two users that were added, we are sure that this is a new chat we need to save. If you step a little further through the code, you can see that the TeamInfo property is empty, meaning we are in a chat. Time to step further and save our user object with the information we need. If you go to the Azure Portal to your storage account and the "Storage Explorer" blade, then we can see the information stored in our table as in Figure 11-1. You can also use the Storage Explorer for Windows if you prefer to work with a client application (`https://azure.microsoft.com/en-us/features/storage-explorer/`).

Figure 11-1. *The user information stored in our table storage*

If we visit the lunch tab, we see that the Administration button has appeared. In the admin page, we can click the Notify for Lunch button, and if we wait a few seconds, we should have our bot send us a message like in Figure 11-2.

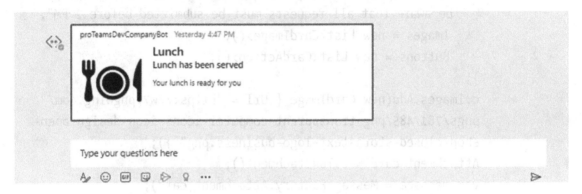

Figure 11-2. *Our bot has sent a proactive message*

Channels

We learned how to send a message to a single user, but what about our channel that needs to get notified? Sometimes, it's just easier to notify an entire channel instead of every user separately. This limits the number of calls we need to make. Back to our LunchController, add the following to the NotifyNews method.

First, again, we need to filter on location; I skipped this again, because well in my development Tenant, there is only one Team. So, that part I am leaving up to you. The beginning is the same as before.

```
var team = _teamsObjectRepository.GetAllAsync(Constants.TeamDataPartition,
1).Result.ToList()[0];
```

```
        ConnectorClient _client = new ConnectorClient(new Uri(team.
        ServiceUrl),
            new MicrosoftAppCredentials(
                _configuration["MicrosoftAppId"],
                _configuration["MicrosoftAppPassword"],
                new HttpClient()));

        ThumbnailCard c = new ThumbnailCard()
        {
            Title = "News",
            Subtitle = "Belgian Office is closing early",
            Text = "Since the Belgian office is closed early today please
            be aware that all requests must be submitted before 2 PM",
            Images = new List<CardImage>(),
            Buttons = new List<CardAction>(),
        };
        c.Images.Add(new CardImage { Url = "https://w7.pngwing.com/
        pngs/781/485/png-transparent-computer-icons-icon-design-open-
        shop-closed-store-text-logo-business.png" });
        Attachment card = c.ToAttachment();
        var message = MessageFactory.Attachment(card);
```

We create the connectorClient and our card that we want to send out. The part is a little different

```
  var conversationParameters = new ConversationParameters
        {
            Bot = new ChannelAccount(team.BotId, team.BotName),
            IsGroup = true,
            ChannelData = new TeamsChannelData
            {
                Channel = new Microsoft.Bot.Schema.Teams.
                ChannelInfo(team.Id),
            },
            Activity = (Activity)message,
            TenantId = _configuration["TenantID"]
        };
```

In our conversation parameters, we need to specify our bot, with its ID and name. We define the channel we want our message to appear, our Tenant ID, and our message. Now the only thing left is to trust our service URL and send out the word.

```
AppCredentials.TrustServiceUrl(team.ServiceUrl, DateTime.MaxValue);

var response = await _client.Conversations.CreateConversationAs
ync(conversationParameters);
```

We aren't doing anything with the response we get back this time, but you can save this somewhere, for instance, if you need to know afterward which channel you have already messaged. This is important in some cases. In our development Tenant, we just send a few messages, but there are throttling limits in place if you start messaging everybody in large Tenants. If you have a large Tenant, you should consider the rate limits (https://docs.microsoft.com/en-us/microsoftteams/platform/bots/how-to/rate-limit). These limits are in place so that you don't have a performance impact on your Tenant and are, with some simple backoff strategies, easily avoided. The most critical limit that is not that hard to hit is 8000 operations within 30 minutes. If you have more than 8000 users in your Tenant and you want to notify them all, then you are surely going to hit this limit. This means you need to spread out the requests over time. Because of these limits, notifying users that lunch is ready is doable, but using a Teams bot to inform a large company that there is a fire in the building might not be such a good idea.

If we run our code and ngrok and leave the breakpoints, we can see that when we add a bot to a Team (Figure 11-3) information is added to out table storage.

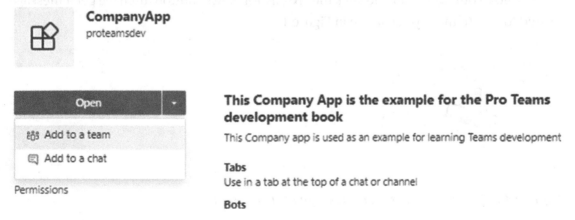

Figure 11-3. *Add our app to a Team*

Make sure that you add the bot and not the tab, like in Figure 11-4.

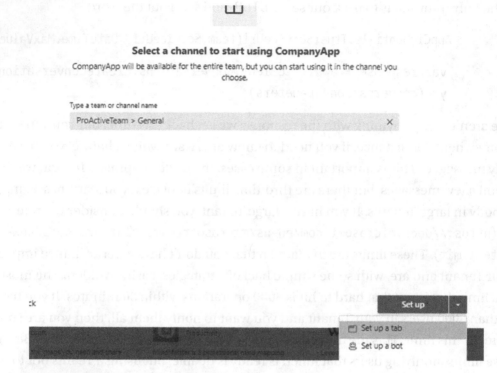

Figure 11-4. *Make sure you select "Set up a bot"*

The information when we add the bot is stored in the same table storage as before. If we now go to our lunch tab and click the "Notify for News" button, then we get a message posted to our Team as you can see in Figure 11-5.

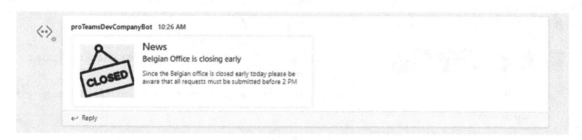

Figure 11-5. *Our bot posted a message to a channel*

Next steps

Now that we know how we can post messages to channels and users proactively, we should also take into consideration that a user can react to our messages. They can type back a message which we get in our bot and can handle there, but what if the user responds with a like? For this, we have a separate event receiver. The problem with this is it's not typed, meaning you just get a string, and you need to figure out what the user's reaction was. I've summed them up for you here. Should Teams ever get more reactions, then this list would need to be updated. Until now, we only have the ones you see in Figure 11-6.

- Like

- Laugh

- Surprised

- Angry

- Sad

- Heart

Figure 11-6. *Reactions available in Teams*

To get notified about reactions, you can use the following code:

```
protected override async Task OnReactionsAddedAsync(IList<MessageR
eaction> messageReactions, ITurnContext<IMessageReactionActivity>
turnContext, CancellationToken cancellationToken)
{
    foreach (var reaction in messageReactions)
    {
        var newReaction = $"You reacted with '{reaction.Type}' to
        the following message: '{turnContext.Activity.ReplyToId}'";
        var replyActivity = MessageFactory.Text(newReaction);
```

```
        var resourceResponse = await turnContext.SendActivityAsync(
        replyActivity, cancellationToken);
    }
}
```

It could be possible that multiple reactions come in at the same time; that is the reason we get a list of message reactions. The Bot Framework can bundle them together to minimize the calls to our bot. But from this list of reactions, we can still determine which users send over what reaction.

There are even more Teams-specific events. We have already covered TeamRenamed and ReactionAdded, but there is also a channel created, renamed, and deleted—and a reaction removed event.

Final thoughts

In this chapter, we learned that we could change our bot to be very Teams specific. Although this can have an impact on the different channels that we can then use our bot on, it's my opinion that having a bot in Teams is more than enough sometimes. Bots in Teams are usually used inside a company, and therefore having them where people work is preferred. We discussed how to get our bot to send messages to users all by themselves without the user's need to start a conversation. This can be an excellent way to notify people of changes. We can, in fact, even go further with this train of thought. You know about webhooks in Teams; if not, no worries, we are going to cover them in one of the next chapters. Well, those are by nature not authenticated, meaning if you have the URL of the webhook, then you can post data into Teams. We could, therefore, not allow webhooks and turn them off, but create our API, protected with our security implementation, and use our proactive bot to send messages to channels and users for us. You could then even create a tab where users can subscribe different channels to specific notifications, a kind of RSS feed into Teams that is powered by the bot we just built.

We are almost at the end of using Bots inside of Teams, or at least "real" bots, as you will find out later. But the next chapter I didn't want to hold you out on. Let's explore the power of bots in Teams when we give them the ability to call, get called, or join meetings.

CHAPTER 12

Calling and media bots

As a final chapter on bots, I could not miss the opportunity to discuss calling and media bots in Teams with you. In my opinion, they are the ones that have the most future potential. Chatbots are indeed cool and have their use cases, but bots where we can have actual live discussions are just on another level. But we aren't there yet. The technology is not advanced enough for most use cases, which means that, except for some cool demos, it's way too difficult (meaning expensive) to build these. Some parts are even still in preview. There are so many steps to take and things to take into consideration that projects like these are the opposite of what we have seen with the QnA bot. But still, very cool stuff to play with so let's dive in.

Change of scenery

First, I want to start with a warning; this chapter is as it is working at the time of writing. Since some parts are still in preview, they can be changed by Microsoft without warning. Therefore, I have no control if this information is still valid when you are reading this chapter. But since it's so much fun to play around with media bots, this chapter needed to be in this book.

When starting with calling and media bots, there is a fundamental principle we must understand. We, as humans, can have different types of calls. I could just call you suddenly, and we would have an ad hoc call. Or I could schedule a meeting with you. Or we could have a call with multiple people ad hoc or a meeting (scheduled call) with multiple people. There are lots of possibilities.

For a bot, this is not the case. A bot has two types of calls, a one-on-one call or a multiparty call. If it's a meeting or not, the bot doesn't care; that's just metadata of a call, just like the meeting ID or the join URL. Another thing we need to take into consideration is that we can have an audio call with our bot or an audio and video call. This can have a significant impact on the performance of our bot, and we should

229

© Rick Van Rousselt 2021
R. Van Rousselt, *Pro Microsoft Teams Development*, https://doi.org/10.1007/978-1-4842-6364-8_12

consider this when planning the underlying infrastructure. Operating with audio and video streams can get quite complicated. You want to have the best experience for your end user. You can compare it with a phone call with your mobile phone. When the connection is bad and you can hardly understand the other person, then this is not a good experience and our user is not going to like calling our bot. As you can imagine, if a user turns on their camera, then our bot shall be receiving a video stream, which must get decoded. If we want our bot to speak, it's not like we can program that behavior, so we must anticipate this and make sure that we prepare to send a .WAV file over.

With media bots, we can make a distinction between two types: service-hosted media bots and application-hosted media bots. Service-hosted media bots are the best way to start. Microsoft has provided us with a solution so that they do the heavy lifting. They provide a platform to do the processing. So, if you want to start recording, then you give the command to record. Your code will wait for the callback from the platform until the recording is done, and you get a URL where you can download that recording file. Since we don't do any processing of the media ourselves, we can even make the bot stateless. But there are, of course, limitations. Recording is just x-amount of seconds, without being able to interact with the things the user says. You will have to wait until the recording is finished or until the user has given an instruction that the recording can stop, for instance, with pressing the pound key. Since service-hosted media bots are also the easiest to debug, we are going to start with those.

Application-hosted media bots are different. In this scenario, we, as developers, must manage everything. We get a constant stream of video and audio, and we must program what to do with it. And as you can imagine receiving 50 audio frames per second where each frame contains 20 milliseconds of audio, that takes quite the CPU power. So be prepared if you go down this route that you will need some heavy compute power. Still, Microsoft has tried to make it as simple as possible for us. In the Bot Framework and especially the part for media bots, they have created a socket-like API, meaning we can register to what we want to send and receive, and this also does the encoding and decoding for us. This way, we don't have to waste our time writing H.264 video encoding software, but we can just send our content to this socket-like API.

The main advantage of application-hosted media bots is that we are in full control. This means that we can immediately do something with the data as it comes in. When a user is talking, we can instantly send that data to the speech-to-text cognitive service API and to QnA or LUIS, and we can understand the intent of our user. We get the video stream of their webcam (if it's turned on of course) so we can take a screenshot of that and send it immediately to the Vision Cognitive Services API to see what the emotional state of our user is.

Although the application-hosted media bots are cool, they are also a pain to set up. As you know by now, I've always said that bots are just APIs, and the only thing they do is send JSON over the wire. Well, not in this case. Media bots also use TCP connections to send information around. Audio and video streams would be impossible to convert into JSON, so they use a lower-level type of network connection where they can send the bits and bytes of a stream directly over the wire. Because they use direct TCP connections, those connections also must be secured. You will even need, when setting up application-hosted media bots, to make DNS changes and get an SSL wildcard certificate. If you are not using Let's Encrypt (`https://letsencrypt.org/`), it can be quite costly. Even debugging can get quite expensive because, until now, we have been using the free version of ngrok. Changing a URL in the portal when you start your tunnel is not that much work, but changing the URL of your endpoint inside of your domain's DNS settings is and also can take some time to get pushed through the rest of the Internet.

You should also know that we have two types of signals when using media bots. When a call is made to a bot, that is what we call an incoming call signal. We also have in-call signals that can occur. For instance, when a bot wants to mute itself or share its screen, then it needs to call an API during the call to achieve this.

Microsoft Graph

Calling and meeting bots use the Microsoft Graph to call the APIs they need. As you know by now, calling the Graph means you need an app registration but also consent given to you by a global administrator. Because the bot cannot do these calls on behalf of a user, it needs application permissions. The following table shows which permissions we need:

Permission	Display String	Description	Admin Consent Required
Calls.Initiate.All	Initiate outgoing 1:1 calls from the app (preview)	Allows the app to place outbound calls to a single user and transfer calls to users in your organization's directory, without a signed-in user.	Yes
Calls.InitiateGroupCall. All	Initiate outgoing group calls from the app (preview)	Allows the app to place outbound calls to multiple users and add participants to meetings in your organization, without a signed-in user.	Yes
Calls.JoinGroupCall.All	Join Group Calls and Meetings as an app (preview)	Allows the app to join group calls and scheduled meetings in your organization, without a signed-in user. The app will be joined with the privileges of a directory user to meetings in your tenant.	Yes
Calls. JoinGroupCallasGuest. All	Join Group Calls and Meetings as a guest (preview)	Allows the app to anonymously join group calls and scheduled meetings in your organization, without a signed-in user. The app will be joined as a guest to meetings in your tenant.	Yes
Calls.AccessMedia.All	Access media streams in a call as an app (preview)	Allows the app to get direct access to media streams in a call, without a signed-in user.	Yes

Microsoft Documentation: `https://docs.microsoft.com/en-us/microsoftteams/platform/bots/calls-and-meetings/registering-calling-bot`

These are the permissions required so that your bot can do calls. If you want our bot to participate in meetings, we are going to need even more permissions.

Permission	Display String	Description	Admin Consent Required
OnlineMeetings. Read.All	Read Online Meeting details from the app (preview)	Allows the app to read online meeting details in your organization, without a signed-in user.	Yes
OnlineMeetings. ReadWrite.All	Read and Create Online Meetings from the app (preview) on behalf of a user	Allows the app to create online meetings in your organization on behalf of a user, without a signed-in user.	Yes

Microsoft Documentation: `https://docs.microsoft.com/en-us/microsoftteams/ platform/bots/calls-and-meetings/registering-calling-bot`

When searching for documentation regarding media bots, they are not located in the normal docs.microsoft.com location. The team responsible for creating calling bots has their document repository straight into their GitHub repository with samples. You can view the documentation here: `https://microsoftgraph.github.io/microsoft-graph- comms-samples/docs/articles/index.html.` You can also use that repository to view some of the examples Microsoft provides regarding media bots. I'm only going to show you how a service-hosted media bot works in Teams; an application-hosted bot would be a hassle for you just to fire up and debug to see what it does. But I do recommend that you take a look at some of the examples of Microsoft just to know what they are capable of.

Service-hosted

Let's get started with our service-hosted bot. If you look in the examples, you can see that I have converted our company bot into a calling bot. I even broke the chat functionality, which could also just be my client that is acting up, because if you want to play around with media bots, you cannot use the web client. You cannot even just use the Teams client. You must set it to developer preview to also have the possibility to upload the Teams app package as in Figure 12-1. And most of the time, an administrator on your production tenant has disabled most of the required settings, so it's best that you try these things first on your own developer tenant. And the developer preview is definitely a preview; it's sometimes impossible to do your daily Teams communications in it because it can break, which, of course, is no problem since new features in Teams also must get tested.

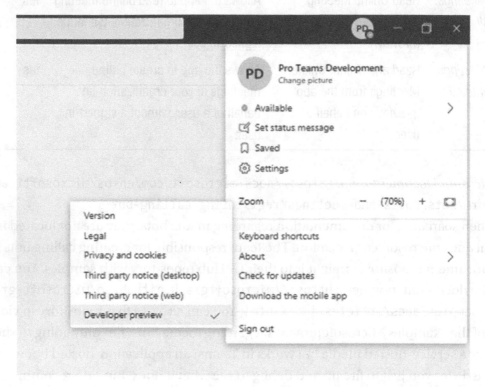

Figure 12-1. *Setting your Teams desktop client to developer preview mode*

When you upload your app package, the Teams client, in the browser or on your PC, does a verification before it really uploads it to your environment. It scans the manifest to see if there are errors. Well, since media bots are still in preview, just getting them uploaded is not simple. I ended up creating a new app package with App Studio like we did in the beginning of the book and upload it that way. Even when you download the app from App Studio, you get a warning that this app has preview features and that you are not able to submit it for publication as in Figure 12-2.

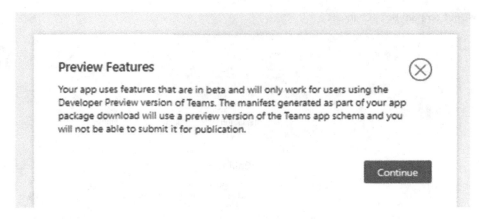

Figure 12-2. *The warning you receive when downloading an app package from App Studio with preview features*

You can see the manifest of that app in the examples. It also helps that I don't have any other stuff like tabs in our manifest. This way, you can immediately see what the setting is that we need, and that's this one.

```
"supportsCalling": true,
"supportsVideo": false
```

These two settings that we can add to the bot part of the manifest will tell Teams that it needs to show either a calling icon or a calling with video icon. And showing this is step 1 in having our bot enabled to receive calls.

The second thing we need to do is configure in the Azure Portal that our bot is enabled for calls. The manifest just tells Teams to show the calling icons; nothing tells the Bot Framework that this bot can call. So open up the Azure Portal, and under your bot registration, where you configured the Teams channel so that we could chat with our bot in Teams, we need to activate the calling feature. If you look at Figure 12-3, you can see that you need to check the box and give a calling endpoint.

proTeamsDevCompanyBot | Channels
Web App Bot

arch (Ctrl+/)   «

verview

ctivity log

ccess control (IAM)

gs

anagement

uild

st in Web Chat

nalytics

hannels

ttings

beech priming

t Service pricing

ervice Settings

onfiguration

l App service settings

rt + troubleshooting

ew support request

Messaging   Calling   Publish

Calling Learn more

These settings determine whether Calling is enabled for your bot, and if
enabled, whether IVR functionality or Real Time Media functionality is to be
used.

Calling

☑ Enable calling

These settings determine whether Calling is enabled for your bot. Note that
some Calling features require elevated permissions from an organization's
Teams Administrator. To add permissions, go to your bot in the Application
Registration Portal, locate the Microsoft Graph Permissions section, and
then add the permissions that your app requires.

Webhook (for calling)

https://proteamsdev.ngrok.io/api/call

***Figure 12-3.** Enable the calling feature in Azure and enter your webhook*

We need to enter our calling endpoint for the same reason as we needed to enter
our messaging endpoint. When a user hits the call button, Teams will contact the Bot
Framework to see where it needs to redirect that call to, just like with a chat message. As
you can see from the URL, I created a new controller for this and a new bot code section,
just to keep the code separated.

We also are going to need the permissions we discussed earlier from the Microsoft
Graph calling APIs. Head over to your app registration from your bot in the Azure
Active Directory section and grant application permissions to all the calling APIs as in
Figure 12-4.

Figure 12-4. *Adding all the Microsoft Graph calling APIs and granting them consent*

Don't forget to click the consent button afterward or the permissions are not going to work.

Breaking it down

Now there is a lot of boilerplate code that comes into play when working with media bots. The easiest way I learn how things work is to debug the code and look at what happens next. If you do that, take note of the multitude of calls going back and forward. This is a snapshot of my ngrok web interface (`http://localhost:4040`) for this simple bot who just says a few words.

All Requests		Clear
POST /api/call	502 Bad Gateway	1.97ms
POST /api/call	202 Accepted	19.32s
GET /audio/346f6ae2-096b-4b03-936c-107953ba8331.wav	200 OK	4ms
POST /api/call	202 Accepted	101.04ms
POST /api/call	202 Accepted	128.05ms
POST /api/call	202 Accepted	161.53ms
POST /api/call	202 Accepted	98.16ms
POST /api/call	202 Accepted	107.66ms

Figure 12-5. *A lot of calls happen when a bot answers a call*

Let's break down what happens here, and remember the bottom call that you see in Figure 12-5 is the first one that happened, and it works its way up from there. The first thing that happens when you click the call button is Teams calling our endpoint with an incoming call request. With this, our bot just answers with a 202 telling Teams it's alive and will accept the call. Next up, the call will be in an establishing state; this, of course, is also communicated to your bot. Once the call is established, which is the third request from the bottom you see in Figure 12-5, our bot will want to say something to our user, so it must notify via the Graph endpoint that it wants to do that. Then the framework will download the media file and will play that; once played, the bot is again informed that the audio file has completed playing. Don't worry about the last one; the "bad gateway error" was because I stopped my Visual Studio too fast, and I left this in on purpose to show you that not all errors are code errors, but sometimes it can just be that the connection was terminated.

As you can see, my WAV file has a weird name; that's because I'm not using audio files I already prepared, but I am rendering them on the fly with the Azure Cognitive speech-to-text service (`https://azure.microsoft.com/en-us/services/cognitive-services/text-to-speech/`). This service, in combination with calling bots, is a very dynamic combination. This is again an API like our QnA maker service, and we need a key to call it. Also, take note that while we use most of the keys inside our code, if we would ever go to production with this app, we would be storing our keys in a configuration file. If you go to the Azure Portal and search for speech, you can find the service and create one. If you look at Figure 12-6, then you can see that I just needed to specify a name, pricing level, and resource group. Pick a location that is close to you because voice bots are sensitive to latency, and going to the other side of the planet is going to have a negative impact on your performance.

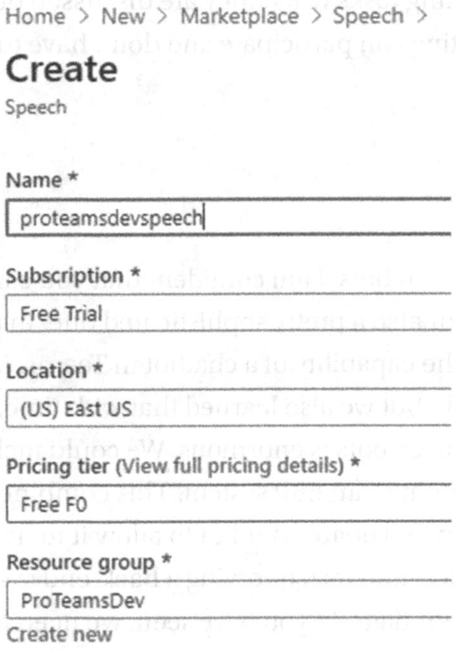

Home > New > Marketplace > Speech >

Create
Speech

Name *

proteamsdevspeech

Subscription *

Free Trial

Location *

(US) East US

Pricing tier (View full pricing details) *

Free F0

Resource group *

ProTeamsDev

Create new

Figure 12-6. *Create a text-to-speech resource in Azure*

This can then be easily achieved by entering a message and a file where the spoken text must be saved to with the following code:

```
var config = SpeechConfig.FromSubscription("646cf1c565854d24b691a0abce444f
bc", "eastus");

        using (var fileOutput = AudioConfig.FromWavFileOutput(fileName))
        {
            using (var synthesizer = new SpeechSynthesizer(config,
            fileOutput))
```

```
        {
            var result = await synthesizer.SpeakTextAsync(message);
        }
    }
```

Too bad that I cannot add a video here of the bot answering the call, talking, and waiting for a key to be entered in the keypad of Teams. I recommend that you play around with the solution, debug it, and see the potential that media bots have. I immediately can think of several use cases where a bot can take away the repetitive tasks of a meeting, such as creating tasks when they are discussed or taking meeting minutes so that people in the meeting can participate and don't have to worry about writing things down.

Summary

Now with this final chapter on bots, I am confident that you can build not only a basic bot for Microsoft Teams but also a pretty sophisticated one. In this chapter, we learned that we could go beyond the capability of a chatbot in Teams. Media bots in Teams are fun to play around with, but we also learned that with time, when the technology matures, the potential of these bots is enormous. We could include all kinds of APIs into our bot such as a CRM system or an ERP system. This combined with voice-to-text and text-to-voice capabilities would enable our bot to allow it to have live conversations, converting that conversation into text, querying a back-end system, and providing a spoken answer with relevant data. As you have seen, we need the power of the Microsoft Graph to get these bots working, so be sure to check out Chapter 17 to learn more about it. In the next chapter, we are going to learn one of my favorite features that a developer can build on the Teams platform, and those are messaging extensions.

PART 4

Webhooks

CHAPTER 13

Incoming webhooks

Now that you are an expert on Bots in Teams, it's time to start with webhooks. Webhooks are also known as connectors which is just a fancy name for webhooks. Because of this, I will switch between these both names; also keep in mind that if you ever have a problem and you search for your issue online, then use both these names, and you might find the correct answer using either webhooks or connectors. In the next two topics, we will see how they work and how we can utilize them inside of Teams.

Webhooks

Connectors are webhooks, and webhooks are, in fact, also just APIs. The difference between connectors and what we have seen so far, is that instead of we initiating a request to call an API or our API gets called as the information is needed, is that webhooks are event based. They are triggered when a configured event occurs. I will explain the difference with a little example.

Take our company app; we created a bot that will notify users when there is a new news item. We created an API for the notification. Well, we created a button, but the button can change quickly to an API. But how about the system calling our notification API? How is it going to get triggered? Do we build an application for our news managers where they can click a button, and the notification happens? Or do we check on a regular basis if a news item is added and then notify our users? Checking on a regular basis is called polling. We need to pull the information from our news repository (probably from another API) every x-amount of time and then trigger our API if required. Wouldn't it be much easier that the news repository (whatever that is) contacts us when there are changes? This is where webhooks come into the picture. This is similar to the observer pattern (`https://en.wikipedia.org/wiki/Observer_pattern`) we use in the software design, where the subject is our third party and the observer is Teams. As soon as something changes, the subject informs the observers.

We turn the flow around with webhooks. We create an API, and so does everybody else who needs to be informed if a new news item gets created, and the news repository

R. Van Rousselt, *Pro Microsoft Teams Development*, https://doi.org/10.1007/978-1-4842-6364-8_13

notifies all those APIs that a change occurred. I can hear you already thinking, doesn't this provide additional work for the developers who maintain the news repository? Well, it does, a little. But now their system doesn't get continuously slammed with API requests from us and all others wanting to see if there is a new news item.

Breakdown

In Teams, we have got two kinds of webhooks: incoming and outgoing. In this chapter, we will focus on the incoming ones. There is also a partial third one, an Office 365 Connector. It's also an incoming webhook, but it gets a configuration page, and we can package it into our Teams app. Let us start with the incoming webhook.

An incoming webhook is where Teams is the system waiting for us to notify that a change has occurred. Teams is just going to take one action; it's just going to relay the information we send to the correct channel, nothing more. Setting one up is quite straightforward; it's also an app in Teams so that it can get added in the same way. Go to your Team's settings by navigating to the "Manage Team" page and select Apps, and then "More Apps" to add an app to the Team. Or you go to a channel and click the three dots in the top-right corner and click connectors. Once you have the list of apps, search for "incoming webhook" as in Figure 13-1.

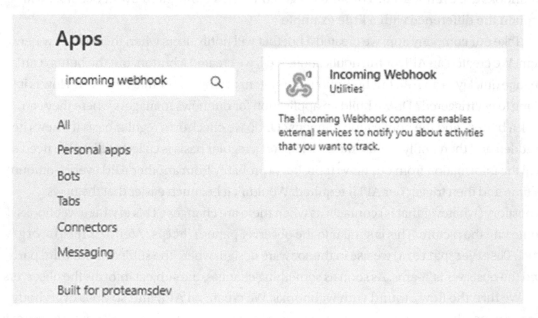

Figure 13-1. *An Incoming Webhook app in the store*

244

We first must add the webhook to the entire Team; notice how it already displays "setup a connector." This already gives us a clue that they are one and the same. Give it a name, and if you like, you can also give it another icon. This icon is going to be used in the channel as the avatar for the connector, so consider this "the face" of your webhook. For now, the same icon is fine, and just call the incoming webhook ProTeamsDev like in Figure 13-2. Now, when you hit the create button, this is where the logic starts.

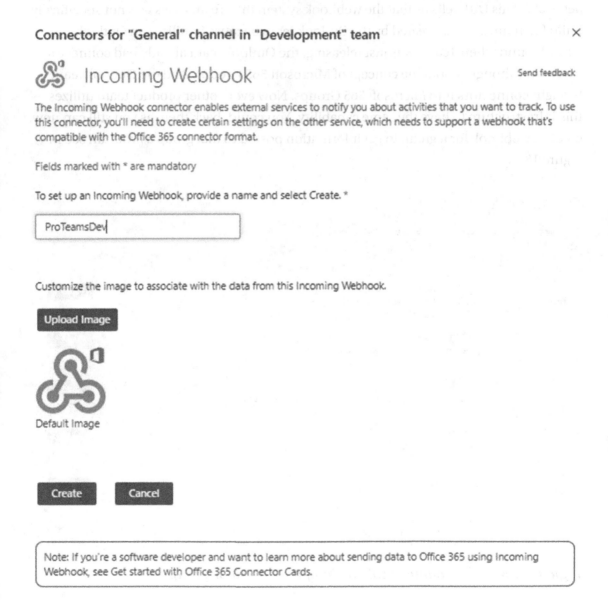

Figure 13-2. Name the incoming webhook and click create

You will see that you receive a URL; don't forget to copy it somewhere because we are going to need it later. Mine looks like this:

`https://outlook.office.com/webhook/9a792aa1-489d-4485-b4c1-d6e9662bc854@` `c1df480e-6f75-4ba5-97a6-efcca25423ee/IncomingWebhook/4ca18db10781479c8d7861` `91f2069274/ee61283f-5214-4ddc-8f0d-596740fc439f`

Let us break this URL into pieces. First up is the "`https://outlook.office.com/` `webhook`." This URL tells us that the webhook system that Teams uses was not specifically build for Teams. It was created by the Outlook team because it utilizes an Outlook URL. Around when Teams was just releasing, the Outlook team already had connectors when they thought about the concept of Microsoft 365 Groups. And the Outlook team brought connectors into Microsoft 365 Groups. Now every other product team utilizes this infrastructure to have the same capability. You could, back then, as you still can now, create a webhook for a group to get information posted to that group as you can see in Figure 13-3.

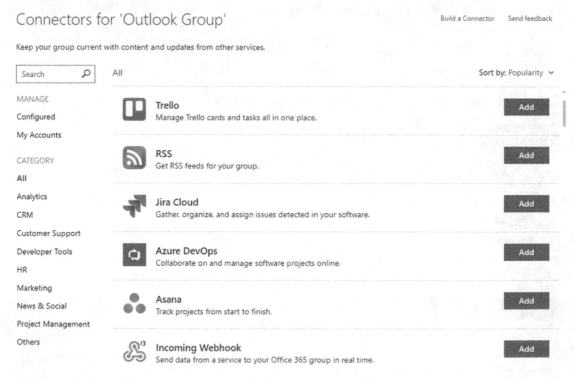

Figure 13-3. *An incoming webhook but for an Outlook group*

The rest of the URL looks like only GUIDs, although sometimes with a dash in between, sometimes without, so can we make sense of them? The first GUID is the ID of our Team. To be sure, let us open the Microsoft Graph explorer and sign in with your developer tenant credentials; use the short link aka.ms/ge. I always use this one, and it's easy to remember and will take you straight to the correct page. If you don't know what the Graph Explorer is, then don't panic. We will get deeper into the Microsoft Graph and the explorer in Chapter 17. For now, just log in with the same credentials as for your developer tenant. If you have never used this tool before, then you must also consent. As in Chapter 6, this is using OAuth as well, and it needs your consent to get the information from your tenant.

On the left side, you will see some examples of requests. If you scroll down, you will find the one that shows you all the groups that you belong to. Since a Team is a Microsoft 365 group, we should see our Teams and their IDs in the information sent back. We can see like in Figure 13-4 that the ID of our Team is 9a792aa1-489d-4485-b4c1-d6e9662bc854, which is the same as in the URL.

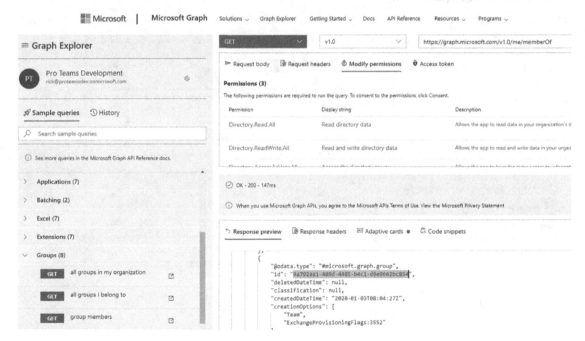

Figure 13-4. *Using the Graph Explorer to find our Team ID*

The second GUID, right after the @, already looks familiar. It's our Tenant ID. If we go to the Azure Portal where we created our App Registrations, we can see that our Tenant ID is c1df480e-6f75-4ba5-97a6-efcca25423ee as in Figure 13-5. We could also utilize a free tool at www.whatismytenantid.com/ to get our Tenant ID.

Tenant ID

c1df480e-6f75-4ba5-97a6-efcca25423ee

Figure 13-5. The Tenant ID of my environment

The next GUID, after the /webhook/ part (4ca18db10781479c8d786191f2069274), is an always random one; I've looked everywhere to see if there was a pattern or that I could match it somewhere, and this must be the unique ID of the webhook. The next one is a GUID that identifies me, the user who created it. If you go to the Graph Explorer again, and you get the information about your profile (https://graph.microsoft.com/v1.0/me/), then you can see that your user also has an ID. This ID is the same as the one in the URL, as in Figure 13-6.

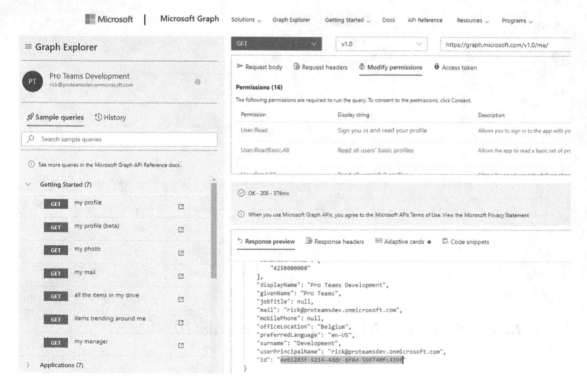

Figure 13-6. Using the Graph Explorer to find my user's ID

Considering all this, a URL for an incoming webhook has most parts fixed and just one random identifier. Now from a security standpoint, this is not so great. It's called security through obscurity, meaning that the security is implemented through hiding the information. An incoming webhook is open, meaning you don't need to authenticate to send data to it. If you have somebody smart enough, they will probably be able to figure out the endpoint to the webhook you created. And this could potentially be a security issue. You don't want phishing messages to end up in your Team's client. Therefore, as discussed in Chapter 11, you could build a bot and have it relay the information, and you can then protect it with an Azure Active Directory login. Now that we know how a webhook works and how to create one, let us send some data to it.

Posting information

The information that we need to send to this endpoint is always going to be in JSON format. We need to create an HTTP Post message and send this over. The easiest way to do this is with Postman (`www.postman.com/`), or at least that's my favorite tool to play around with incoming webhooks. There are also others, so pick your favorite one and prepare a POST request to the URL you received from the incoming webhook. I've also included a Postman collection with all the requests so that you don't need to copy/paste them.

The information that is going to get sent to the channel is going to get posted as a card. There are different options with cards, and we will go through the various possibilities. But the simplest one is just text only. Try adding the following JSON as a body and send out the request:

```
{"text": "An alert from Pro Teams Development"}
```

As you can see in Figure 13-7, when we send out the request, we get an HTTP status of 200 back, meaning that the request was successful.

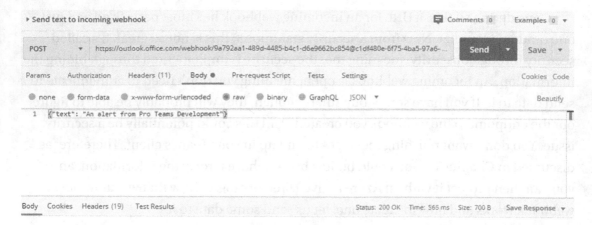

Figure 13-7. *Sending data to our incoming webhook in Teams*

The cool thing about Postman is that you can let it generate the same request in a different variety of languages. If you click "code" on the right-hand side, you can select your language of choice, and the correct code will be shown to repeat this request (see Figure 13-8).

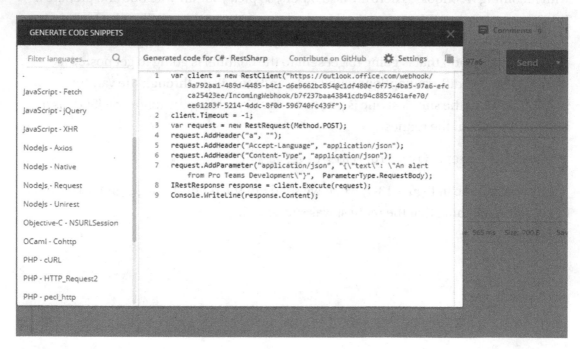

Figure 13-8. *Postman providing us with example code*

Sending a piece of text can sometimes be enough, but not always; we have even more options available.

Cards

Let's go through all the different cards available to us. These cards are mostly universal within Teams and the Bot Framework. As we have already seen in the previous bot chapters, we can also send out the JSON that composes a card as a message from a bot, but also as incoming webhooks. When you start with cards, be sure to use the card section in App Studio to get you going. The only downside with using cards is the different versions that exist and the differences in supportability. Some are only available for Teams but not in the Bot Framework and vice versa. Some versions are not yet supported in Teams, but others are. It's challenging to keep up with the different services from Microsoft that support the different versions of cards. When you start implementing them, it's always good to test out the card(s) you want to use in your project. It might be that the one you need is not available yet or doesn't appear in the form that you want it to look. The Bot Framework itself supports eight different kinds of cards, and you can find more information here: `https://docs.microsoft.com/en-us/azure/bot-service/ rest-api/bot-framework-rest-connector-add-rich-cards?view=azure-bot- service-4.0#types-of-rich-cards`. Teams supports seven cards, but they are different sometimes; let us see what they are and how they work.

Hero card

The hero card is the most basic card to use. You might have seen in previous chapters the use of a hero card. It typically contains a single large image, a small amount of text, and some buttons. They can be used in Bots and in messaging extensions (Chapters 15 and 16) in Teams. So, we cannot use them with connectors, meaning incoming webhooks. It has the following properties.

Property	Type	Description
title	Rich text	Title of the card. Maximum two lines; formatting not currently supported
subtitle	Rich text	Subtitle of the card. Maximum two lines; formatting not currently supported
text	Rich text	Text appears just below the subtitle.
images	Array of images	The image displayed at the top of the card. Aspect ratio 16:9
buttons	Array of action objects	Set of actions applicable to the current card. Maximum six
tap	Action object	This action will be activated when the user taps on the card itself

Microsoft Documentation: https://docs.microsoft.com/en-us/microsoftteams/ platform/task-modules-and-cards/cards/cards-reference#hero-card

The raw JSON that will need to go over the wire will be

```
{
    "contentType": "application/vnd.microsoft.card.hero",
    "content": {
        "title": "Pro Teams Dev Hero Card",
        "subtitle": "Hero card example",
        "text": "This is an example of a Hero card JSON",
        "images": [
            {
                "url": "https://statics.teams.cdn.office.net/evergreen-
                assets/apps/teams_dev_app_largeimage.png"
            }
        ],
        "buttons": [
            {
                "type": "openUrl",
                "title": "Open link 1",
                "value": "https://www.rickvanrousselt.com"
            },
            {
```

```
            "type": "openUrl",
            "title": "Open link 2",
            "value": "https://www.apress.com/"
          }
      ]
    }
}
```

In C#, we would use

```
Activity reply = activity.CreateReply();
HeroCard card = new HeroCard
{
    Title = "Pro Teams Dev Hero Card",
    Subtitle = "Hero card example",
    Text = "This is an example of a Hero card JSON",
    Images = new List<CardImage>(),
    Buttons = new List<CardAction>(),
};
card.Images.Add(new CardImage { Url = "https://statics.teams.cdn.office.
net/evergreen-assets/apps/teams_dev_app_largeimage.png" });
card.Buttons.Add(new CardAction
{
    Title = "https://www.rickvanrousselt.com"
});
card.Buttons.Add(new CardAction
{
    Title = "https://www.apress.com/"
});
reply.Attachments.Add(card.ToAttachment());
```

and in Node we would use:

```
var msg = new builder.Message(session);
msg.attachmentLayout(builder.AttachmentLayout.carousel);
var attachments = [
  new builder.HeroCard(session)
    .title("Pro Teams Dev Hero Card")
```

```
    .subtitle("Hero card example")
    .text("This is an example of a Hero card JSON")
    .images([
      builder.CardImage.create(session, "https://statics.teams.cdn.office.
      net/evergreen-assets/apps/teams_dev_app_largeimage.png"),
    ])
    .buttons([
      builder.CardAction.imBack(session, "https://www.rickvanrousselt.com",
      "https://www.rickvanrousselt.com"),
      builder.CardAction.imBack(session, "https://www.apress.com/",
      "https://www.apress.com/"),
    ])
];
msg.attachments(attachments);
```

Once we send out the card, it will look something like in Figure 13-9.

Figure 13-9. *An example of a hero card*

List card

List cards are something that I have never had to need to use. There are newer and better ways to have a list of items as a card. Since this is a very undocumented type of card, without integration in the SDKs for C# and Node, it's also not easy to implement. But it could be that this is just the one you need, so let's see how this one works. List cards are not available in messaging extensions and connectors, so only usable with a bot. There is also no example that you can build within App Studio. List cards have the following properties:

Property	Type	Description
title	Rich text	Title of the card. Maximum two lines; formatting not currently supported
items	Array of list items	*undocumented
buttons	Array of action objects	Set of actions applicable to the current card. Maximum six

Microsoft Documentation: https://docs.microsoft.com/en-us/microsoftteams/ platform/task-modules-and-cards/cards/cards-reference#hero-card

Since the items property from above is still undocumented, these are its properties:

Property	Type	Description
title	Rich text	Title of the card. Maximum two lines; formatting not currently supported
id	Rich text	ID of the item
type	Array of objects	This can be file, resultItem, or person
subtitle	Rich text	Subtitle of the card. Maximum two lines; formatting not currently supported
tap	Action object	This action will be activated when the user taps on the card itself

Microsoft Documentation: https://docs.microsoft.com/en-us/microsoftteams/ platform/task-modules-and-cards/cards/cards-reference#list-card

The JSON you would use will look something like this:

```json
{
  "title": "List Card Example",
  "items": [
    {
      "type": "file",
      "id": "https://proteamsdev.sharepoint.com/teams/new/Shared%20
      Documents/Report.xlsx",
      "title": "Team Excel file",
      "subtitle": "Open a URL",
      "tap": {
        "type": "openUrl",
        "value": "https://contoso.sharepoint.com/teams/new/Shared%20
        Documents/Report.xlsx"
      }
    },
    {
      "type": "resultItem",
      "icon": "https://cdn2.iconfinder.com/data/icons/social-icons-33/128/
      Trello-128.png",
      "title": "A generic result",
      "subtitle": "This is a generic result item",
      "tap": {
        "type": "imBack",
        "value": "generic result returned"
      }
    },
    {
      "type": "section",
      "title": "Manager"
    },
    {
      "type": "person",
      "id": "rickvanrousselt@proteamsdev.onmicrosoft.com",
      "title": "Rick Van Rousselt",
```

```
      "subtitle": "Author",
      "tap": {
        "type": "imBack",
        "value": "rickvanrousselt@proteamsdev.onmicrosoft.com"
      }
    }
  ],
  "buttons": [
    {
      "type": "openUrl",
      "title": "Open link",
      "value": "https://www.apress.com/"
    }
  ]
}
```

Since there is no support in the SDK for C# and Node, the only thing you can do in code is send this response back as one JSON as we already did in the company app. Finally, you end up with something looking like Figure 13-10.

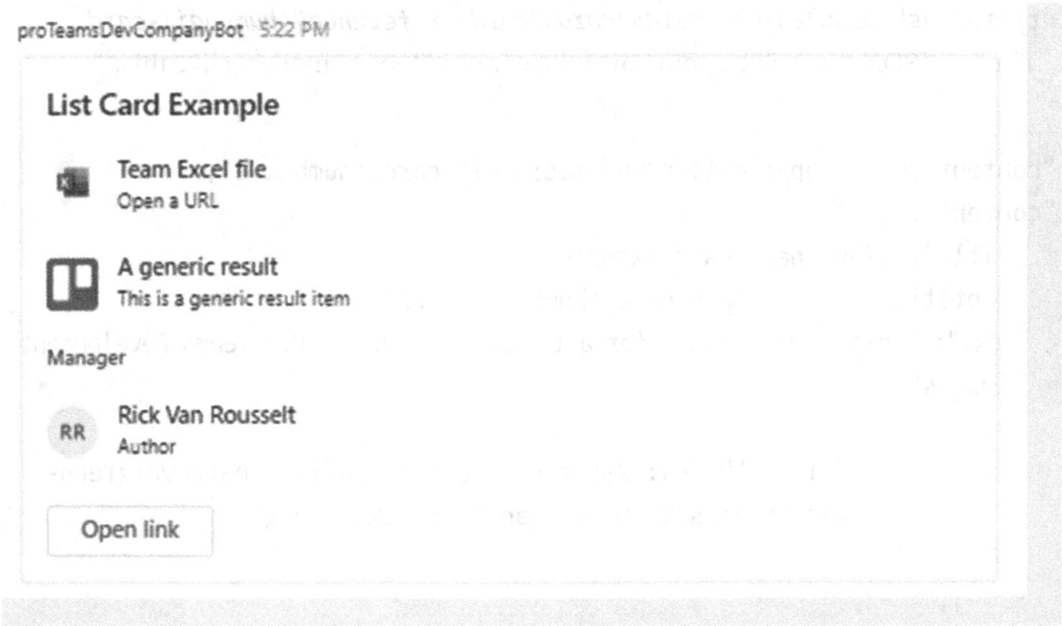

Figure 13-10. *A list card example*

Thumbnail card

Thumbnail cards are like hero cards but smaller. They do not have an image that takes up all the space. They are used the same as hero cards, in bots and messaging extensions but not in webhooks. They have the following properties:

Property	Type	Description
title	Rich text	Title of the card. Maximum two lines; formatting not currently supported
subtitle	Rich text	Subtitle of the card. Maximum two lines; formatting not currently supported
text	Rich text	Text appears just below the subtitle
images	Array of images	Image displayed at the top of the card. Aspect ratio 1:1 (square)
buttons	Array of action objects	Set of actions applicable to the current card. Maximum six
tap	Action object	This action will be activated when the user taps on the card itself

Microsoft Documentation: https://docs.microsoft.com/en-us/microsoftteams/ platform/task-modules-and-cards/cards/cards-reference#thumbnail-card

The raw JSON that will be going over the wire will look something like this:

```
{
  "contentType": "application/vnd.microsoft.card.thumbnail",
  "content": {
    "title": "Thumbnail Card example",
    "subtitle": "An example of a thumbnail card",
    "text": "This is an example for a thumbnail card for Pro Teams Development",
    "images": [
        {
            "url": "https://statics.teams.cdn.office.net/evergreen-
            assets/apps/teams_dev_app_largeimage.png"
        }
    ],
```

```
    "buttons": [
        {
            "type": "openUrl",
            "title": "Open link 1",
            "value": "https://www.rickvanrousselt.com"
        },
        {
            "type": "openUrl",
            "title": "Open link 2",
            "value": "https://www.apress.com/"
        }
    ]
}
```

Card combinations

You can also combine more cards if you would like that. We have already seen a carousel collection where we were sending out multiple hero cards. Not only do we have the possibility to create a carousel, but we can also create a list of cards. Now this only works for adaptive cards, hero cards, and thumbnail cards. Nothing we can use in our webhook. But as we have seen in the bot chapters, they can be convenient sometimes to let the user scroll between the right card and do an action on that one.

Receipt card and sign-in card

You must have seen receipt cards somewhere. They are widely used in the demos that Microsoft gives about the Bot Framework, and they can be used as a receipt for a purchase. Usually, in Teams, we won't use this card, or you must work for a company that sells products to its employees. This card can be looked at as a legacy card. Adaptive cards are again the way forward here. And this is the same story for the sign-in card. It is a legacy type of card that used to be for signing in users from your bot. It also was a watered-down version of the Bot Framework.

Office 365 connector card

The Office 365 connector card is one we could already describe as a legacy. You might call it the predecessor of the adaptive card. We can use the Office 365 Connector card in our webhook and in messaging extensions and bots, but only in Bots for Teams. This card, like an adaptive card, is very powerful because users can immediately take action from within the card. You don't need to trigger the opening of a website to have the user act on something. We won't go any deeper into this one because, as already stated, an adaptive card is the next generation and has a lot more functionality. But this was the only card we were able to use with an incoming webhook. All the others until now are only available in your Teams bot and maybe in a messaging extension.

Adaptive cards

I'm a massive fan of adaptive cards. They are versatile to use, and Microsoft has made them platform independent. It's a separate team within Microsoft who is responsible for these, which means that we are not forced to use them only in Teams, but we can use them in the Bot Framework or even with email. Like all the other cards, they are composed of JSON. Because adaptive cards replace so many different types of other cards and can do more, we are not going to go over all the options, and you don't need to know them by heart. There is a designer available for you at `https://amdesigner.azurewebsites.net/`. Now, wouldn't it be easy if we could just use these adaptive cards everywhere? Well, we can. Even in incoming webhooks, we can use adaptive cards.

Actionable messages

To get started with actionable messages, there is an old designer, which we can still use (`https://messagecardplayground.azurewebsites.net/`). This designer helps us to construct the JSON in a visual way. Be aware that the card editor you get in App Studio is for adaptive cards and not actionable messages, so for our incoming webhook, it's not helpful.

Let's start by constructing our message. We are going to keep triggering the incoming webhook from Postman. But you could change this to anything that suits your business case, like a scheduled task in Windows or a PowerShell script. Let's not wander too far away from our original use case, our lunch and news intranet. We already had an option to notify users with our proactive bot, but we could also do this with an incoming webhook, at least to a channel. Let's notify our users that a birthday is coming up and that we are going to eat a birthday cake after work. Users can then choose to accept with comments, decline, or view the news item in our company app to get more information. Let's construct our message card. This is the basic JSON:

```
{
    "@type": "MessageCard",
    "@context": "https://schema.org/extensions",
    "summary": "Happy birthday",
    "themeColor": "0078D7",
    "title": "Birthday alert: \"Time to eat cake\"",
    "sections": [
        {
            "activityTitle": "Rick Van Rousselt",
            "activitySubtitle": "20/04/1983",
            "activityImage": "https://images.freeimages.com/images/large-
            previews/dbc/happy-birthday-1326522.jpg",
            "facts": [
                {
                    "name": "Office Location:",
                    "value": "Belgium"
                },
                {
                    "name": "Time & place",
                    "value": "17:30pm"
                }
            ],
            "text": "Do you want to have cake at the company restaurant
            after hours"
        }
    ],
    "potentialAction": [
        {
            "@type": "ActionCard",
            "name": "Accept and add a comment",
            "inputs": [
                {
```

```
                "@type": "TextInput",
                "id": "comment",
                "title": "Enter your comment",
                "isMultiline": true
            }
        ],
        "actions": [
            {
                "@type": "HttpPOST",
                "name": "OK",
                "target": "https://6da5e407772b.ngrok.io/api/
                BirthdayConfirmation",
                "body": "{{comment.value}}"
            }
        ]
    },
    {
        "@type": "HttpPOST",
        "name": "No",
        "target": "https://6da5e407772b.ngrok.io/api/BirthdayConfirmati
        on?answer=no"
    },
    {
        "@type": "OpenUri",
        "name": "View news item",
        "targets": [
            {
                "os": "default",
                "uri": "https://teams.microsoft.com/l/entity/1f1167eb-
                517c-465b-bf52-6de75a2f4cad/CompanyNews?context=%7B%22c
                hannelId%22%3A%20%2219%3A1473566abaf444e4a2e59b94959982
                0f%40thread.tacv2%22%7D"
            }
        ]
    }
]
}
```

You should end up with an actionable message looking like Figure 13-11.

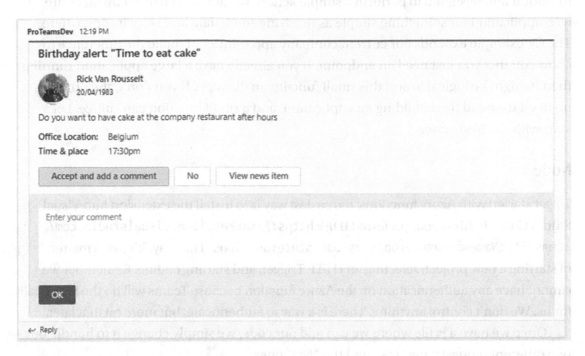

ProTeamsDev   12:19 PM

Birthday alert: "Time to eat cake"

Rick Van Rousselt
20/04/1983

Do you want to have cake at the company restaurant after hours

Office Location: Belgium
Time & place   17:30pm

Accept and add a comment   No   View news item

Enter your comment

OK

← Reply

Figure 13-11. *An actionable message in Teams with the comment section already open*

I have tried to add the different functionalities we can do with an actionable message. The first part is where we define the type which is "MessageCard" and some default information like type and context. For more information, you can look in the documentation about message cards: `https://docs.microsoft.com/en-us/outlook/actionable-messages/message-card-reference`.

The cool stuff is in the potential action part. In this card, I have added three actions: two HttpPost actions and one OpenUri. They do what their name already describes. The HTTP post action will call an HTTP endpoint that you configure and will post information back. This request is taken care of by Teams. The only thing we need to do is configure the target URI. As you can see, I have already added an ngrok URL. If you start running ngrok, you will of course get a different URL, so that must be changed. As you can see in the first potential action, we can even ask for comments, and those will be included in the body of the POST call.

The only thing we need is something to receive this POST call. I have included two examples. The Node one is using an Azure function. Azure functions match perfectly with these actions from our message card because they are small functions that run in the cloud and designed to perform a simple action. We don't need to set up an entire web application for something simple as receiving some data and store it somewhere. The C# example expands our current company app solution. I made the difference to show you that you just need an endpoint. If you already have a large application running, then it might be logical to add this small function to that app. If you don't, then there is no need to spend time building an application, and a small function can suffice. Let's start with the Node one.

Node

To get started with Azure functions, the easiest way is to install the extension into Visual Studio Code (if this is your preferred IDE): https://marketplace.visualstudio.com/items?itemName=ms-azuretools.vscode-azurefunctions. This way, it's just a matter of starting a new project, selecting an HTTP Trigger, and starting coding. Remember we cannot have any authentication on the Azure function because Teams will do the POST call for us. We don't control anything. There is a way to authenticate, but more on that later.

Once we have a js file where we can add our code, we simply change it to handle our two different requests: the "OK" and the "NO" ones.

```
module.exports = async function (context, req) {
    context.log('JavaScript HTTP trigger function processed a request.');
    var responseMessage = {"text": "Sorry you can not make it" }
    const name = (req.query.name || (req.body && req.body.name));
    if(req.query.answer != "no"){
        responseMessage = {"text": "Thanks for registering and giving the
        following comment: " + req.body }
    }
        //Here you should save this data to a repository. This can be a
        simple SharePoint list or a CosmosDB or SQL instance.
    context.res = {
        // status: 200, /* Defaults to 200 */
        headers: {
            "CARD-UPDATE-IN-BODY":"true"
        },
```

```
      body: responseMessage
  };
}
```

As you can see, this doesn't do very much. We check if the query string contains "answer=no" to verify if the NO button was clicked. The cool logic is in what we send back. We could just send back a status of 200 and be done with it. But we can also update the card again. If we add another JSON that represents a card, and send that back, then the card gets updated like in Figure 13-12. In the example, we used the simplest form of a card, but you could also use a hero card or a thumbnail card. In theory, you could also use an actionable message again, but that's not really recommended because then you are replacing questions with even more questions and that could confuse the user. To get this working, we have to add an extra header to the answer we send back "CARD-UPDATE-IN-BODY" with the value of true.

Figure 13-12. *Actionable message card is updated with our response from our Azure function*

To debug this piece of code, we have the option in Visual Studio Code to "Attach to Node Functions." If we hit the play button, we can start debugging. Of course, like always, this is running on our localhost. So we should use ngrok to connect our localhost with a public reachable URL. The port for debugging Azure functions is different than what we have used so far, so use the following command (but be sure to check if the endpoint has not changed with your version of Visual Studio Code):

```
ngrok http 7071 --host-header localhost
```

Replace the URL you receive inside the JSON that we use to create the actionable message so that Teams does the call to the correct URL. Now there is one thing we are not doing, and that is authentication. If you debug the code, you can see that there is a lot more to send over the wire than just our comment. If you look at Figure 13-13, you can also see that a bearer token is added to the headers. This token is to make sure that its Teams does the call and not somebody else. So, to get the code safe, we should

265

add a check to verify this token and only do something when this is OK. This is highly recommended in production environments. You can find an example on how to do this here: https://github.com/OfficeDev/outlook-actionable-messages-node-token-validation.

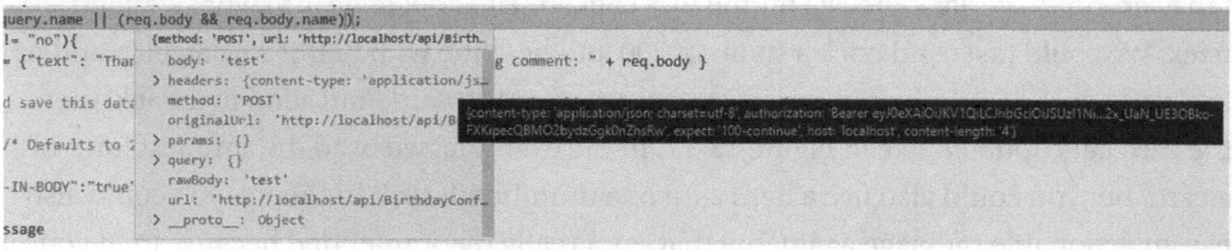

Figure 13-13. *A bearer token is sent automatically to our endpoint*

C#

For C#, it's the same story. We provide an endpoint; this time, I have included it in the news controller. We need to check if it was a "No" response and send back the correct information accordingly.

```
[HttpPost]
    public IActionResult BirthdayConfirmation()
    {
        using (StreamReader reader = new StreamReader(Request.Body,
        Encoding.UTF8))
        {
            var userResponse = reader.ReadToEndAsync().Result;
            var responseMessage = "{\"text\": \"Sorry you can not make
            it\" }";
            Request.Query.TryGetValue("answer", out var answer);

            if (answer != "no")
            {
                responseMessage = "{\"text\": \"Thanks for registering
                and giving the following comment: " +
                                    userResponse + "\"}";
            }
```

```
    Response.Headers.Add("CARD-UPDATE-IN-BODY", "true");
    return StatusCode(200, responseMessage);
    }
}
```

As you can see, it's a simple code. You could of course extend this with a save to a back end or with additional other logic. Just make sure that the response does not take too long; otherwise, you are going to get timeouts. And of course as in Node, make sure that you check the bearer token if it is indeed a request coming from Teams.

One more thing

As you might have noticed, we haven't discussed the last action in our actionable message. This was the OpenUri. We could make this a simple URL and let the browser open a website somewhere, but I wanted to explain the concept of deep links inside of Teams. If, like in our company app, we want the user to interact with something in our app, we have the possibility to direct the user straight to an app, a part of an app, a tab, or a channel. This is called deep linking because it's not just a link to Teams that we provide. But it's a link to something a few clicks away inside of Teams. As you can see here, I have created a link that goes to an entity inside of Teams. That entity is our app, identified by its app ID from the manifest. Then we want to direct the user not only to our app but to a tab that our app provides, the "CompanyNews" tab. We chosen this name ourselves with the entityID when our tab was configured. The last part is to let Teams know that our tab resides in a certain channel; I've extracted the channel ID, which you can do easily with the "Get channel Link" from the context menu of a channel in Teams, or you could do this in code. This provides us with a unique opportunity to notify users that something has happened, and we then, if a comment section or a button won't do the trick, navigate them immediately within Teams to the correct location. Deep links are very simple yet powerful to be used. If you want to test the one provided in the request, then don't forget to update your channel ID. As you can see, the channel ID is provided in the query string with the parameter context, and don't forget to URL encode this or Teams will not be able to find the channel ID. You can find more information about deep linking here: https://docs.microsoft.com/en-us/microsoftteams/platform/concepts/build-and-test/deep-links.

Connector

The other item we haven't discussed is the Office 365 connector. We discussed the card but not the connector itself. Adding a webhook is a manual job, and we don't want to work that way. We want a way to automate the deployment of our webhook. And this is where an Office 365 connector comes in. To get started, first we need to visit `https://outlook.office.com/connectors/home/login/#/publish` and create a new connector. Here, you can determine from the URL again that these connectors were born in Exchange and then found their way into Teams. These connectors work in a similar fashion as a configurable tab. We get an iFrame created by Teams that loads a page that we provide; we use the SDK to let Teams know that our part of the configuration was completed, and Teams creates the webhook for us.

First, let's fill out the web page. In this particular case, Microsoft does not differentiate if you want to publish your connector to AppSource (name for the app store) or if you just want to use it inside your tenant. You always have to register it here. The main part here is to fill out the correct values for the domains and the configuration page. We can add a page later both for C# and for Node, since we already know how to do that. And the ActionsUrl field should also not be a problem since we just created an action in our actionable message card. Once we have filled in the values like in Figure 13-14 and we hit the save button, our connector is registered and ready to use. Be aware that here the valid domains section must be the full URL, including HTTPS. If you download the example manifest, then this URL will also be in the valid domains section, but that is wrong because there we cannot add HTTPS or HTTP in the URL. This small difference can have you searching for hours for the error, because the error message returned when you try to save your connector and if the valid domain is not correct is not really helpful as you can see here: `https://stackoverflow.com/questions/52654310/empty-exception-when-saving-a-connector-configuration-in-microsoft-teams`.

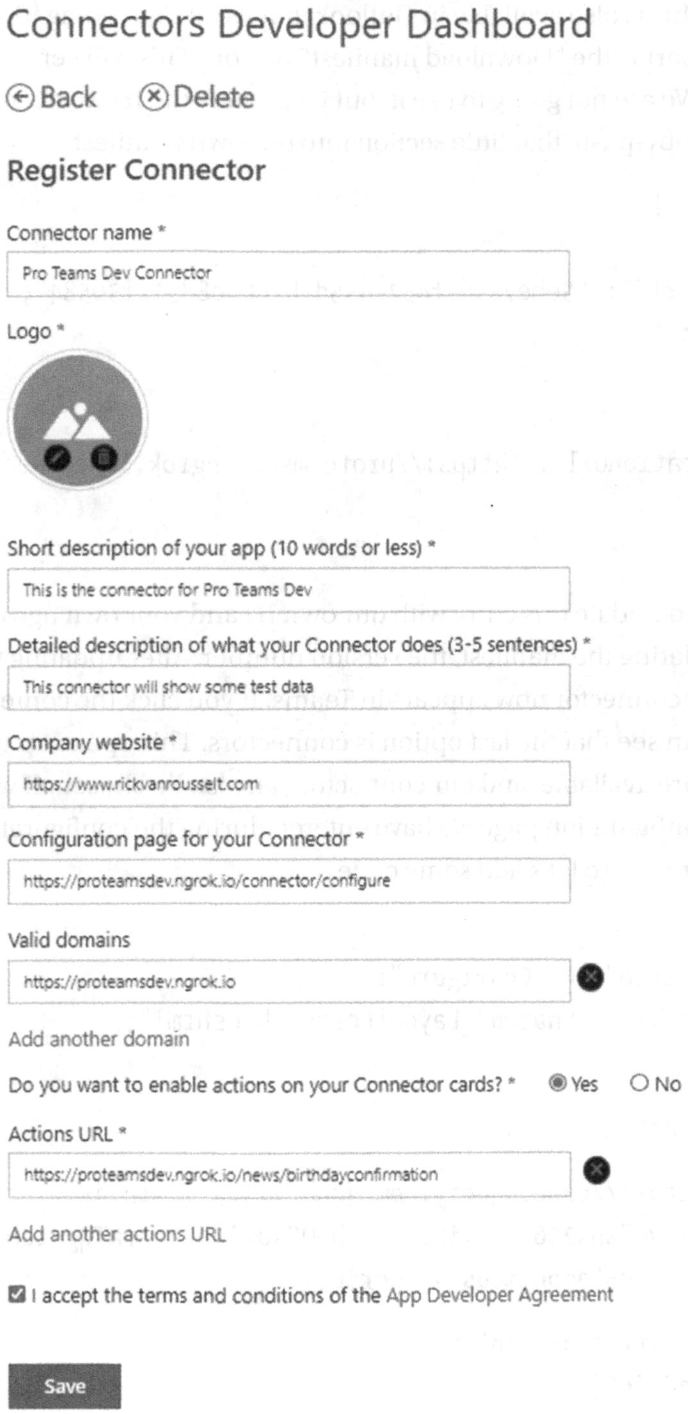

Connectors Developer Dashboard

◉ Back   ⊗ Delete

Register Connector

Connector name *

> Pro Teams Dev Connector

Logo *

Short description of your app (10 words or less) *

> This is the connector for Pro Teams Dev

Detailed description of what your Connector does (3-5 sentences) *

> This connector will show some test data

Company website *

> https://www.rickvanrousselt.com

Configuration page for your Connector *

> https://proteamsdev.ngrok.io/connector/configure

Valid domains

> https://proteamsdev.ngrok.io   ⊗

Add another domain

Do you want to enable actions on your Connector cards? *   ◉ Yes   ○ No

Actions URL *

> https://proteamsdev.ngrok.io/news/birthdayconfirmation   ⊗

Add another actions URL

☑ I accept the terms and conditions of the App Developer Agreement

Save

Figure 13-14. *The configuration page for our Office 365 connector*

You can see this is also available in Outlook, but we are not going to use that. The most important part is the "Download manifest" button. This will generate an example manifest for us. We are not going to use it, but it contains the ID we need that identifies our connector. Copy-paste that little section into our own manifest.

```
"connectors": [
  {
    "connectorId": "5ebe783d-f432-435d-b3d6-c8891ff30584",
    "scopes": [
      "team"
    ],
    "configurationUrl": "https://proteamsdev.ngrok.io/connector/configure"
  }
],
```

Don't forget to update this entry with our own ID and your own ngrok URL and, as always when updating the manifest, the version number. After updating the app, you can see that your connector now appears in Teams. If you click the context menu of a channel, you can see that the last option is connectors. This opens up the different connectors that are available, and our connector can also be chosen. If we select our connector, the configuration page we have entered during the configuration is opened. Now this is still empty, so let's add some code.

```
@{
    ViewData["Title"] = "Configure";
    Layout = "~/Views/Shared/_LayoutForLunch.cshtml";
}

<h1>Configure</h1>

<script src="https://code.jquery.com/jquery-3.5.1.min.js"
        integrity="sha256-9/aliU8dGd2tb6OSsuzixeV4y/faTqgFtohetphbbjo="
        crossorigin="anonymous"></script>

<script type="text/javascript">
    function onClick() {
        microsoftTeams.settings.setValidityState(true);
    }
```

```
microsoftTeams.initialize();
microsoftTeams.settings.registerOnSaveHandler(function (saveEvent) {
    microsoftTeams.settings.setSettings({
        entityId: "CompanyConnector",
        contentUrl: "https://proteamsdev.ngrok.io/connector/configure",
        configName: "CompanyConnectorConfig"
    });
    microsoftTeams.settings.getSettings(function (settings) {
        document.getElementById('webhookUrl').textContent = settings.
        webhookUrl;
        // We get the Webhook URL in settings.webhookUrl which needs to
        be saved.
        $.ajax({
            url: '/Connector/Save',
            type: 'post',
            contentType: 'application/json',
            data: JSON.stringify({
                webhookUrl: settings.webhookUrl,
                eventType: eventType
            }),
            success: function (data, textStatus, jQxhr) {
                console.log('webhook created successfully.');
            },
            error: function (jqXhr, textStatus, errorThrown) {
                console.log('error', errorThrown);
            }
        });
    });
    saveEvent.notifySuccess();
});
microsoftTeams.settings.registerOnRemoveHandler(function (removeEvent)
{
    var removeCalled = true;
});
</script>
```

```
<p id="webhookUrl"></p>
<div class="col-md-8">
    <section id="configSection">
        <form id="configForm">
            <input type="Button" name="startConfig" value="Start"
            onclick="onClick()" />
        </form>
    </section>
</div>
```

As you can see, all the logic happens when you click the start button. This is similar to a configurable tab, but here we must do an extra call with the name "getsettings." This returns the webhook URL we can use to post to the channel. Here, we place it back on the screen, but that would not help much. Therefore, we must save the URL to a back end somewhere so that we have a list of webhook URLs we can call. In our controller, I don't save the URL; for this example, I just need to copy-paste it to Postman, so we can do this while debugging.

```
[HttpPost("Save")]
public async Task<HttpResponseMessage> Save()
{
    using (StreamReader reader = new StreamReader(Request.Body,
    Encoding.UTF8))
    {
        var jsonString = reader.ReadToEndAsync().Result;
        return new HttpResponseMessage(HttpStatusCode.OK);
    }
}
```

As you can see in Figure 13-15, we can extract the URL, and when we copy that to Postman, we have the same result as with a manually configured incoming webhook.

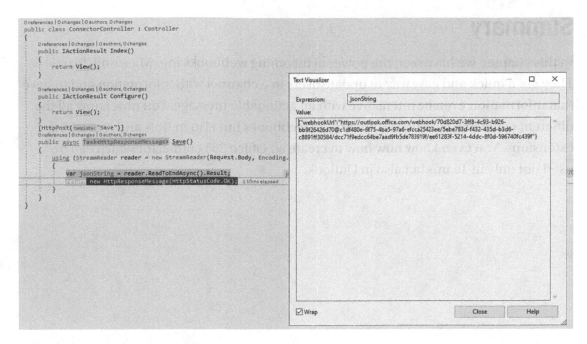

Figure 13-15. *Get the webhook URL to use in Postman*

The nice thing about these connectors is although they work in a similar way as the generic incoming webhook. The difference is that here you can add some of your own styling and branding, and that users can be more guided during the setup, instead of having to manually configure a generic webhook and give you the URL.

Figure 13-16. *Our custom connector and in the back end an actionable message sent to that connector with the URL we got in our API*

Summary

In this chapter, we have seen the power of incoming webhooks into Microsoft Teams. They are a quick and easy way to update users in a channel with information and to have that information even be interactive with an actionable message. You now know all the different cards that we can use, not only in webhooks but also in Bots and messaging extensions. You even know now how to create an Office 365 connector which can be used not only in Teams but also in Outlook.

CHAPTER 14

Outgoing webhooks

Now that we have extensively discussed incoming webhooks, it's time to turn the tables around and talk about outgoing webhooks. Outgoing webhooks work the same as incoming webhooks, just the other way around. This time, Teams is going to call our API when an event occurs, so let's see how we set up that API.

Breakdown

An outgoing webhook can be compared in usability best to a bot. Users have to at-mention it to trigger the event, and triggering the event is what we need for our API to get called. That's why with incoming and outgoing webhooks, we can build a bot-like solution. Bots use APIs and send JSON over the wire, and so do webhooks. They both need to be at-mentioned, and they are scoped to a Team. The only difference is the authentication and the number of events that get triggered. A bot, for example, has access to the Team member list (also known as the member roster); a webhook doesn't. Using webhooks to mimic bots is called custom bots.

As with actionable messages, we need to provide an endpoint. We again have the choice where to integrate this endpoint. We can use an Azure function as the Node example shows or build it into a more extensive solution as the C# example shows. We could even make an endpoint running on a Raspberry Pi. We must make sure that our endpoint exists and that it executes our logic and responds. Bear in mind that outgoing webhooks are currently not supported yet in private channels or in a personal scope (a 1:1 chat), but we can use cards as an answer-back, which is mostly a better solution than just some text.

Let's start with a simple API.

R. Van Rousselt, *Pro Microsoft Teams Development*, https://doi.org/10.1007/978-1-4842-6364-8_14

C#

For the C# example, we keep building on top of our company app. Just create a new controller named OutgoingWebhook and add the following method:

```
[HttpPost]
    public Activity AnswerBack()
    {
        using (StreamReader reader = new StreamReader(Request.Body,
        Encoding.UTF8))
        {
            var userResponse = reader.ReadToEndAsync().Result;
            var newReaction = $"You send" + userResponse;
            var replyActivity = MessageFactory.Text(newReaction);
            return replyActivity;
        }
    }
```

This method will read the information sent over and will respond with some text back.

Node

For Node, we are going to add another Azure function to the project, read what the user's message was over, and send that back.

```
module.exports = async function (context, req) {
    context.log('JavaScript HTTP trigger function processed a request.');

    var receivedMsg = req.body.text;
    var responseMessage = '{ "type": "message", "text": "You typed: ' +
    receivedMsg + '" }';

    context.res = {
        // status: 200, /* Defaults to 200 */
        body: responseMessage
    };
}
```

Webhook creation

Now that we have our endpoint ready, we need to hook it up with our outgoing webhook. First off, as you know by now, fire up ngrok because our webhook needs a public URL. This is just so that we can debug our endpoint. Once we go to production, we would have this code running on a real URL. Once you got your public URL, you can find the configuration of an outgoing webhook on the "Apps" tab in the manage Team section in the bottom-right corner. When you click it, you need to name it and provide the URL you just configured and a description as you can see in Figure 14-1.

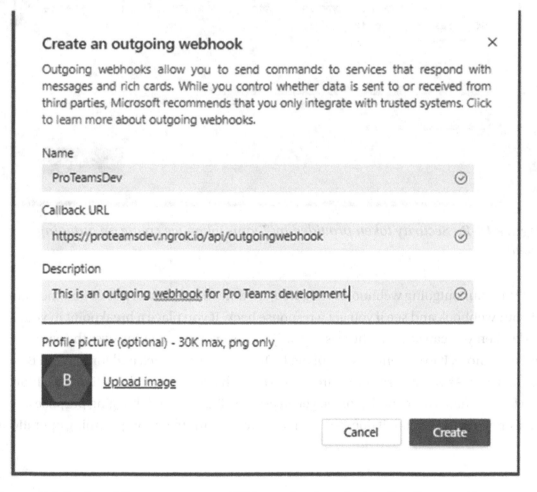

Figure 14-1. Provide a name, your URL, and a description for the outgoing webhook

Once we have filled in this information, we get presented with a second screen, as in Figure 14-2. This series of characters is a security token and is an answer to the security challenge that we are creating. Because I am sure you were already wondering that now anybody could call your API because it's publicly available. Teams is providing you with a token that only Teams and you know. Don't forget to save this token somewhere; we are going to need it later.

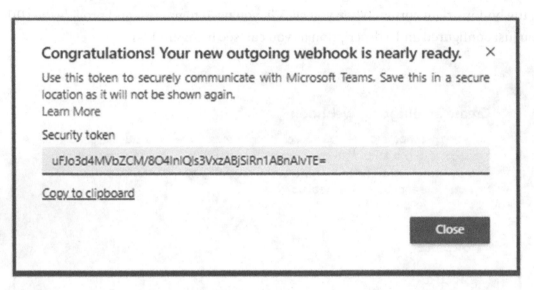

Figure 14-2. *Security token provided by Teams when we create an outgoing webhook*

With our outgoing webhook configured, it's time to test it out. At-mention the name of your webhook and see if you get a response back. If you place a breakpoint in your code, then you can see that there is not only the text you typed going over the wire but a lot more. It even reminds me of the JSON that we send back and forth in the Bot Framework. As you can see in Figure 14-3, we also have to respond in a timely fashion (no longer than five seconds), or we get an error in Teams. For debugging purposes, that's not a problem, but it does tell us that there is no room for long-running operations.

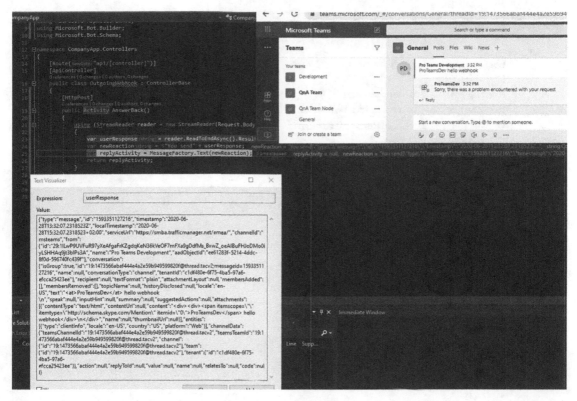

Figure 14-3.   *There is a lot of information sent with an outgoing webhook, and we have to respond in a timely fashion, or we get an error in Teams*

Let's have a look at what is inside the JSON. What I usually do is open any online JSON viewer that helps me visualize the data. As you can see in Figure 14-4, there is a lot of information available.

Figure 14-4. *JSON that gets sent to our API by an outgoing webhook*

Some things are normal to be in there—a type of message, a timestamp, a way to identify the tenant, channel, and team. It's data we might need at some point. We could use the same API for different tenants, so it would be convenient if we could identify the origin of the message. Some are not needed, but I'm happy that the team who developed this added them, like the platform where the Teams client was running.

Other information is weird that they have included it since it's always going to be empty. I already told you that an outgoing webhook doesn't have access to the Teams roster, yet in the JSON, there are the "membersAdded" and "membersRemoved" properties. These never get used. An outgoing webhook does not get triggered when you remove or add members, only if you at-mention it. So why this is in there is a mystery. I guess that they reused the activity class from the Bot Framework to speed up development.

As you can see, the message that we need also has the at-mention in there, so if you need to do something with that message, then don't forget to remove the at-mention. The only thing that we don't see is our secret string that we received from Teams when creating the webhook. That's because it's added as a header to the request and not in the body. It's added as an HMAC token. An HMAC is a hash created from the contents of the message we got from Teams. If we have the same hash calculated with our secret and the contents as the one Teams sends over, then we can be sure that the call came from the webhook we configured. More information on HMAC tokens can be found here: `https://en.wikipedia.org/wiki/HMAC`.

We can update our code with some additional code to calculate and compare the hashes. I didn't write the code myself; boilerplate code like this usually gets provided by Microsoft, and you can find it online. It can be, however, that you need to adjust it a little bit. Remember, at the beginning of this book, we discussed that you could use ngrok to replay messages. An outgoing webhook is a perfect example to use it. Or you can type the same message over and over again in Teams, or you can replay the last message. To me, the last one seems easier. Let's add the authentication part for our code.

C#

```
var userResponse = reader.ReadToEndAsync().Result;
            var teamsIncomingInformation = Newtonsoft.Json.JsonConvert.
            DeserializeObject<Activity>(userResponse);

            var newReaction = $"You send" + userResponse;
            var replyActivity = MessageFactory.Text(newReaction);

        var header=  Request.Headers["Authorization"];

        var authResponse = AuthProvider.Validate(
            authenticationHeaderValue: header,
```

```
                messageContent: userResponse,
                claimedSenderId: teamsIncomingInformation.From.Name);

        if (authResponse.AuthSuccessful == true)
        {
                // authentication ok, if not we could throw an exception.
        }

        return replyActivity;
```

As you can see, we can convert the JSON we receive into an activity. Having the information strongly typed makes it easier to handle. The bulk of the authentication logic is in the Authprovider class. You can look in the completed sample at the code. It just creates the hash and compares it.

Node

For Node, we are going to use a library called crypto (version 1.0.1). Add it with npm to your solution and change the code of our Azure function to the following:

```
context.log('JavaScript HTTP trigger function processed a request.');
const crypto = require('crypto');
const sharedSecret = "jKCFTZeeyZoqV6tupFLbu77gKTmAUlYd8OFvBm8YQN8="; //
e.g. "+ZaRRMC8+mpnfGaGsBOmkIFt98bttL5YQRq3p2tXgcE="
const bufSecret = Buffer(sharedSecret, "base64");

var auth = req.headers['authorization'];
var msgBuf = Buffer.from(context.req.rawBody, 'utf8');
var msgHash = "HMAC " + crypto.createHmac('sha256', bufSecret).
update(msgBuf).digest("base64");

var receivedMsg = req.body.text;
var responseMessage = '{ "type": "message", "text": "You typed: ' +
receivedMsg + '" }';

if (msgHash === auth) {
    //authentication ok
} else {
```

```
    responseMsg = '{ "type": "message", "text": "Error: message sender
    cannot be authenticated." }';
}

context.res = {
    // status: 200, /* Defaults to 200 */
    body: responseMessage
};
```

As you can see, we calculate the hash again on the contents that got sent over the wire. If that hash matches the hash that Teams calculated, then we can be sure that this is originating from our configured webhook.

Summary

In this chapter, we discussed outgoing webhooks. They have a simple setup, which makes them easy to develop. Although they cannot do as much as bots, sometimes we don't need to have all that functionality. They are secured so we can trust that the call originates from Teams and even from the channel that we configured the outgoing webhook on. This concludes the part about incoming and outgoing webhooks, and I'm sure that you now have the skill to build a custom bot as they get called.

PART 5

Messaging Extensions

CHAPTER 15

Search-based extensions

It is time that we tackle the last type of customization we can do on the Teams platform: messaging extensions. Messaging extensions are divided into two categories, search based and action based. In this chapter, we will go deeper into the search-based messaging extensions. A search-based extension provides you with the capability to search for information right from within Teams and then use that information inside of your conversation. Let's assume, for instance, we have a CRM system, then we could create a search-based extension that would allow our users to search the information in our CRM system. But that is not the added value; the added value of a search-based extension will be in a card that we can then provide with the result and what will be added to the chat conversation of the user and therefore enriching this chat with valuable information.

Location, location, location

Messaging extensions have the best location to interact with end users. Instead of being buried in a tab somewhere, or the need to at-mention them, they have a place right in the center of the user's field of vision. If you look at Figure 15-1, then you can see that they are easily accessible.

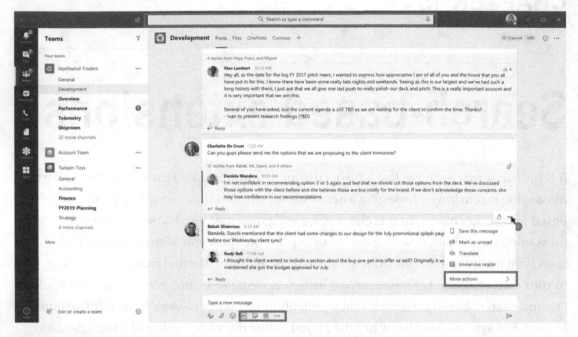

Figure 15-1. *Messaging extensions are easily accessible by users*

Image from the Microsoft documentation: `https://docs.microsoft.com/en-us/microsoftteams/platform/messaging-extensions/what-are-messaging-extensions`

But with this capability also comes a great deal of responsibility. It's best not to get these locations overcrowded with applications. We only have that amount of space, and if you start adding a lot of applications there, you are getting into the risk that users get overwhelmed by choice.

Messaging extensions are based on the Bot Framework. They utilize the same authentication and JSON schemas to share information between your app and Teams. Therefore, they are also built like bots and need the same amount of setup and configuration as a bot. If you have a bot for Teams, then adding a messaging extension is the next logical step. A messaging extension can hold up to ten different commands. Those commands are search based or action based and need to be configured for a location. These locations are the compose message area, command bar, and/or message (as seen in Figure 15-1). Messaging extensions used to be called compose extensions, so as a tip, if you ever need to find information about it, sometimes you will find more information using the old name. And even in code and in the manifest, you will see the compose extension name used a lot. Microsoft does have to provide a backward compatibility, so changing a name in the documentation can be done; telling everybody that their code will not work anymore is something else. So, you must also forgive me that I use both these names for the same item. Now let's get started with our search-based messaging extension.

Manifest

For our search-based messaging extension, we must let Teams know that we want to use that functionality. This is done inside the manifest.

```
"composeExtensions": [
    {
        "botId": "6ae6e155-6dce-4133-ab9a-ece0416e451d",
        "canUpdateConfiguration": true,
        "commands": [
            {
                "id": "searchCmd",
                "description": "Search our knowledge repository",
                "title": "Search",
                "initialRun": false,
                "type": "query",
                "context": [ "compose", "commandBox" ],
                "parameters": [
                    {
                        "name": "searchKeyword",
                        "description": "Enter your search keywords",
                        "title": "Keywords"
                    }
                ]
            }
        ]
    }
],
```

As you can clearly see here, messaging extensions use the Bot Framework because you need to add a botId. You can reuse the same bot from the previous chapters or create a new one; that's up to you. For the Node example, I started from a fresh template; for the C#, I just kept adding on top of our company app. The "canUpdateConfiguration" is something we will touch later in the chapter. The bulk of the logic is in the commands section. This tells Teams that we want a search-based extension by specifying the type to "query." We give it an ID, title, and description. The "initialRun" parameter is if you want to prepopulate the results already; this way, you can launch a query the moment a user opens the app. We also must configure where we want our extension to be usable. Both options are specified here; compose, as you can see in Figure 15-1, is the bottom red box. The three dots need to be clicked by the user, and then your app will show up as in Figure 15-2.

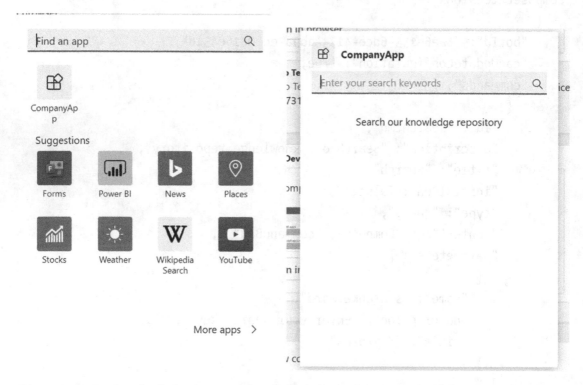

Figure 15-2. *On the left, our compose extension when you click the three dots; on the right, the view for a search-based compose extension*

The other option we have is that our app appears in the command box as you can see in Figure 15-3. In my opinion, this is too much hidden, and very difficult for users to find. You have to at-mention your app in the command bar, which then provides a different experience than your bot does (if you have a bot), and except for a copy-to-clipboard function, there isn't much that users can do with the search results.

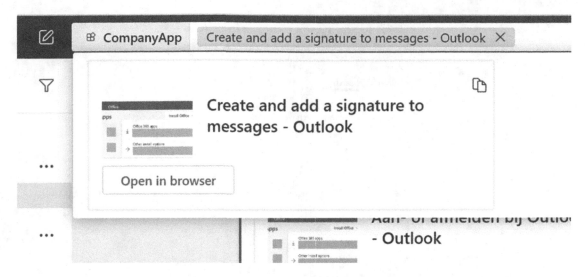

Figure 15-3. *Our search-based messaging extension used in the command bar*

The next item we can configure is what is shown in the search box where users need to type their query. It helps to guide our users in explaining what this extension can do. We also have the possibility to have multiple search areas by adding more commands as in Figure 15-4. They will be distinguished by their name when they call our code so that we have a way to know where the search originated from. We can have up to ten different commands, and they can be a mix of search commands and action commands.

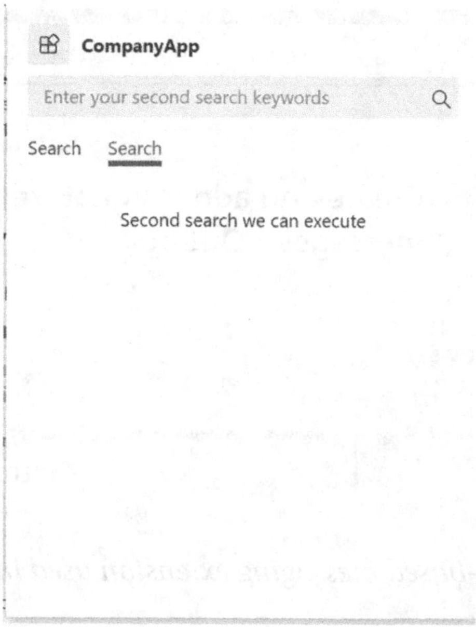

Figure 15-4. *Multiple commands into one search-based extension*

Time to code

Now that we have our configuration complete, we do need a bot API to receive the requests. When developing extensions, you are going to see a lot of error messages. These errors occur because we get five seconds from Teams to respond to the request. Now, I don't know how fast you can debug your code, but in my case, I'm always late. But don't worry; it's not because Teams gives an error that your code will stop running. But this also implies that your search query must be faster than five seconds when not debugging. So, it's best not to search some old SQL database with millions of records, or even SharePoint for that matter. If you do have a use case like this, then I can recommend you investigate a Redis cache (`https://azure.microsoft.com/en-us/services/cache/`). It's not a Microsoft technology, but you can create one in Azure. I have several customers using this, and the results are incredibly fast.

For Node, I started out with the Microsoft Teams Toolkit again. You can also start with the Teams generator. The main objective is that we have a bot and that we implement the two functions that are responsible for handling search-based messaging extensions. Our first method is to get the search query as an input parameter and to provide a list of search results.

Node

```
async handleTeamsMessagingExtensionQuery(context, query) {
    const axios = require('axios');
    const querystring = require('querystring');
    const request = require("request");
    const searchQuery = query.parameters[0].value;

    var subscriptionKey = '5c00e48b0d034ecebc333d89e0234bfb';
    var customConfigId = '4fb85d73-afae-4aed-b7da-a7ff6c4ce11a';

    const response = await axios.get(https://api.cognitive.microsoft.
    com/bingcustomsearch/v7.0/search?' +
    'q=' + searchQuery + "&" + 'customconfig=' + customConfigId, {
        headers: {
            'Ocp-Apim-Subscription-Key': subscriptionKey
        }
    });

    const attachments = [];
    response.data.webPages.value.forEach(obj => {
        const heroCard = CardFactory.heroCard(obj.name);
        const preview = CardFactory.thumbnailCard(obj.name);
        var imageUrl = this.CheckImageUrl(obj.snippet);
        preview.content.tap = { type: 'invoke', value: { name: obj.
        name, snippet: obj.snippet, link: obj.url, img: imageUrl } };
        preview.images = CardFactory.images([imageUrl])
        const attachment = { ...heroCard, preview };
        attachments.push(attachment);
    });

    return {
        composeExtension: {
            type: 'result',
            attachmentLayout: 'list',
            attachments: attachments
        }
    };
}
```

C#

```csharp
protected override async Task<MessagingExtensionResponse>
OnTeamsMessagingExtensionQueryAsync(ITurnContext<IInvokeActivity>
turnContext, MessagingExtensionQuery query, CancellationToken
cancellationToken)
        {
            var text = query?.Parameters?[0]?.Value as string ?? string.
            Empty;
            var _searchClient = new CustomSearchClient(new ApiKeyService
            ClientCredentials(_configuration["SearchSubscriptionKey"]));
            var _customConfigId = _configuration["SearchConfigurationId"];
            var results = _searchClient.CustomInstance.SearchAsync(_
            customConfigId, text).Result;

            var attachments = results?.WebPages?.Value?.Select(result =>
            {
                var imageUrl = HelperMethods.CheckImageUrl(result.Snippet);
                var extensionSearchResult = new ExtensionSearchResult() {
                Title = result.Name, ImageUrl = imageUrl, Snippet = result.
                Snippet, Link = result.Url };
                var previewCard = new ThumbnailCard { Title = result.
                Name, Tap = new CardAction { Type = "invoke", Value =
                extensionSearchResult } };
                previewCard.Images = new List<CardImage>() { new
                CardImage(imageUrl, "Icon") };

                var attachment = new MessagingExtensionAttachment
                {
                    ContentType = HeroCard.ContentType,
                    Content = new HeroCard { Title = result.Name },
                    Preview = previewCard.ToAttachment()
                };
                return attachment;
            }).ToList();

            // The list of MessagingExtensionAttachments must be
            wrapped in a MessagingExtensionResult wrapped in a
            MessagingExtensionResponse.
```

```
return new MessagingExtensionResponse
{
    ComposeExtension = new MessagingExtensionResult
    {
        Type = "result",
        AttachmentLayout = "list",
        Attachments = attachments
    }
};
}
```

As you can see, we needed something to query. In this case, I have reused our custom Bing Search from Chapter 10. We get our search query, we configure our Bing endpoint with the subscription key and our configuration key we received when configuring the service, and we perform a GET request to get back our results. Then it is just a matter of processing the results.

Our search results we have to send back are formed as JSON. You could skip the entire Bot Framework and construct the results yourself, but let's keep to the framework provided. The result that must be returned is a compose extension, and the most common one used is of type result, meaning a list of search results. We also have the possibility to authenticate the user on their first query, if this would be needed, or to run a configuration page. These results we are sending back most commonly are cards, thumbnail cards, hero cards, connector cards, or adaptive cards, as we discussed in the previous chapter.

The reason why you are seeing two cards generated in the code is because when using a connector or adaptive card, we have the possibility to choose the way it's previewed by the user. They can become quite long and complex, so not something we want to fit inside a small results view. If we use a hero or a thumbnail card, Teams will create its own preview out of the title, text, and image. So basically, we are doing the same thing twice in our code, but I still wanted to show you that it's possible. The reason why this exists is if you would like to reuse, for instance, an adaptive card from your bot, you don't need to redesign your application, but you can just add a little preview that looks better on this narrow screen space. Our result is a list, therefore it consists out of a series of cards that we send back as attachments to our compose extension. Now, the only thing left is to have an action when the user selects a result; this is our second function.

Node

```
async handleTeamsMessagingExtensionSelectItem(context, obj) {
    const thumbnailCard = CardFactory.thumbnailCard(obj.name,
        CardFactory.images([obj.img]),
        CardFactory.actions([{
            type: ActionTypes.OpenUrl,
            title: 'Open in browser',
            value: obj.link
        }])
    );

    return {
        composeExtension: {
            type: 'result',
            attachmentLayout: 'list',
            attachments: [thumbnailCard]
        }
    };
}
```

C#

```
protected override Task<MessagingExtensionResponse>
OnTeamsMessagingExtensionSelectItemAsync(ITurnContext<IInvokeActivity>
turnContext, JObject query, CancellationToken cancellationToken)
    {
        var article = query.ToObject<ExtensionSearchResult>();
        var card = new ThumbnailCard
        {
            Title = $"{article.Title}",
            Subtitle = article.Snippet,
            Buttons = new List<CardAction>
                {
                    new CardAction { Type = ActionTypes.OpenUrl, Title
                    = "Open in browser", Value = article.Link}
```

```
            },
        };

        card.Images = new List<CardImage>() { new CardImage(article.
        ImageUrl, "Icon") };
        var attachment = new MessagingExtensionAttachment
        {
            ContentType = ThumbnailCard.ContentType,
            Content = card,
        };

        return Task.FromResult(new MessagingExtensionResponse
        {
            ComposeExtension = new MessagingExtensionResult
            {
                Type = "result",
                AttachmentLayout = "list",
                Attachments = new List<MessagingExtensionAttachment> {
                attachment }
            }
        });
    }
```

As the name already describes, the "handleTeamsMessagingExtensionSelectItem" function is responsible for handling what happens when a user clicks a result item. In this case, if you look at the extensionQuery function, you can see that we can add our own values to the "value" property in the preview like so:

```
preview.content.tap = { type: 'invoke', value: { name: obj.name, snippet:
obj.snippet, link: obj.url, img: imageUrl } };
```

This tells Teams what to send back as a value. Now this is going to get converted again into JSON so you cannot go freewheeling with the information you put in there. In this case, you can try it with the entire result you get back from the Bing Search API, and that isn't going to work. It's just too much data and probably not convertible into decent JSON. As you can also see in glancing at both the Node and the C# version, the Bot Framework team has done an excellent job again to keep the code in sync. You can immediately read the code, even if you have never written the other language, because of the same naming and structures used. Now that we can construct a decent card in our second function, we send that back to the user, and it will appear into their compose area, ready to be posted as in Figure 15-5.

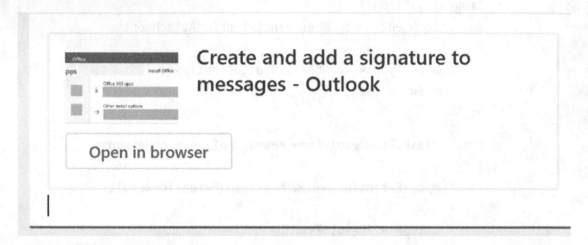

Figure 15-5. *The result of our messaging extension in the compose area of the user*

There is just one method that's not in here, and it's a reuse of the one we used in our bot to match an image to the result, so that we have something visual for the user. As we have already seen, there is also the possibility to have settings with your search-based extension.

Settings

Sometimes, it's just easier to have the user configure some settings, instead of working with multiple search tabs. This is possible with a search-based extension although a bit hard to find. To allow for configuration, we must set the manifest to allow configurations as we did before with the following entry:

```
"canUpdateConfiguration": true,
```

This creates an additional settings menu item if you right-click your extension as you can see in Figure 15-6.

Figure 15-6. *Settings menu item for my search-based messaging extension*

When you look at Figure 15-6, you should also notice that there is a loading icon next to the settings button. This is because, although we have told the manifest to have the button appear, it has no idea where to direct the user. And a link in a button should be available for the button to work properly. During this loading period, Teams is already calling your extension to query what the URL is. We can accept this request by implementing the "OnTeamsMessagingExtensionConfigurationQuerySettingUrlAsync" function. This is where it gets a little weird how Microsoft implemented this feature. They had to stick to the messaging extension framework, so this method needs to return the type "MessagingExtensionResponse." But Teams doesn't need a card or a list of results, it just needs the URL to use behind the settings button. That's why a type called "config" has been added. We already used the type "result" to return our search results. When we change this type to config then this is will tell Teams that this is going to be used for configuration. Together with a card action of openUrl, Teams can figure out the URL for the settings button. We could just write our function like this:

```
protected override async Task<MessagingExtensionResponse> OnTeams
MessagingExtensionConfigurationQuerySettingUrlAsync(ITurnContext
<IInvokeActivity> turnContext, MessagingExtensionQuery query,
```

```
            CancellationToken cancellationToken)
        {

            return new MessagingExtensionResponse
            {
                ComposeExtension = new MessagingExtensionResult
                {
                    Type = "config",
                    SuggestedActions = new MessagingExtensionSuggestedAction
                    {
                        Actions = new List<CardAction>
                        {
                            new CardAction
                            {
                                Type = ActionTypes.OpenUrl,
                                Value = $"https://proteamsdev.ngrok.io/
                                extension/index",
                            },
                        },
                    },
                },
            };
        }
```

As you can see in the code, we just return the response with the URL in it, and our settings button will know that it needs to point the user to the /extension/index page. But let's make it a little bit smarter. We could use our bot state as we did in the previous bot samples to save the information that the user enters in our settings page. If we add a few more lines of code, we can utilize the state of our bot as a storage to save configuration changes.

```
protected override async Task<MessagingExtensionResponse> OnTeamsMessagin
gExtensionConfigurationQuerySettingUrlAsync(ITurnContext<IInvokeActivity>
turnContext, MessagingExtensionQuery query,
        CancellationToken cancellationToken)
    {
        // The user has requested the Messaging Extension Configuration page.
```

```
        var escapedSettings = string.Empty;
        var userStateAccessors = UserState.CreateProperty<ExtensionSett
        ing>(nameof(ExtensionSetting));
        var setting = await userStateAccessors.GetAsync(turnContext, ()
        => new ExtensionSetting(), cancellationToken);

        if (!string.IsNullOrEmpty(setting.Source))
        {
            escapedSettings = Uri.EscapeDataString(setting.Source);
        }

        return new MessagingExtensionResponse
        {
            ComposeExtension = new MessagingExtensionResult
            {
                Type = "config",
                SuggestedActions = new MessagingExtensionSuggestedAction
                {
                    Actions = new List<CardAction>
                    {
                        new CardAction
                        {
                            Type = ActionTypes.OpenUrl,
                            Value = $"https://proteamsdev.ngrok.io/
                            extension/index?settings={escapedSettings}",
                        },
                    },
                },
            },
        };
    }
```

By adding the first four lines of code, we are checking to see if our custom object, the ExtensionSetting, which is a basic class with one property exists on the state object of the users.

```
public class ExtensionSetting
    { public string Source { get; set; } }
```

The Bot Framework will automatically retrieve and save the state for us in the repository we defined in the startup.cs class. In our case, this is still in the memory, but we could easily change that to a Blob storage so that the state would be persistent. You should know that there are different types of state maintained by your bot. You can divide them into three buckets:

- Conversation state: For saving the context of the conversation

- User state: For saving information about the user

- Private conversation state: For saving specific user and conversation information in group conversations

Depending on the type of state you use when you save your information defines how long your information is stored and how it's stored. You can imagine, for instance, that saving specific presets that a user once made like language can best be stored in the user state because this information needs to be used over multiple conversations.

Actually, there are only two lines necessary, where we create the property and retrieve it, but it could be that our configuration is not properly URL encoded, and to pass it along to our configuration page in the query string, we need to encode it first.

When we click the link, we don't have a page yet; let's quickly create a new controller and add a view. I have called the controller extension, and it has only one index method; that doesn't do any logic. The main logic will be in the view by using once again the Teams Client JavaScript SDK. Let's just add two checkboxes and save the data back to our user state, and because we retrieve the user state to see if the user already filled out the settings once before and send those along in the query string, we also need some code to activate the correct checkbox.

```
@{
    ViewData["Title"] = "Index";
    Layout = "~/Views/Shared/_LayoutForLunch.cshtml";
}

<h1>Index</h1>

<form>
    <fieldset>
        <legend>What would you like to search?</legend>
        <input type="radio" name="includeInSearch" value="microsoft">Micros
        oft<br>
```

```
        <input type="radio" name="includeInSearch" value="qna">Company
        knowledge base<br>
    </fieldset>

    <br />
    <input type="button" onclick="onSubmit()" value="Save"> <br />
</form>

<script type="text/javascript">

    document.addEventListener("DOMContentLoaded", function () {
        var urlParams = new URLSearchParams(window.location.search);
        var settings = urlParams.get('settings');
        if (settings) {
            var checkboxes = document.getElementsByName("includeInSearch");
            for (var i = 0; i < checkboxes.length; i++) {
                var thisCheckbox = checkboxes[i];
                if (settings.includes(thisCheckbox.value)) {
                    checkboxes[i].checked = true;
                }
            }
        }
    });

</script>

<script type="text/javascript">

    microsoftTeams.initialize();

    function onSubmit() {
        var newSettings = [];

        var checkboxes = document.getElementsByName("includeInSearch");

        for (var i = 0; i < checkboxes.length; i++) {
            if (checkboxes[i].checked) {
                newSettings.push(checkboxes[i].value);
            }
        }
```

```
        microsoftTeams.authentication.notifySuccess(JSON.stringify(newSettings));
    }
```

```
</script>
```

Let's start from the top. As you can see, by utilizing the same layout once more, we don't have to worry about adding a reference to our Teams SDK. Then we add our two checkboxes with a setting; in this case, these are simple checkboxes, but you can make this settings page as complex as you want to. The first piece of JavaScript will get the information from the query string and will select the correct checkbox. The second piece is our save action; as you can see, this is where the Teams SDK comes into play. To notify our back end which checkbox the user selected, there is nothing we can utilize, unless we utilize the same method we used when doing authentication in our tabs. As you can see, we use the authentication part of the SDK to notify Teams that the save action succeeded, and we can send data back with it. It's kind of a misuse of the function because it was, as the name specified, designed for authentication, but we can also use it to send data back and forth.

Once the user hits the save button, we are going to need a method that will accept this information and save it to the user state. For this, we have the "OnTeamsMessagingExtensionConfigurationSettingAsync" method which we can override.

```
{
        // When the user submits the settings page, this event is fired.
        var state = settings["state"];
        if (state != null)
        {
            var setting = new ExtensionSetting();
            setting.Source = state.ToString();
            var userStateAccessors = UserState.CreateProperty<Extension
            Setting>(nameof(ExtensionSetting));
            await userStateAccessors.SetAsync(turnContext, setting,
            cancellationToken);
        }
    }
```

As you can see, not much is going on inside this method; we get the information inside of a JSON object, convert that information to our custom class we created, and save it in the user state. As you can see in Figure 15-7, we now have a settings page with two checkboxes that's shown the moment we click the settings button, and it even remembers our previous selection.

Figure 15-7. Our custom settings page for our messaging extension

As you can see, we can use this settings page to have the user select if they want to search our own knowledge base or search the Microsoft knowledge base with the Bing Custom Search API we implemented. This is an alternative to showing the two tabs with the different search options. If you want, you can as an exercise adjust our search-based extension to retrieve the settings before we execute our search and make a decision based on that to see what API should be called, the Bing API or the QnA maker API.

Summary

In this chapter, we have built our own search-based messaging extension, and you now know that you can even have a custom settings page linked to it. The usability of the settings page is something that's still up for debate because we have seen that it's not easy to find the settings button and that we probably need to train our users to find it. But in some use cases, it can be very helpful that it exists. By now, you have a vast knowledge of how messaging extensions work in Teams, and in the next chapter, we are going to find out how to build an action-based extension.

CHAPTER 16

Action-based extensions

In the previous chapter, we discussed search-based extensions, but what if we don't need our users to search for something? Think of action-based extensions more in the context of a form for data input that then triggers a business process further along. Or maybe we want to present the user with a training video. We can even show a PowerApp application where the user can perform various actions. Then our search-based extension is not going to help, and that's where action-based extensions come into the picture. In this chapter, we are only going to work with C# because, as already stated, the differences between C# and Node are so small that you can easily convert the code yourself.

Differences

Action-based messaging extensions are not just one single solution; it's a group name for several different options we have. They all look the same and are based on the same functionality (invoke an action), but they work a little bit differently from each other. The basis of an action-based message is a pop-up or modal dialog as the official name is. In Teams, we refer to them as task modules. But we have a choice of what is going to get rendered inside this pop-up. The simplest and fastest way to create an action-based extension is by providing a static list of parameters; we define them in the manifest (which you can easily do with App Studio), and Teams will perform all the rendering for us. We just need to implement a save functionality. If we don't like the way Teams renders the properties, we can go a level higher and provide an adaptive card. Adaptive cards give us more flexibility, but we need to create an adaptive card as well as implement the save functionality. Our last two options are the embedded web view and a SharePoint Framework web part. In the case of an embedded web view, Teams provides us with an empty screen that we are free to fill with whatever we want. Embedded web views are the most flexible solution but also the most work to implement. Should you have more

© Rick Van Rousselt 2021

R. Van Rousselt, *Pro Microsoft Teams Development*, https://doi.org/10.1007/978-1-4842-6364-8_16

experience in building SPFx web parts or you already have an existing one then since version 1.11, you can even show that as a messaging extension. I think with the four alternatives provided to us, the Teams team did their best to hear developer demands and have different levels of customizations available depending on your experience and the time and effort you are willing to spend on your messaging extension.

Our user will have the same options and more as the search-based extensions where they can activate our action. By at-mentioning the app with it's name from the command bar, in the button that get's added below the compose message area but also directly from a message by using the context menu on the message. If you remember Figure 16-1 from the previous chapter, then you can see the locations again where our extension can get surfaced.

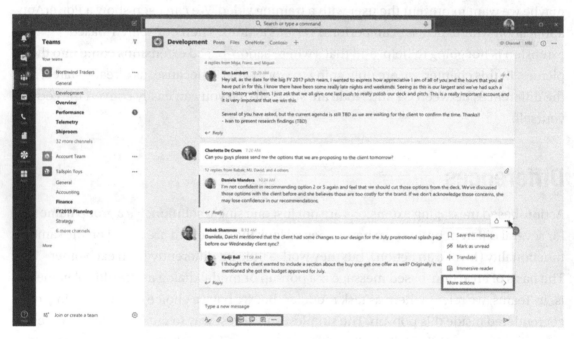

Figure 16-1. *Action-based messaging extensions can be invoked from three places*

Image from the Microsoft documentation: `https://docs.microsoft.com/en-us/microsoftteams/platform/messaging-extensions/what-are-messaging-extensions`

As with search-based messaging extensions, action-based extensions utilize the Bot Framework as a means of communication between Teams and our app. But let's first have a deeper look into our pop-up mechanism. These task modules are widely used inside of Teams, and we haven't discussed them until now.

Task modules

In Teams, we have the possibility to show a modal dialog, sometimes with data that is rendered by Teams, sometimes with data rendered by us. These task modules can be used in extensions but are not limited to extensions. We haven't used them so far, but we could also use them in our bots, tabs, or deep links. Theoretically, we do have already worked with task modules because they are based on tabs and adaptive cards. They use the same iFrame mechanism and the same Teams Client JavaScript SDK to get things done. They are just not shown as a tab but as a pop-up. So, with the experience you now have building tabs and cards, you are already 95% prepared for building task modules. One thing you should keep in the back of your head when working with task modules is the supportability on the Teams mobile client. They are not fully supported yet so don't automatically assume that your task module is going to work on the mobile client. To define a task module, we have an object called "TaskInfo." This needs to be sent over to our Teams client so that Teams knows what we are trying to achieve. Throughout this chapter, we will use different task modules so that you can see how to implement them.

Static action-based extension

But let's go one step back to our static action-based extension and see how a task module is rendered without our help by Teams. By adjusting the "ComposeExtensions" part of our manifest, we can add our extensions. Add the following command to the compose extension in the manifest:

```
{
        "id": "orderLunchOnSaturday",
        "description": "If you are working on Saturday's you can order
        lunch here.",
        "title": "Order Saturday lunch",
        "type": "action",
        "context": [ "commandBox", "message", "compose" ],
        "fetchTask": false,
        "parameters": [
          {
            "name": "Name",
            "description": "Your name",
```

```
              "title": "Title",
              "inputType": "text"
          },
          {
              "name": "Choice",
              "description": "Which sandwich would you like",
              "title": "Choice",
              "inputType": "choiceset",
              "choices": [
                  {
                      "title": "BLT",
                      "value": "BLT"
                  },
                  {
                      "title": "Cheese",
                      "value": "Cheese"
                  },
                  {
                      "title": "Ham",
                      "value": "Ham"
                  }
              ]
          },
          {
              "name": "Date",
              "description": "What Saturday are you working",
              "title": "Date",
              "inputType": "date"
          }
      ]
  }
```

This will enable our static action-based messaging extension, and as you can see in Figure 16-2, when we upload a new version of the manifest, the link to it is immediately visible. Only in the compose message box, I find it a bit hard to find. A little plus icon appears, and your extension is hidden behind it. This again makes it difficult for users to find. That's why I usually just go for the "actions on a message" location. This is much easier to find for users.

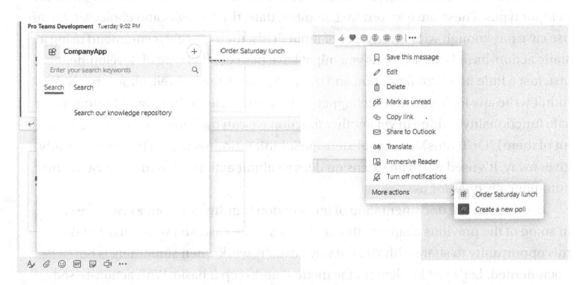

Figure 16-2. *Our static extensions is available after we update the manifest and upload a new version*

The cool thing about these static extensions is not that after changing the manifest, we immediately get a button extra but also the functionality of the button already works. A pop-up is automatically generated with our configured questions as you can see in Figure 16-3.

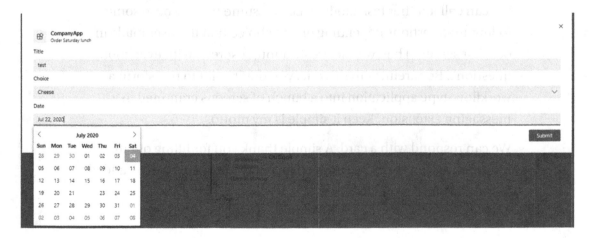

Figure 16-3. *Our static extension renders a page with our configured questions*

As you can also see in Figure 16-3, for some types of fields, there is automatically an additional functionality available—in this case, a date picker when we have a date field, or if we have a choice field, a list of choices. We are however limited to a given set of input types. These are text, textarea, number, date, time, toggle, and choiceset. If your use case has enough with these types of input fields, then I surely recommend using a static action-based extension. As you might have noticed, this type of development is fast. Just a little bit of configuration and our extension is ready. Well, almost ready. We didn't write any logic yet on what happens when a user clicks the submit button. The safe functionality is done in yet another function we can override (I know there are a lot of them) "OnTeamsMessagingExtensionSubmitActionAsync." As the name already gives away, it's used when an extension does a submit action, what in this case Teams automatically does for us.

In this case, the documentation of the function is quite clear, but as we have seen in some of the previous chapters, that is not always the case, so I would like to take this opportunity to share with you the way I usually work when something is not documented. Let's just implement the method and keep it basic. With action-based extensions, we have several options in our response. We can

- Send no response: It's entirely possible to not send a response back. It's best that we of course let the user know that their action did do something, but it's not required. This can be a valid option if we use an action-based messaging extension to call another application or service, and that service notifies the user by, for example, sending them a mail.

- We can call another task module. Let's assume that we have some follow-up questions depending on the choice that the user made in our first screen. Then we can create another screen with even more questions. Be careful with this one; you don't want to transform a workflow-type application into a bunch of screens crammed in a messaging extension. Keep it simple is my motto.

- We can respond with a card. A simple thank you for filling out the information can easily be wrapped in a hero card. This will be added to the compose box of the user.

– We can start an authentication flow. This could be like the authentication flow we did in our configurable tab.

– We can initiate a settings page, like we did with our search-based extension when a user clicked the settings button.

As you can see, we have plenty of options to choose from. Luckily, we don't need to respond so let's keep our method empty for now.

```
protected override async Task<MessagingExtensionActionResponse>
OnTeamsMessagingExtensionSubmitActionAsync(ITurnContext<IInvokeActivity>
turnContext, MessagingExtensionAction action, CancellationToken
cancellationToken)
    {
        return null;
    }
```

If we start ngrok, run our code, place a breakpoint on our return statement, and fill out the form and press submit, we can see what is being sent over the wire as you see in Figure 16-4. Don't forget that we only have five seconds to respond, so when debugging, Teams is going to show an error screen, but you don't need to worry about it.

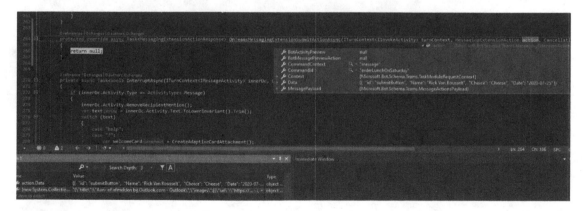

Figure 16-4. *When we debug our empty function, we can see what is actually in all the properties provided*

The information we need is in the "action" property. It tells us that I have used the messaging extension on a command context, the command ID that I configured was "orderLunchOnSaturday," and the information that I filled in. As a bonus, because I activated it on a message and not from the compose box, the message content on which I activated the extension is also provided. We can also use ngrok to see the full JSON message sent over by the Bot Framework. Navigate to our ngrok inspection url (`http://127.0.0.1:4040/inspect/http`), and we can see the full request. And remember, don't waste time filling out the same form repeatedly while testing. Just hit the replay button in ngrok to trigger the same event. As you can see in Figure 16-5, the "value" property is converted into our messagingextensionaction object.

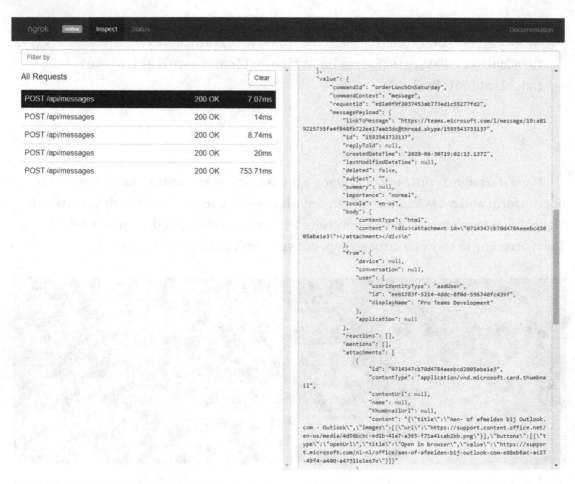

Figure 16-5. *The JSON data sent over to ngrok when we fill out our static action-based messaging extension*

Now let's take a look at the data value from our action object that is sent over in code.

```
{
    "id": "submitButton",
    "Name": "rick",
    "Choice": "Cheese",
    "Date": "2020-07-11"
}
```

This looks interesting. This is the information that our user has entered in the form. You can simply take this JSON and in Visual Studio use the "copy JSON as classes" functionality (under edit menu ➤ paste special). Now we have a class to cast our information to.

```
public class StaticSaturdayLunchResponse
{
    public string id { get; set; }
    public string Name { get; set; }
    public string Choice { get; set; }
    public string Date { get; set; }
}
```

We also need to implement a switch because this is not the only action-based extension we are going to build. And of course, we need to let our users know that we got the information successfully, so let's send back a hero card saying thanks. Let's change our "OnTeamsMessagingExtensionSubmitActionAsync" method:

```
protected override async Task<MessagingExtensionActionResponse>
OnTeamsMessagingExtensionSubmitActionAsync(ITurnContext
<IInvokeActivity> turnContext, MessagingExtensionAction action,
CancellationToken cancellationToken)
    {
        switch (action.CommandId)
        {
            case "orderLunchOnSaturday":
                return CreateCardResponse(turnContext, action);
            default:
```

```
                    throw new NotImplementedException($"Invalid CommandId:
                    {action.CommandId}");
            }
        }
```

Our card response is going to look like this:

```
private MessagingExtensionActionResponse CreateCardResponse(ITurnContext<IInvokeActivity> turnContext, MessagingExtensionAction action)
        {
            var formInformation = JsonConvert.DeserializeObject<StaticSaturdayLunchResponse>(action.Data.ToString());
            var card = new HeroCard
            {
                Title = "Success",
                Subtitle = "You lunch has been ordered",
                Text = $"Dear {formInformation.Name}. Your lunch
                {formInformation.Choice} is ordered and will be ready for
                your on {formInformation.Date}",
            };

            var attachments = new List<MessagingExtensionAttachment>();
            attachments.Add(new MessagingExtensionAttachment
            {
                Content = card,
                ContentType = HeroCard.ContentType,
                Preview = card.ToAttachment(),
            });

            return new MessagingExtensionActionResponse
            {
                ComposeExtension = new MessagingExtensionResult
                {
                    AttachmentLayout = "list",
                    Type = "result",
                    Attachments = attachments,
                },
            };
        }
```

Here, we cast our action.data into our custom class to have the information more easily accessible from code. We then use this to send back a hero card. As you can see from Figure 16-6, the return message is added to the compose box of the user. In this case, not very in line with what we are trying to do, just send a thank you message. The user is not going to post this inside a channel.

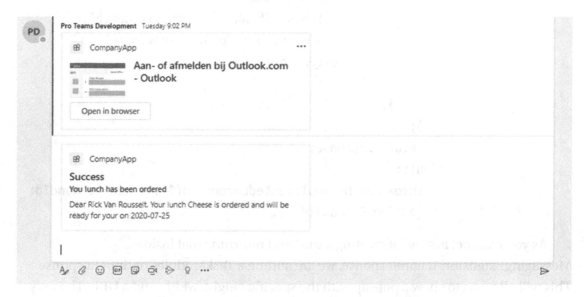

Figure 16-6. *The response hero card from our form is added to the compose box*

In this case, it would have been better to send back nothing and inform the user in another way. The proactive bot we build could be very useful for this, because it has the possibility to contact the user in a one-on-one message. But if we would change the form that a user has the possibility to order lunch for their entire team, then a draft message would be helpful because then the user can let their team members know that the user ordered lunch for all of them. This was a card response; let's see if we can create a task module response and control what is being shown.

First, let's change our submitAction method so that it doesn't send back a hero card but a task module.

```
case "orderLunchOnSaturday":
        //    return CreateCardResponse(turnContext, action);
        var response = new MessagingExtensionActionResponse()
        {
```

```
                    Task = new TaskModuleContinueResponse()
                    {
                        Value = new TaskModuleTaskInfo()
                        {
                            Height = "small",
                            Width = "small",
                            Title = "Thanks for your feedback",
                            Url = "https://proteamsdev.ngrok.io/
                            extension/thanks",
                        },
                    },
                };
                return response;
            default:
                throw new NotImplementedException($"Invalid CommandId:
                {action.CommandId}");
```

As you can see, instead of creating a card and returning that inside a MessagingExtensionActionResponse, we are adding a TaskModuleContinueResponse. This will allow us to show a pop-up with the specific height, width, and a URL. The only thing left to do is to create a web page that displays a thank you message. Add another method to our Extension controller called Thanks, add a view to it, and display our thank you message. If all goes well, you should see a result as in Figure 16-7.

Figure 16-7. *A task module showing a simple thank you message*

This could be one solution to give feedback directly to our user instead of placing information that's not useful into their compose box. You can also imagine that we can use a page like this should the user enter the wrong information in our original form. Since the form to order lunch is autogenerated by Teams, there is also no logic in there that supports our use case. Nothing stops the user from entering a date in the past, for instance, or entering the name of somebody else. Let's see what the other option is, if we are responsible for rendering everything.

Embedded web view

To have an action-based messaging extension where we control what happens, we need to add another command to our manifest. At this point, we are faced with two options that will eventually have the same result, but we have a choice on how to implement them. The goal is to have a pop-up appear with a web page from our application. This way, we have complete control over the input fields. But how the web page will be triggered can be done in different ways. We could add a control to the manifest like this:

```
{
    "id": "orderLunchControlled",
    "description": "If you are working on Saturday's you can order
    lunch here.",
```

```
        "title": "Order Saturday lunch",
        "type": "action",
        "context": [ "commandBox", "message", "compose" ],
        "fetchTask": true
    }
```

This specifies that the command will be visible, but because we now set the "fetchtask" to true, we tell Teams, just call our code and we will tell you what to render in code. We could also configure it this way.

```
{
        "id": "orderLunchWithFetch",
        "description": "If you are working on Saturday's you can order
        lunch here.",
        "title": "Order Saturday lunch no Fetch",
        "type": "action",
        "context": [ "commandBox", "message", "compose" ],
        "fetchTask": false,
        "taskInfo": {
          "title": "Order lunch",
          "width": "medium",
          "height": "medium",
          "url": "https://proteamsdev.ngrok.io/lunch"
        }
```

In this configuration, we tell Teams, don't bother asking our code for the URL and the size. Just render this page. As you can see in Figure 16-8, because we have already built a lunch tab, this gives an instant result in a task module.

Figure 16-8. *Our lunch tab shown as a task module without a fetch and a taskinfo provided in the manifest*

You would assume that the second option is the best; well that depends. Of course, this is built faster, but the additional bonus we have when specifying the taskinfo parameters in code and not in the manifest is that we can apply additional logic to it. As you can see in Figure 16-8, the location is not filled in, because, as you can remember from our tab, we get that when the user is authenticated from their profile. We left our authentication on the silent authentication, but even if we switch back to a button to authenticate, it doesn't work. Well, that's because we cannot have pop-ups inside of pop-ups. So, if we want to authenticate, we should chain our task modules after each other. Also, it sometimes is just convenient that the URL to our lunch controller is fetched when a user clicks the button. This way, we manage the endpoint in our back-end code, and we can update this endpoint without the need to update the manifest and have users install a new version or admins install a new version for all users. Let's see how we would achieve the correct result with option 1. We need to tell Teams our taskinfo object; we can do that in the "OnTeamsMessagingExtensionFetchTaskAsync" method. We already did this with our "Thanks" page, so the result looks similar.

```
protected override async Task<MessagingExtensionActionResponse>
OnTeamsMessagingExtensionFetchTaskAsync(ITurnContext<IInvokeActivity>
turnContext, MessagingExtensionAction action, CancellationToken
cancellationToken)
    {
        var response = new MessagingExtensionActionResponse()
        {
            Task = new TaskModuleContinueResponse()
            {
                Value = new TaskModuleTaskInfo()
                {
                    Height = "medium",
                    Width = "medium",
                    Title = "Order lunch",
                    Url = "https://proteamsdev.ngrok.io/lunch",
                },
            },
        };
        return response;
    }
```

This now matches option 1 with option 2. Either way we choose, configuration in the manifest or by code, we get the same result. But we still don't get the location of the user. It's time to add some authentication. As you can remember, we already did authentication in our tab (see Chapter 6), so we already have an app registered in Azure that will enable us to use OAuth to authenticate our users. Let's open up the Azure Portal once more and adjust our app registration. As you remember from authentication from inside the tab, we needed to specify our redirect URL. In this case, we are not going to handle the redirect, but the Bot Framework will handle that for us. Add the following URL to the redirect URLs in the Azure Portal under the API permissions blade of your app, as in Figure 16-9. Be careful not to add it as a single-page application URL but as a web URL.

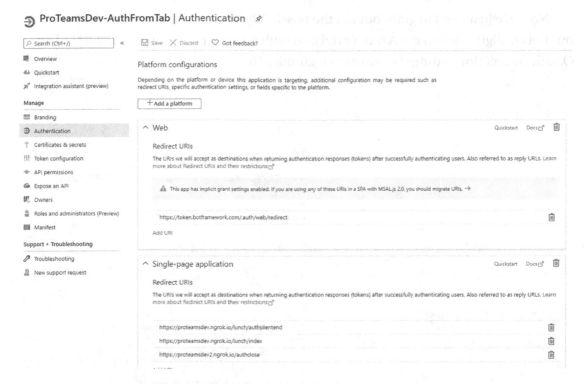

Figure 16-9. *We add the authentication link from the Bot Framework to our redirect URLs*

The reason for this is that we are not in control of the entire authentication flow. Inside the Bot Framework is already a mechanism provided to authenticate a user. Now, I can already hear you thinking: but wait, this is not a bot we are building, it's an action-based messaging extension? And that's correct, but it does use the Bot Framework as a base on which extensions run, and so the authentication part is the same. The next item on our list is a secret. Until now, we worked with the implicit flow and didn't need a client secret. Our authentication happened in the browser, so a client secret would have been useless since everybody can read our JavaScript code. In this case, it's different. The Bot Framework will authenticate to our app registration on behalf of the user, meaning the user will authenticate to the bot, and the bot will authenticate with the token from the user and in combination with the client ID and secret of our app to our tenant to get information. Under the certificates and secrets, you can create a new client secret. Give it a name and don't forget to copy your secret to somewhere safe so that you don't lose it.

Now, we just need to grant our bot the possibility to authenticate our users. Go to our bot configuration in the Azure Portal and under the settings blade, you can find an OAuth connection settings button as in Figure 16-10.

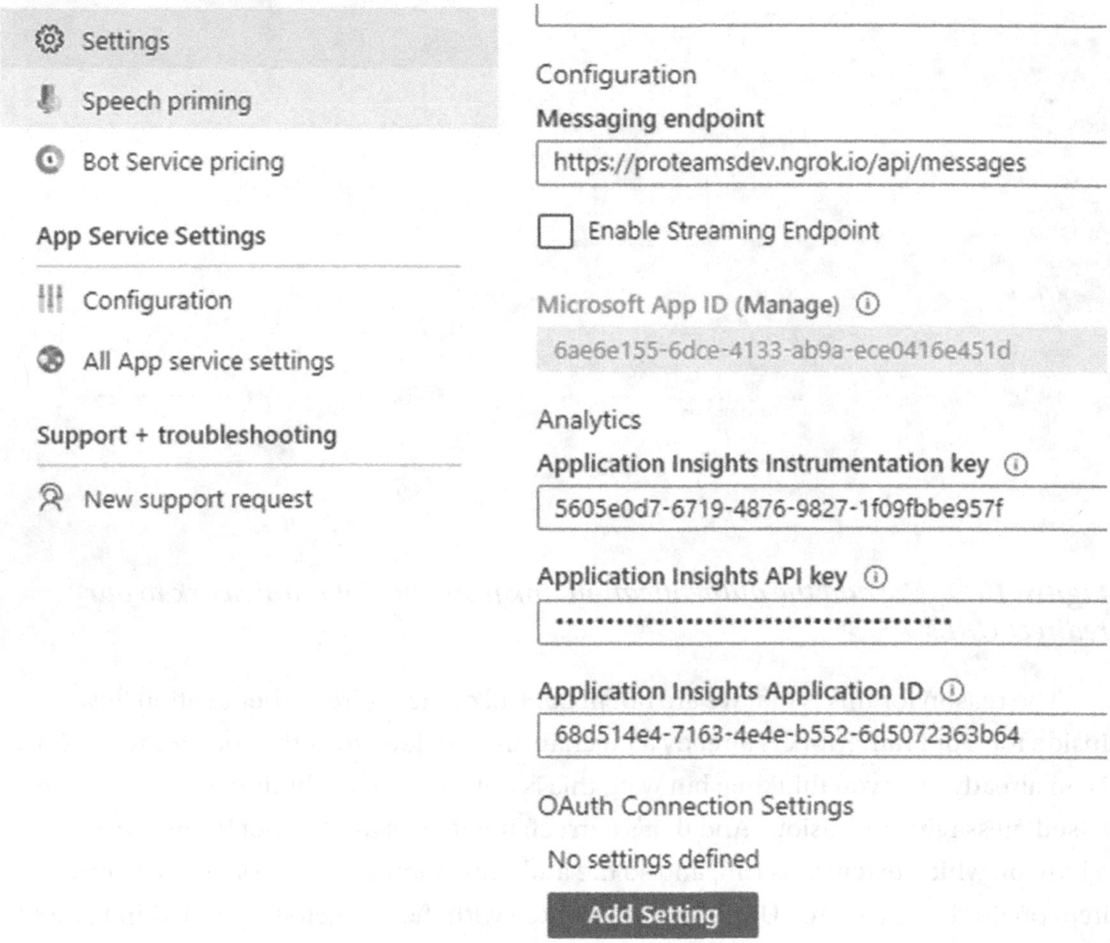

Figure 16-10. *Under the settings blade of our bot configuration in Azure, we can add OAuth connection settings*

Give our connection a name like "GetLocation" and choose as a service provider "Azure Active Directory V2." I don't need to explain to you the difference anymore between V1 and V2, so it's entirely possible you select the V1. Then we need to fill out our basic information. Except for the secret, this information is the same as we used in our tab authentication: same Client ID and Tenant ID. As you can remember from the authentication in the tab's section, we had to do two calls to Azure, one to get an open id token and then to get the bearer token to the Microsoft Graph. Since this is not a single-page application and our secret is safe, the Bot Framework doesn't need to do two calls, and we can combine our scopes here. If you filled out the information, then we can test our connection with the "test connection" button, and we should receive a token. The token exchange URL can be empty; you don't need one for this flow. When you hit the test connection button, you should see a similar result to Figure 16-11.

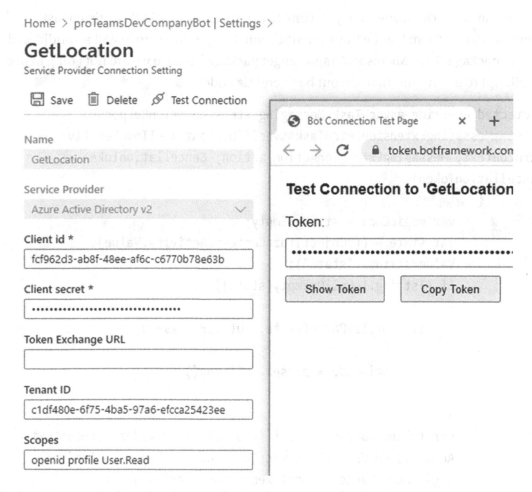

Figure 16-11. *Authentication configuration on our bot in Azure*

Now, one very important item that we haven't done yet is to add the Bot Framework domain to our valid domains section in our Teams app manifest. We have added the redirect URL from the Bot Framework to our app registration in Azure, but Teams will refuse to link to any domain that we do not approve of in the manifest. Update the version of the manifest and adjust the valid domains section to the following:

```
"validDomains": [
  "proteamsdev.ngrok.io",
  "token.botframework.com"
]
```

We haven't written any code yet. Time to get going. Let's adjust our FetchTask function so that it can handle the authentication. First, we need to install an additional NuGet package. The "Microsoft.Graph" nuget package because we are not going to use JavaScript to get our information but back-end C# code.

```
protected override async Task<MessagingExtensionActionResponse>
OnTeamsMessagingExtensionFetchTaskAsync(ITurnContext<IInvokeActivity>
turnContext, MessagingExtensionAction action, CancellationToken
cancellationToken)
        {
            var magicCode = string.Empty;
            var state = ((JObject)turnContext.Activity.Value).
            Value<string>("state");
            if (!string.IsNullOrEmpty(state))
            {
                if (int.TryParse(state, out var parsed))
                {
                    magicCode = parsed.ToString();
                }
            }
            var tokenResponse = await ((IUserTokenProvider)turnContext.
            Adapter).GetUserTokenAsync(turnContext, "GetLocation",
            magicCode, cancellationToken: cancellationToken);
            if (tokenResponse == null || string.
            IsNullOrEmpty(tokenResponse.Token))
            {
                var signInLink = await (turnContext.Adapter as
                IUserTokenProvider).GetOauthSignInLinkAsync(turnContext,
                "GetLocation", cancellationToken);
```

```
return new MessagingExtensionActionResponse
{
    ComposeExtension = new MessagingExtensionResult
    {
        Type = "auth",
        SuggestedActions = new MessagingExtensionSuggestedAction
        {
            Actions = new List<CardAction>
            {
                new CardAction
                {
                    Type = ActionTypes.OpenUrl,
                    Value = signInLink,
                    Title = "Sign in Please",
                },
            },
        },
    },
};
}
var accessToken = tokenResponse.Token;
if (accessToken != null || !string.IsNullOrEmpty(accessToken))
{
    var client = GetGraphServiceClient(accessToken);
    var user = await client.Me
        .Request()
        .GetAsync();

    var response = new MessagingExtensionActionResponse()
    {
        Task = new TaskModuleContinueResponse()
        {
            Value = new TaskModuleTaskInfo()
            {
                Height = "medium",
                Width = "medium",
```

```
                    Title = "Order lunch",
                    Url = $"https://proteamsdev.ngrok.io/lunch?
                    name={user.OfficeLocation}&context=teams",
                },
            },
        };
        return response;
    }
    return null;
}
```

Now there is a lot going on in this method; let's break it into pieces. The first part checks if there is a magic code available. The way the authentication flow works is that after you are presented with the login screen, the token is sent back. But to be sure that it is the correct user that logged in to your bot that is also in the chat (the authentication happens in another page and so could be intercepted), the Bot Framework team implemented something that's called a magic code. With the old version of the Bot Framework, the user even had to log in and copy-paste that magic code back into the bot to prove that they where the one logging in. These days, with the new version, users don't have to do that anymore because the magic code is placed in the user state object of the bot. But it still exists. Well, if there is no magic code, we also cannot get the token, so if that fails, we present the user with a suggested action response. This just contains the request to sign in and a button with a URL behind it. The magic happens in the "GetOauthSigninLinkAsync" part. Here, the Bot Framework will look in the configuration of our bot to see what type of OAuth connections we configured and will search the one with the name GetLocation. The Bot Framework will then generate the correct login URL for us. This is a Microsoft-owned URL (token.botframework.com) that we added to our valid domains because that's where we want to authenticate against. As you can see in Figure 16-12, we get a nice sign-in task module.

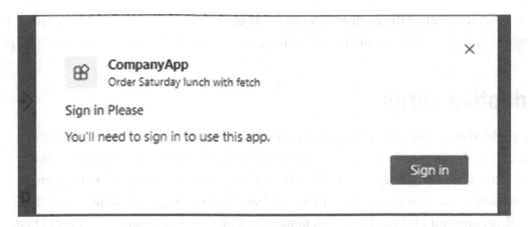

Figure 16-12. *First, we need to sign in to use our action-based extension*

Once the user signs in, the same function is called again, but this time we have a magic code and can get the authentication token. Then it's just a matter of initiating the Microsoft Graph Client and calling information about the logged-in user to get their location. Once we have the location of the user, we can then proceed with our normal flow again. Show the order lunch page with the location added to the query string. As you can see in Figure 16-13, we are running the function twice, and the second time, we have our access token and we can retrieve information about the logged-in user.

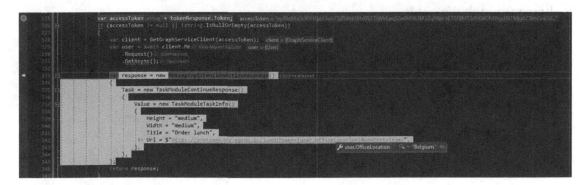

Figure 16-13. *We now have an access token and get the office location of the logged-in user*

Now we are not doing anything with the office location yet in the order lunch page. That was also the case in tab. It's just to show you that it's possible. And even though we now are chaining task modules together, it's still a nice solution to have users authenticate because the normal "pop-up" way isn't possible in task modules, except for single sign-on, but that, at the time of writing, only works with a handful of Graph APIs.

Adaptive cards

We could also respond with an adaptive card. Adaptive cards as you know have the ability that the user can interact with our card. In this scenario, we even take it one step further; we are going to chain the whole lot together. In doing so, I'm trying to demonstrate that you can make your action-based messaging extensions very difficult in a short amount of time. Therefore, make sure that you don't make your flow of task modules and adaptive cards too long to keep it understandable for both you and the user. The following is just an example so don't use it in real-life production scenarios. One thing I should point out here is that Microsoft is investing in making adaptive cards more powerful and easier to manage with the creation of ACMS (Adaptive Card Management System; https://developer.microsoft.com/en-us/microsoft-365/blogs/adaptive-cards-community-call-april-2020/), which allows us to create and store the cards we need into a separate management system. The Adaptive Card management system can then be queried for the correct card, and we don't need to store this in our solution and so decoupling our source code with the actual user interface that is shown through the cards.

Instead of showing our lunch page, we want to add an adaptive card to the compose box of the user. That would result in changing the code after authentication to the following code:

```
var response = new MessagingExtensionActionResponse
            {
                Task = new TaskModuleContinueResponse
                {
                    Value = new TaskModuleTaskInfo
                    {
                        Card = new Attachment
                        {
                            Content = new AdaptiveCard("1.0")
                            {
                                Body = new List<AdaptiveElement>()
```

```
                    {
                        new AdaptiveTextBlock()
                            {Text = "This is your adaptive
                            card", Size = AdaptiveTextSize.
                            Large},
                        new AdaptiveTextBlock()
                            {Text = "Press open URL
                            to open a URL", Size =
                            AdaptiveTextSize.Small}
                    },
                    Height = AdaptiveHeight.Auto,
                    Actions = new List<AdaptiveAction>()
                    {
                        new AdaptiveOpenUrlAction()
                        {
                            Title = "Open",
                            Url = new Uri("https://
                            proteamsdev.ngrok.io/lunch")
                        },
                    }
                },
                ContentType = AdaptiveCard.ContentType
            },
            Title = "Adaptive Card",
            Height = 300,
            Width = 600,
        }
    }
};
return response;
```

This would result in an adaptive card being shown inside a task module as in Figure 16-14.

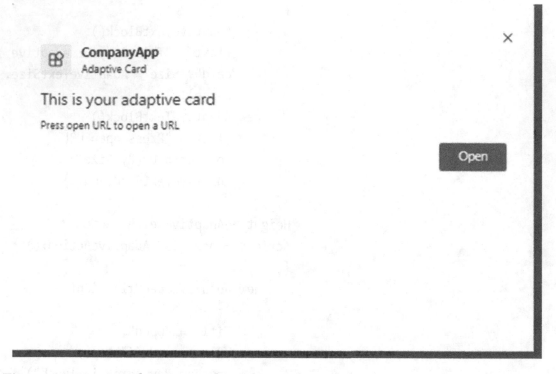

Figure 16-14. *An adaptive card inside a task module*

We also have the capability to use something of type "botMessagePreview." This allows us to show a preview of an adaptive card to the user. Why? Well, let's assume our user needs to fill out a form, and then we create an adaptive card for them that we add to their compose box. But the user made a mistake and now has to start over again. We can have Teams render additional send and edit buttons when using the "botMessagePreview" type. Let's change our adaptive card code a little bit.

```
var response = new MessagingExtensionActionResponse
        {
            ComposeExtension = new MessagingExtensionResult
            {
                Type = "botMessagePreview",
                ActivityPreview = MessageFactory.Attachment(new
                Attachment
                {
                    Content = new AdaptiveCard("1.0")
                    {
```

```
                    Body = new List<AdaptiveElement>()
                    {
                        new AdaptiveTextBlock() { Text =
                        "This is your adaptive card", Size =
                        AdaptiveTextSize.Large },
                        new AdaptiveTextBlock() { Text =
                        "Press open URL to open a URL", Size =
                        AdaptiveTextSize.Small}
                    },
                    Height = AdaptiveHeight.Auto,
                    Actions = new List<AdaptiveAction>()
                    {
                        new AdaptiveOpenUrlAction()
                        {
                            Title = "Open",
                            Url = new Uri("https://proteamsdev.
                            ngrok.io/lunch")
                        },
                    }
                },
                ContentType = AdaptiveCard.ContentType
            }) as Activity
        }
    };
    return response;
```

As you can see, we now send back the "botMessagePreview" type, which results in what you see in Figure 16-15. It's a preview of the adaptive card. If you try to click the "open" button, you will notice that it won't work. This is because it's a preview. More importantly, the user is presented with an edit and a send button.

Figure 16-15. *A bot message preview of an adaptive card*

This gives the user an idea of what they are going to send, because in this case we are not going to add it to their compose box, but our bot is going to send it on their behalf. Of course, those edit and send buttons are going to call our app so we need to implement them if we want them to work. It's time to add a couple more functions. When the edit button is clicked, this triggers the "OnTeamsMessagingExtensionBotMessagePreviewEditAsync" function with the following code:

```
protected override async Task<MessagingExtensionActionResponse>
OnTeamsMessagingExtensionBotMessagePreviewEditAsync(
        ITurnContext<IInvokeActivity> turnContext,
        MessagingExtensionAction action, CancellationToken
        cancellationToken)
    {
        var response = new MessagingExtensionActionResponse
        {
            ComposeExtension = new MessagingExtensionResult
            {
                Type = "botMessagePreview",
                ActivityPreview = MessageFactory.Attachment(new Attachment
                {
                    Content = new AdaptiveCard("1.0")
                    {
                        Body = new List<AdaptiveElement>()
                        {
                            new AdaptiveTextBlock() { Text =
                            "This is your adaptive card", Size =
                            AdaptiveTextSize.Large },
```

```
                          new AdaptiveTextBlock() { Text =
                          "Press open URL to open a URL", Size =
                          AdaptiveTextSize.Small}
                    },
                Height = AdaptiveHeight.Auto,
                Actions = new List<AdaptiveAction>()
                {
                    new AdaptiveOpenUrlAction()
                    {
                        Title = "Open",
                        Url = new Uri("https://proteamsdev.
                        ngrok.io/lunch")
                    },
                }
            },
            ContentType = AdaptiveCard.ContentType
        }) as Activity
    }
};
return response;
}
```

I just want to demonstrate here that we can send another messaging extension response back. This is again a preview page; normally, this should be some place where the user edits the information and then we would send this preview again. But I hope you are seeing the point I'm trying to make here. It can get quite complex fast when chaining screen after screen, and the best tip I can give you is to keep your messaging extensions simple. If you want this amount of changes, then maybe it should not be an extension but a tab, where you have a lot more room and where you can also use task modules if needed.

Now for the send button functionality, this is implemented in "OnTeamsMessagingExtensionBotMessagePreviewSendAsync," and this is one last cool thing I wanted to show you.

```
protected override async Task<MessagingExtensionActionResponse>
OnTeamsMessagingExtensionBotMessagePreviewSendAsync(
        ITurnContext<IInvokeActivity> turnContext,
        MessagingExtensionAction action, CancellationToken
        cancellationToken)
```

```
    {
        var activityPreview = action.BotActivityPreview[0];
        var attachmentContent = activityPreview.Attachments[0].Content;
        var previewedCard = JsonConvert.DeserializeObject<AdaptiveCard>
        (attachmentContent.ToString(),
            new JsonSerializerSettings { NullValueHandling =
            NullValueHandling.Ignore });

        previewedCard.Version = "1.0";

        var responseActivity = Activity.CreateMessageActivity();
        Attachment attachment = new Attachment()
        {
            ContentType = AdaptiveCard.ContentType,
            Content = previewedCard
        };
        responseActivity.Attachments.Add(attachment);

        // Attribute the message to the user on whose behalf the bot is
        posting
        responseActivity.ChannelData = new
        {
            OnBehalfOf = new[]
            {
                new
                {
                    ItemId = 0,
                    MentionType = "person",
                    Mri = turnContext.Activity.From.Id,
                    DisplayName = turnContext.Activity.From.Name
                }
            }
        };

        await turnContext.SendActivityAsync(responseActivity);

        return new MessagingExtensionActionResponse();
    }
```

As you can see in this code, we don't need to create the adaptive card again. That information is already sent back to us by the Bot Framework. But we can post this message as a bot on behalf of a person as you can see in Figure 16-16. This way, you are making it easier for users, not having data stuffed in their compose box and having to press enter once more. If they have reviewed the information in our preview and click send, then it's good to be posted to the channel.

Figure 16-16. *Our company bot posts on behalf of our user*

Link unfurling

One last thing I would like to show is called link unfurling. If you don't know what link unfurling is, then post a link to a YouTube video in your favorite messaging app. You will notice that not only is the link posted but also a little preview of the page. This allows for a more user-friendly experience because users instantly see what the link is about. The actual word "unfurling" means "to spread or shake out from a rolled state." This also works in Teams. If you paste a YouTube video inside of your compose box, you can see that Teams will render it like in Figure 16-17.

Figure 16-17. *If we paste a link to a YouTube video inside the compose box, Teams will render a preview for us*

Now, while this is cool for YouTube videos and other well-known services, Teams is not going to do this for our own links. Let's assume I want to link to my ngrok URL, then Teams is just going to show the link and nothing more. We do however have the possibility to create this preview ourselves. First, we must tell Teams when to contact us for a preview when which URL is entered. We of course do this inside our manifest in our compose extension section. Add the following to your manifest:

```
"messageHandlers": [
    {
       "type": "link",
       "value": {
         "domains": [
            "proteamsdev.ngrok.io"
         ]
       }
    }
  ]
```

Be mindful where you place this inside your manifest; it does not belong to the command section but is a separate section under our compose extension. By implementing this, Teams knows that every link with my proteamsdev domain should be checked against our endpoint to render a preview. I could also add *.ngrok.io if I wanted to; that's up to you to decide. Teams is going to call our app, and the JSON will contain a composeExtension/querylink invoke section. This can be handled in the "OnTeamsAppBasedLinkQueryAsync" function. We once again must answer with a messaging extension response, and like before this can be a thumbnail card, a hero card, a connector card, or an adaptive card. These should be enough to provide you flexibility in how you want your preview to appear.

```
protected override async Task<MessagingExtensionResponse> OnTeamsAppBasedL
inkQueryAsync(ITurnContext<IInvokeActivity> turnContext, AppBasedLinkQuery
query, CancellationToken cancellationToken)
        {
            var card = new HeroCard
            {
                Title = "You are referencing our domain",
                Text = query.Url,
                Images = new List<CardImage> { new CardImage("https://
                upload.wikimedia.org/wikipedia/commons/thumb/c/c9/
                Microsoft_Office_Teams_%282018%E2%80%93present%29.
                svg/1200px-Microsoft_Office_Teams_%282018%E2%80%93prese
                nt%29.svg.png") },
            };

            var attachments = new MessagingExtensionAttachment(HeroCard.
            ContentType, null, card);
            var result = new MessagingExtensionResult(AttachmentLayoutTy
            pes.List, "result", new[] { attachments }, null, "Our domain
            unfurling");

            return new MessagingExtensionResponse(result);
        }
```

This is the most basic the function can be. Normally, you should add some additional logic. As we can see with YouTube, they always use a frame from the video as a screenshot. If we would implement this for our own public website, for example, it's rather easy to write some code that screenshots every page and checks the URL and provides the correct screenshot, but in this case, I've chosen to use a Teams icon as you can see in Figure 16-18.

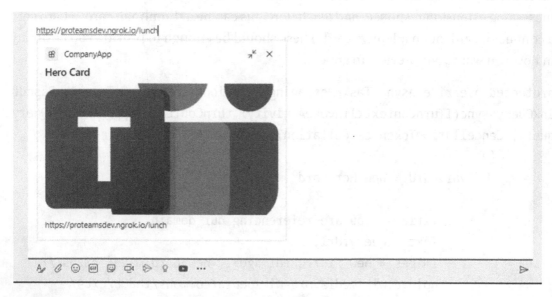

Figure 16-18. *Link unfurling on our own domain*

Now, something to point out here is that it's not because a link from YouTube automatically is unfurled that there is an extension running in our Teams client from YouTube to do this. Most websites already have the information they want to have shown inside the preview prepared and embedded into every web page. Description, images, and other information that they wish to show are added through dedicated HTML meta tags, Facebook's Open Graph tags, or Twitter card tags. There are several systems that provide this, but basically, they all add specific tags to every web page with the information for the preview, like description or images. If you ever need link unfurling for public websites, then this information will probably already be on the page, and you will just need to render it. The power of custom link unfurling in Teams is more that we can immediately have actions added when we do our own link unfurling. Like adding buttons to a product page of a website where the marketing department always orders promotion material, that directly places an order for that product.

Summary

I hope you enjoyed reading this chapter as much as I did writing it. Message extensions are so flexible that we can use them from the simplest of use cases to the most complex ones. I hope you agree with me that the Teams team really did their best in making this one of the most flexible extension points in Teams. By now, you can build not only search-based messaging extensions but also action-based messaging extensions and combine them. We have discussed how to authenticate and the freedom that task modules provide us to really own a piece of real estate on the screen inside of Teams. The task module embedded web view, showed us that it is just an iFrame and allows us to have endless possibilities. There are examples out there of YouTube videos being played in a task module, but also a PowerApp or an SPFx web part can be shown. You now know that in developing Teams messaging extensions, the difficulty is not in the code or in finding workarounds; but it's making sure that you or your fellow developers don't make it too complex. I did a quick count and we have implemented 12 overrides in our QABot class, only counting the Teams-specific ones. So, any decent Teams app is going to be large, and if we don't manage the complexity, we are going to regret it afterward. This concludes the part about messaging extensions and even the part where we truly extend Teams. In the next chapter, we will find out how we can code against and not on the Teams platform with the Microsoft Graph and PowerShell.

PART 6

Developing Against Microsoft Teams

CHAPTER 17

Microsoft Graph for Teams

From now on, we are done with building on top of the Teams platform. It sometimes is necessary that we build a solution against the Teams platform. Provisioning, for example, is a use case most used. Users needing multiple teams with specific settings don't want to create them all manually. A company policy changes, and suddenly all GIF settings must change for all Teams. Doing something like that manually would be impossible. That's the reason we sometimes must develop against Microsoft Teams, and for that we are going to use the Microsoft Graph.

Background

With Teams, we are actually very lucky that the Microsoft Graph already existed when Teams came around. If you look at other services like Azure Active Directory or SharePoint, they already were around and had their own APIs with their own quirks and with their own authentication mechanisms. I used to work solely with SharePoint, and if there was a project that involved Active Directory or Windows, then they would have to bring in people specialized in that area and everybody needed to build their part of the puzzle because we didn't understand how the other product APIs worked. Thanks to the Microsoft Graph, this is not the case anymore. Because of the unification of the different endpoints, meaning same authentication and same filtering or ordering techniques, we can easily understand how to query, for instance, Azure Active Directory. The Teams APIs were directly built on the Microsoft Graph, which gives us only one version to work with and not having to find out if an API is already mapped to the Microsoft Graph, because mapping all the existing APIs is a big undertaking and the Microsoft Graph team is after several years not even done with it. Now, what is the Microsoft Graph? It's called one API to rule them all, and it was created for the reason I specified earlier—to remove all the differences in APIs between the products of Microsoft (`https://developer.microsoft.com/en-us/graph`).

© Rick Van Rousselt 2021
R. Van Rousselt, *Pro Microsoft Teams Development*, https://doi.org/10.1007/978-1-4842-6364-8_17

The Microsoft Graph is easy to use. The endpoints used are very consistent, and the only real struggle is authentication. We have two ways of being authenticated against the Microsoft Graph. One is called delegated permissions, meaning we are logged in as a user, so we delegate our credentials to some code that runs commands in our name, just like the authentication we have used so far. The other is application permissions, meaning we tell Microsoft that we have an application that must execute commands. Application credentials have more access. Delegated permissions work in the name of the user, so if a user doesn't have access to something, then our code also doesn't have access. An application is usually built to work with all the data, and it's up to the developer to see that they handle those super access rights with care.

To get started quickly with the Microsoft Graph, I always go to `https://aka.ms/ge`. This takes you instantly to the Graph Explorer where you can sign in and see examples and results of requests with actual data from your tenant. And don't forget to sign in with your developer tenant. This way, you can try out most capabilities without asking permission from an administrator first.

Permissions

We are going to start with the hardest part, and those are permissions. Once you get the hang of permissions, working with the Graph is a breeze. The first thing we need with working with the Graph is an application registration in Azure. That's something we cannot get around; how easy it would sometimes be that we could just use a username and password without an app registration, but this is an additional security layer. This makes sure that an administrator always knows what is going on inside their environment and that we cannot have rogue users downloading code they find on Google or Bing and running that against the environment. Another benefit is that developers cannot get more information than the admin specified. Remember that when creating an app registration, we need to specify the permissions of that app. Well, those permissions cannot be more than what we specified here. With application permissions, that seems logical; the app has the access permissions that the admin specified. But with delegated permissions, that is sometimes confusing, because let's say the app only specifies access to the users' files, then we cannot access the mails of the users, even with using their credentials. The actual permissions we have are an intersection between what the app registration allows and what permissions the user has, and the least access always wins. This is also continuously evolving; the Microsoft Graph team has announced at Build

2020 that they are working on even more fine-grained permissions for both channels and teams.

Authentication and authorization with the Microsoft Graph use, as you already know, OAuth. We are not going too deep into the different OAuth flows as already mentioned, but I did want to explain the basics. After running through the OAuth flow, we are presented with an access token. This access token or bearer token is a long string. This string is a JSON Web Token (or JWT), and we have the possibility to decode it to see what's in it. But let's start at the beginning. Let's register our application and run through a flow to see what happens. Register an app in Azure and give it user.read permissions; if you don't remember how that's done, then here you can find some guidance: `https://docs.microsoft.com/en-us/azure/active-directory/develop/quickstart-register-app`. We are going to register a single tenant app, with a client secret, and as permissions, we are selecting "Group.ReadWrite.All". Since Teams are using Microsoft 365 groups, getting all the Teams from our Tenant requires us to get all the Microsoft 365 groups. When registering the app, don't forget to grant it permissions. You have no idea how happy I am that this button exists. It hasn't always existed, and when granting permissions, we used to be required to call an endpoint to consent an app. Try explaining that to global administrators of a Tenant in a large enterprise who live in PowerShell the entire day.

Tokens

To get our access token, we need to make a request to `https://login.microsoftonline.com` as you can remember from Chapter 6; to use the V2 endpoint, we need to add something to this URL, namely, our tenant ID. So, the full URL will look like this: `https://login.microsoftonline.com/<YOUR_TENANT_ID>/oauth2/v2.0/token`. Now, we do need to specify our client ID and secret somewhere; this we can do in the body, since we are going to do an HTTP POST call. So add the following values to the body field as form data as you can see in Figure 17-1.

- Key: client_id / Value: The (application) client ID from your app registration

- Key: client_secret / Value: The secret you created in the "Certificates & Secrets" blade

- Key: scope / Value: `https://graph.microsoft.com/.default` (we are requesting access to the Microsoft Graph in this case; should you need, e.g., access to the Outlook REST APIs, then this would have been `https://outlook.office.com/mail.read`)

- Key: grant_type / Value: client_credentials (this is the OAuth flow we are using)

Once you added the information and you click the send button, you can see that we get a token back from our login endpoint as in Figure 17-1.

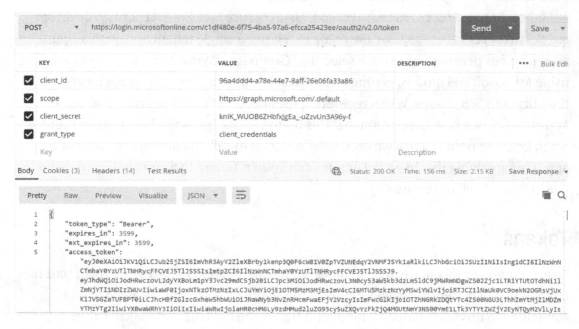

Figure 17-1. *Calling our login endpoint in Postman and getting a bearer token*

If we now take this token and decode it (`https://jwt.io/`), then we can see that this is not a random combination of letters but that it actually holds information about our permissions as in Figure 17-2.

PAYLOAD: DATA

```
    "aud": "https://graph.microsoft.com",
    "iss": "https://sts.windows.net/c1df480e-6f75-4ba5-97a6-
  efcca25423ee/",
    "iat": 1593933333,
    "nbf": 1593933333,
    "exp": 1593937233,
    "aio": "E2BgYLBfsPr/uur68l+ZkawGf3QWAwA=",
    "app_displayname": "MicrosoftGraphAccess",
    "appid": "96a4ddd4-a78e-44e7-8aff-26e06fa33a86",
    "appidacr": "1",
    "idp": "https://sts.windows.net/c1df480e-6f75-4ba5-97a6-
  efcca25423ee/",
    "oid": "6d8e3239-a8de-47a4-8dc5-1fcd9a0342bf",
    "roles": [
      "Group.ReadWrite.All"
    ],
    "sub": "6d8e3239-a8de-47a4-8dc5-1fcd9a0342bf",
    "tenant_region_scope": "EU",
    "tid": "c1df480e-6f75-4ba5-97a6-efcca25423ee",
    "uti": "s4Qp5EKqmEidBR-JGnxBAA",
    "ver": "1.0",
    "xms_tcdt": 1578037952
  }
```

Figure 17-2. *Our access token decoded*

Sometimes, we need to verify this token ourselves; for instance, we can also have our own API protected by Azure, and then we need to check if a token that was issued to a user is valid. Decoding this token, its Base64 encoded, and verifying the contents would then be step 1 that we need to do. When we call the Microsoft Graph, the exact same thing happens on their end. They decode the token, see if the information is correct, and even check with the issuer (in this case, sts.windows.net, so Azure AD) if they recently created this token. If you ever need to do this, then don't write the code for it yourself; there are plenty of helper libraries out there that can help you with this.

Getting information

Now that we have our token, it's just a matter of adding that as a header to all our requests. Since this is to authorize our request, it needs to be in the authorization header, and we need to add the word "bearer" to it because it's a bearer token. Your request is going to look like something in Figure 17-3. Since we want to know all the teams in our tenant, we are going to need to do a GET request to the following endpoint: `https://graph.microsoft.com/v1.0/groups`.

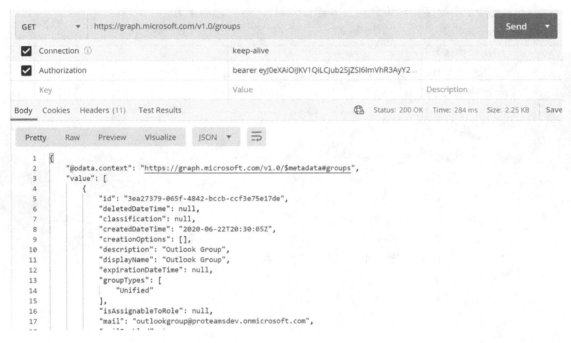

Figure 17-3. *Calling the Graph with our bearer token to get the Microsoft 365 groups of our tenant*

This was an example of how the flow works. Do not go crafting and wasting time with constructing all these calls. The Microsoft Graph team has already prepared a Postman collection for working with the Microsoft Graph. It uses variables so you don't need to copy/paste tokens, and most standard requests are added as an example (`https://docs.microsoft.com/en-us/graph/use-postman`). I have a version of this collection on my workstation ready to be used, and I suggest you do the same. You don't need it that often because there is even an easier solution, and that's the Graph Explorer (`https://`

developer.microsoft.com/en-us/graph/graph-explorer). The Graph Explorer is a website where you can test and execute calls against the Graph. It's like Postman but then as a website. It also has the additional bonus of being able to log in. This does mean that because you log in, it uses delegate permissions. But if you have enough permissions on a tenant, then you should be able to test most calls. While Postman and the Graph Explorer are perfect for testing single calls when developing a solution, using them to execute multiple operations can be hard. Let's say we want to update a setting on all the Teams in our Tenant. That would take forever in the Graph Explorer or in Postman. For this reason, I usually have a solution at hand that I adjust to my needs when I need to do this kind of task. It's a messy collection of requests and logic, but the most important part is that the authentication part is taken care of and that I just need to write my logic, call the endpoint, and run the solution.

Tooling

Depending on the customer where I'm working at that moment, I have different solutions to execute logic toward the Tenant. Some customers provide a little more freedom, and there I can use, for instance, the Microsoft 365 CLI (https://pnp.github. io/cli-microsoft365/). The Microsoft 365 CLI is an open source tool supported by the community, and they are always looking for developers to help support this awesome tool. The Microsoft 365 CLI is perfect for building automation scripts, and if you check out the GitHub repository, you will see that all the calls that it executes are using the Microsoft Graph. Another option would be PowerShell; the PnP PowerShell team which is also community driven has some nice Teams commands (https://docs. microsoft.com/en-us/powershell/sharepoint/sharepoint-pnp/sharepoint-pnp-cmdlets?view=sharepoint-ps). Other customers don't allow me to use anything related to npm or GitHub; in that case, I use my generic C# solution. This solution is a mix of both worlds. The Graph team has provided us with an SDK. While it's easy to use, the flexibility is sometimes not what I want, so I switch between the SDK and just using a pure HTTP client to do different calls.

C#

If you look at my generic solution, then you can see it's a mess of different calls and ways to execute those calls. This is my go-to solution when I want something done fast. As you can see, there are two different ways to get a bearer token. The first one is how we used to do it in .NET Core; the second one is using a new NuGet package called "Microsoft.Graph.Auth" which is still in preview at the time of writing this. These are using application permissions, and we can see that not only because we need a client ID and a client secret but also because we are using the "ConfidentialClientApplicationBuilder" class.

```
var authority = $"https://login.microsoftonline.com/{tenantId}";
        var app = ConfidentialClientApplicationBuilder
            .Create(clientId)
            .WithClientSecret(clientSecret)
            .WithAuthority(new Uri(authority))
            .Build();
```

Once we have our client application, we can request a bearer token in the old way:

```
var scopes = new[] { "https://graph.microsoft.com/.default" };
        var authenticationResult = app.AcquireTokenForClient(scopes).
        ExecuteAsync().Result;

        // Create GraphClient
        var originalGraphClient = new GraphServiceClient(
            new DelegateAuthenticationProvider(requestMessage =>
            {
                requestMessage.Headers.Authorization =
                    new AuthenticationHeaderValue("bearer",
                    authenticationResult.AccessToken);
                return Task.FromResult(0);
            }));
```

Or in the new way:

```
// Create an authentication provider by passing in a client application and
graph scopes.
        ClientCredentialProvider authProvider = new
        ClientCredentialProvider(app);
// Create a new instance of GraphServiceClient with the authentication
provider.
        GraphServiceClient newGraphClient = new GraphServiceClient(auth
        Provider);
```

I kind of like the new way better because it's cleaner, but the old way did gave us an easy access to the bearer token so that we could switch between an HTTP client and the SDK as you can see here.

```
// Call the Graph with the SDK
        var user = originalGraphClient.Groups.Request().GetAsync().Result;

        //Call the Graph with HTTP Client
        HttpClient client = new HttpClient();
        client.DefaultRequestHeaders.Authorization = new Authentication
        HeaderValue("Bearer", authenticationResult.AccessToken);
        HttpResponseMessage response = client.GetAsync(new
        Uri("https://graph.microsoft.com/v1.0/users/rick@proteamsdev.
        onmicrosoft.com")).ConfigureAwait(false).GetAwaiter().
        GetResult();
```

Summary

In this chapter, we looked into coding against the Teams platform instead of on the Teams platform. Coding against Teams is useful, for instance, when we want to provision Teams or when a lot of teams need to have a setting updated. We discussed that it's not the coding part that is hard but that it's working with permissions. We learned that there are, because of the flexibility of the Microsoft Graph, numerous ways to solve the same problem and that we can choose what tooling to use. This flexibility allows us to work with what we like best; if it's PowerShell, C#, the Microsoft 365 CLI, Node, and so on, as long as we can call an endpoint on the Graph with the coding or scripting language of our choice, we are good to go.

CHAPTER 18

PowerShell for Teams

In this chapter, we are going to take a closer look at what we can do with the PowerShell cmdlets for Teams. You can do some things with the Microsoft Graph but not everything. Setting policies, for instance, is one of them. For the most part, the Teams PowerShell modules use the Microsoft Graph under the covers, but not all the time. As a developer, we·don't interact with PowerShell that often, but I did want to give you this information because it's happened to me before that I needed my development tenant to match the production tenant. And having some basic understanding of the PowerShell capabilities for Teams is essential.

Getting started

Let's not spend too much time discussing how to install PowerShell or the PowerShell cmdlets for Teams. But I do want to bring up the topic because you are going to do it often. With Teams for PowerShell, there is a GA (General Availability) version and a Public Preview version. And the difference is enormous. You are going to be switching between versions sometimes so be prepared for that. If we are not using the preview version, then we are also going to need the Skype for Business PowerShell modules.

As you know, some of the calling and meeting parts in Teams are taken over from Skype for Business. The latest preview version at the time of writing doesn't need the Skype for Business PowerShell modules anymore, which is, in my opinion, a great win. So for the moment, it's quite a hassle to switch between versions.

My favorite PowerShell editor is Visual Studio Code. You can just run your script with pressing F5, and with the integrated terminal, you can also run a command directly in there. If you are using Visual Studio Code to run PowerShell, I can recommend the PowerShell extension from Microsoft (`https://github.com/PowerShell/vscode-powershell`). Another tip I can give you is something I need right away. Since the release of PowerShell 7, which I installed of course immediately, there have been registered

R. Van Rousselt, *Pro Microsoft Teams Development*, https://doi.org/10.1007/978-1-4842-6364-8_18

issues with the Teams cmdlets, so the recommendation is to revert to the 5.1 version. When you are in VS Code, then hit the Ctrl+Shift+P button (which opens the menu) and type "PowerShell: Show session menu." This gives you the ability to change the PowerShell version, or you can click the icon on the bottom right of the page to switch as in Figure 18-1.

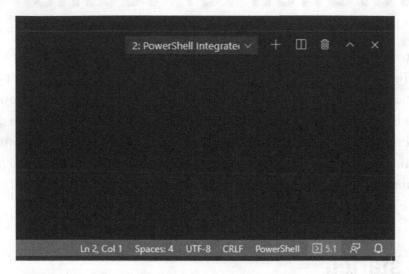

Figure 18-1. *The green PowerShell icon in the bottom-right corner will allow you to switch between PowerShell versions*

Now there is a lot more that I did with my VS Code; there are a bunch of tips and tricks out there, but if you are getting started, then I recommend you take a look at the ones from Microsoft (`https://github.com/microsoft/vscode-tips-and-tricks`). The first thing we always must do is to connect; we can do that with these simple commands:

```
$UserCredential = Get-Credential
Connect-MicrosoftTeams -Credential $UserCredential
```

Once we are connected, we can execute our commands against our Tenant. Don't forget to use the `Disconnect-MicrosoftTeams` cmdlet after you are done. But what are the commands? Well, we can get a list of all possible commands available by running this command:

```
Get-Command -Module MicrosoftTeams
```

Currently, I'm running the preview version 1.1.3, and there are 7 functions available and 35 cmdlets. Let's start simple by creating a new team. Enter the following command:

```
New-Team -DisplayName "My New Team"
```

As you can see in Figure 18-2, our new team is created.

```
PS C:\ProTeamsDevGit\ProTeamsDev\Chapter 18\Teams PowerShell> c:\ProTeamsDevGit\ProTeamsDev\Chapter 18\Teams PowerShell\CreateTeam.ps1

GroupId                               DisplayName      Visibility  Archived  MailNickName    Description
-------                               -----------      ----------  --------  ------------    -----------
70def4c3-3e13-4843-b428-17a5c8a99fae  My New Team      Private     False     msteams_7e194e
```

Figure 18-2. *Our new team is created*

When you look at the output of our new team, you can immediately see that this command doesn't do what we want. It sets a team default to private, which, according to the documentation, is expected. Now I usually try to persuade customers that I work for to have their Teams public. I know there are valid reasons for having private Teams, and I have nothing against them. But I have seen the difference in enterprises that are more open in their daily work and the ones that keep everything locked down. In the more open ones, there is a more collaborative atmosphere, and isn't that one of the key points of Teams, to have more collaboration? So, it's time to create a new team, but let's set all the settings to our liking from the start. Now be careful not to switch classification with visibility. The visibility setting is what determines if a Team is public or private; the classification is an internal Microsoft use.

```
New-Team -DisplayName "My Configured Team" -Description "This is a
configured team" -MailNickName "configured" -Visibility "Public"
-AllowGiphy $true -GiphyContentRating "Moderate" -AllowStickersAndMemes
$true -AllowCustomMemes $true -AllowGuestCreateUpdateChannels
$true -AllowGuestDeleteChannels $true -AllowCreateUpdateChannels
$true -AllowDeleteChannels $true -AllowAddRemoveApps $true
-AllowCreateUpdateRemoveTabs $true -AllowCreateUpdateRemoveConnectors
$true -AllowUserEditMessages $true -AllowUserDeleteMessages
$true -AllowOwnerDeleteMessages $true -AllowTeamMentions $true
-AllowChannelMentions $true
```

I know that this is a long cmdlet to execute, but at least we now have a fully configured team, with all the parameters that we can set. To remove this team, again we just need the Microsoft 365 group ID that is behind the team to delete it.

```
Remove-Team -GroupId 'f94f7ae9-5172-45c2-8a77-54a5601b1595'
```

Now that we can create a Team, let's add a user. The default settings add the user as a member, but we could specify the "-role" to "owner" to add this user as an owner.

```
Add-TeamUser -GroupId '45b99352-d287-402e-adb0-07356c68f669' -User 'MeganB@proteamsdev.onmicrosoft.com'
```

To remove a member, it's the same cmdlet; just replace "Add" with "Remove". I have also taken the liberty to add a small script that will create a team with some channels and some members to the examples provided. Should you ever need to provision a few teams for testing purposes, then this is a good starting point. Now it's time to start using something that we are going to use more often, installing and upgrading our app. First, we need to add our Teams app package to our Tenant.

```
New-TeamsApp -DistributionMethod "organization" -Path "C:\Users\RickVanRousselt\Downloads\UserGroupPackage.zip"
```

This command takes two parameters, the location of the zip file and the distribution method. Here, we have the option to use "organization" or "global." According to the documentation, we need to use the organization for Line of Business Apps. I tried to use the "global" parameter, but it just returns an error. So it's best to stick with the "organization." Now, after installing, it can take a while for your app to show up, so if you don't see it immediately in your Teams environment, then don't panic and give it a few minutes. Mine showed up after about five minutes. This is important to know; when using the PowerShell cmdlets for Teams, even though they complete quite fast and return no error, that doesn't mean that your Team is already provisioned, that the app is added, or that a user is added. You should take this into consideration when building more advanced scripts that you double check if a command completed successfully. The new team app command returns an ID, well actually two IDs, an ID and an externalID. The externalID is the ID we have given our app inside our manifest. This way, it's easily recognized. The other ID is the ID it gets when being installed in the Tenant. And it's this ID that we need to install our app in a team with the command:

```
Add-TeamsAppInstallation -AppId '0d582118-0869-42f1-a97f-768aad803f2c'
-TeamId '45b99352-d287-402e-adb0-07356c68f669'
```

Now all that's left is for us to be able to update our app. Unfortunately, there is no Update-TeamsApp cmdlet, so we are stuck with removing the app and then adding it again, which is a hassle. Therefore, I recommend if you want to update your app that you do this through the Microsoft Graph.

Other ways

While most of this chapter is about the specific PowerShell modules for Teams released by Microsoft, it's only fair to mention other initiatives. One we already mentioned briefly in the previous chapter is the PnP PowerShell initiative. This open source community–led PowerShell library also has a variety of commands especially for Teams (`https://docs.microsoft.com/en-us/powershell/sharepoint/sharepoint-pnp/sharepoint-pnp-cmdlets?view=sharepoint-ps`). This library initially was created to work with SharePoint, but they have numerous commands in there to interact with teams, channels, tabs, messages, and much more.

Another great initiative is Microsoft365DSC (`www.youtube.com/watch?v=mDCuZgvCWWc`). This was initially created by Microsoft engineers but is now also open source and maintained by the community. Microsoft365DSC goes way beyond Teams and is a way to use configuration-as-code for your Tenant, which means that you can write a definition on how your Tenant should be configured and monitor that definition. It's incredibly easy when working with large enterprises where administrators must keep multiple large Tenants in sync and configured correctly. Microsoft365DSC uses a combination of several frameworks and components like our Teams PowerShell module to configure a Tenant.

Since both of the preceding tools are open source, if you ever have a problem coding or scripting, then you can always have a look on their GitHub pages how they solved that specific problem, if you are not already using these tools. Another recommendation I cannot make enough is that should you use these tools and there is a bug, then look at the code, fix the problem, and do a commit to the repository on GitHub. You are not only helping yourself by fixing the problem but you are helping out the entire community.

These kinds of initiatives are based on people from the community helping each other, and since we can use all these tools for free and they make us spend less time coding ourselves, we can always give back by donating a little time.

Summary

In this chapter, we learned that we can also use PowerShell to do actions against the Teams platform. We discussed that the current version of the Teams PowerShell cmdlets is still using the Skype for Business cmdlets, and the preview is not. And from that, we learned that Teams and Skype are still under the covers linked together somehow. The Teams cmdlets can help you speed up repetitive tasks that you sometimes must do, and it's always convenient to have some basic scripts laying around just in case. As a final part, we learned that various open source initiatives, like PnP PowerShell or Microsoft365DSC, can help us with doing actions against Teams and even other parts of our Tenant.

APPENDIX A

Advanced Teams development

Now that you know all the different ways to build on top of or against the Microsoft Teams platform, I wanted to end this book with some final thoughts on more advanced topics. Converting an application to run inside of Teams or building one from scratch in Teams should not be a problem anymore. But in some use cases, there are still some quirks in the system that you should know. This chapter contains some of the compelling real-life use cases I've come across, and I wanted to share my thoughts on them. The solutions provided are by no means the best and could be solved differently, but they do get the job done.

CI and CD

CI and CD stand for Continuous Integration and Continuous Deployment (sometimes replaced with Delivery), and you should have heard of it. If not, it's explained pretty quickly. It's where we build software, and instead of building big pieces and releasing them every few months, we build in short cycles and release it with a lot more speed to the point where we make weekly or even daily updates in production. This implies that we need to automate as much as we can and will make us more comfortable with releasing. Therefore, implementing small incremental updates allows us to reduce cost, time, and risk with every release.

CI/CD is tied together with DevOps, which is all the hype these days. Let's not go too deep into the benefits of CI/CD and DevOps; if they are not clear to you, then I recommend you look up some information on it. I must say I'm a huge fan. But how does this work in Teams development? As you know, Teams development consists of

© Rick Van Rousselt 2021
R. Van Rousselt, *Pro Microsoft Teams Development*, https://doi.org/10.1007/978-1-4842-6364-8

our two most essential items, our code and our manifest. Doing CI/CD with our code is straightforward and can be compared to how you do it on other development platforms that use Azure.

Source control

We can work with various source control platforms that give us the possibility to do CI/CD. We could stay in the Azure realm and use Azure DevOps, or we could steer more toward GitHub. Both have their positives and negatives, and which one you want to use depends on your personal preference and usually also the company where you work. The decision to use one of these two or even a different one is often tied to the culture of the company. A company with a track record of .NET development usually used Team Foundation Server a long time ago and moved, therefore in the direction of Azure DevOps, while a company more focused on open source development often leans more in the direction of GitHub. But this can change over time; even Microsoft is now using GitHub for the development of Windows and thus having one of the largest GitHub repositories ever created (`https://devblogs.microsoft.com/bharry/the-largest-git-repo-on-the-planet/`).

Let's start with Azure DevOps. I created a repository and uploaded a new project in it. For this one, I started with the Microsoft Teams Toolkit for Visual Studio (`https://marketplace.visualstudio.com/items?itemName=TeamsDevApp.vsteamstemplate`). At the time of writing, it has just released in preview, and I wanted to test it. The toolkit is created to help with Teams development in Visual Studio and to simplify the process of creating a Teams application directly from Visual Studio. I just selected a static tab because what the Teams app does is not important. We just need some code running in my app to use as an example to deploy items automatically. Once the project gets created, we can commit and sync it to our Azure DevOps repository. Having something that does source control is a vital part of CI/CD because we want different versions deployed to different environments. The most common way that I have seen until now is that there are different Tenants used to do acceptance testing. Most enterprises have test, acceptance, and production Tenants. This way, the development lifecycle is guarded, and before a new feature is released, it gets validated by testers. After going through this cycle, the new feature gets to a production environment. And as you know in an ideal world, a developer never installs software in a production environment.

These days, it's tough to keep up with this approach because we are using different Tenants. When everything was still in databases and self-managed data centers, this was easier to do; you took a copy of the production database and moved that to the test and acceptance environments, and those environments resembled the production environment. These days, it's not that simple anymore; you cannot ask Microsoft to move a database from one tenant to another. You can write code to do it, but that's a lot of work. So, these days you more and more see that both acceptance and test environments (and maybe more environments in between) get merged into one and that it's just there to validate the technical side of a feature (to make sure that you don't have developers saying the famous words: "It works on my machine"). Testers spend more and more time re-creating data on the test and acceptance environments; then, they do testing features. Therefore, the need to test with production data is getting higher. To do this, you, of course, need a small containerized environment for your testers within your production environment. This is something that we are going to do so that you can have your testers and test your app with real data, and you don't waste time with writing code and scripts to keep tenant data in sync.

One significant help in this area is the Teams app policies. We already touched this a little bit at the beginning of the book. With these policies, we can make sure that only testers have the app available in their Team's client. This is perfect for a new app. You create the app, upload it to the tenant, and configure the policies so that only your test audience has the app available, and they can start testing. The problem is when you need to update your app. You can only have one version of the app installed in your tenant, meaning that if you update your app that's used by the entire organization, then the whole organization gets the new features and not only the test audience. I know that Microsoft is working on a solution, but until that is released, we need an alternate approach. And this comes in the form of a second app.

The way I currently do it is that we create a second Teams app package that directs to another web application in Azure where our new feature is running. We then, through policies, direct this app to our test user base, as you can see in Figure A-1.

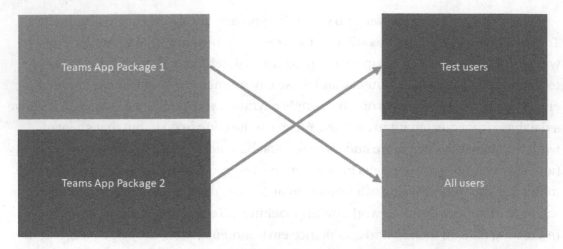

Figure A-1. *We create a new Teams app package and target this to our test users*

Now the key here is that when creating our second Teams app package, we keep everything the same as in the first one, meaning the same icons, same name, same everything. The only things that change are the Teams app ID and the endpoints used in the various extension points such as the URL of a tab or the bot ID. The first time you set this up, it's a hassle, because you need to double everything, two web applications or two bots. But once the setup is complete, you can switch between apps, and the users will not notice it. After you have turned them around, you can have the second app package exposed to all users and the first one back to the test users, as in Figure A-2. And you can keep this cycle going on every time you develop a new feature.

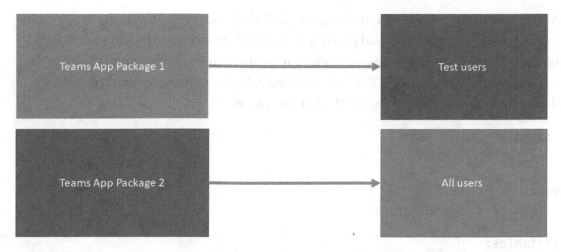

Figure A-2. *When releasing a new version, our second app package gets targeted against all users and our first app package to our test users, ready to receive new features*

It does require you to maintain which app is currently in "production," but it does allow test users to test in the same tenant as they are working with real data. Now I can already hear you thinking, why don't you use blue/green deployments that are available in Azure? Well, the problem here is that we also need to update our manifest from time to time. While blue/green deployments let you swap your back-end code between slots, the app manifest doesn't get updated. But let's take a step back and see how we first can create a simple pipeline to deploy our code automatically.

Pipeline

We have an Azure DevOps repository with our code already in it. It's time to set up automatic deployment to our Azure web application that will be hosting the code. Start by going to the "Pipelines" section and create a new pipeline. Since our code is in Azure DevOps, we select the Azure Repos Git option. This will allow us to work with YAML-based pipeline. There used to be a more UI-based solution to create build pipelines inside of Azure DevOps, but YAML-based pipelines are slowly replacing them. The most significant advantage of a YAML-based pipeline for me is that your build (and deploy if you want) gets described inside a file that gets added to your repository. This way, you also have source control over your builds, and should you ever move your code, then because the build pipeline is described in a file in the solution, this just follows along.

And in case something needs to change to the build pipeline, it follows the same logic as your code, with commits and pull requests. YAML-based build pipelines can also be used to deploy and release your code, but this is somewhat debatable. I still like the release section of Azure DevOps, and I still use it, but you are more than welcome to deploy with YAML as well. My YAML file looks like this:

```yaml
trigger:
- master

pool:
  vmImage: 'ubuntu-latest'

variables:
  buildConfiguration: 'Release'
  solution: '**/*.sln'
  nugetVersion: '5.6.0'

steps:
- task: UseDotNet@2
  displayName: ".NET Core 3.1.x"
  inputs:
      version: '3.1.x'
      packageType: sdk

- task: NuGetToolInstaller@1
  inputs:
    versionSpec: $(nugetVersion)
    checkLatest: true

- task: NuGetCommand@2
  inputs:
    command: 'restore'
    restoreSolution: $(solution)

- task: DotNetCoreCLI@2
  displayName: Build
  inputs:
    command: build
    projects: '**/*.csproj'
```

```
      arguments: '--configuration $(buildConfiguration)'
- task: DotNetCoreCLI@2
  inputs:
    command: 'publish'
    publishWebProjects: true
    zipAfterPublish: true
    arguments: '--configuration $(BuildConfiguration) --output $(Build.
    ArtifactStagingDirectory)'

- task: ArchiveFiles@2
  inputs:
    rootFolderOrFile: '$(Build.SourcesDirectory)/ProTeamsDev.CICD/
    ProTeamsDev.CICD/Tabs/TeamsAppDev'
    includeRootFolder: false
    archiveType: 'zip'
    archiveFile: '$(Build.ArtifactStagingDirectory)/development.zip'
    replaceExistingArchive: true

- task: ArchiveFiles@2
  inputs:
    rootFolderOrFile: '$(Build.SourcesDirectory)/ProTeamsDev.CICD/
    ProTeamsDev.CICD/Tabs/TeamsAppProd'
    includeRootFolder: false
    archiveType: 'zip'
    archiveFile: '$(Build.ArtifactStagingDirectory)/production.zip'
    replaceExistingArchive: true

- task: PublishBuildArtifacts@1
  displayName: "Upload Artifacts"
  inputs:
      pathtoPublish: '$(Build.ArtifactStagingDirectory)'
      artifactName: 'proteamsdevapp'
```

As you can see, there are already a lot of steps, even without deploying. The first step is simple; it specifies that whenever there is an update on the master branch, this should run. Normally, you would have a master and a development branch at the very least if you use the Gitflow workflow (`https://nvie.com/posts/a-successful-git-branching-model/`). This flow is one of the most popular flows to do version control and already exists for ten years now, which in today's world seems like an eternity. There is a variety of different flows out there, and, like also stated in the article, take one that fits your team and your work habits. But in my case, I like this one, especially for big projects.

The second step in the build pipeline is the agent we will be using. Because this is a .NET Core app, we can run our build on Ubuntu, and we will get some increase in build time because of this. Depending on your choice of framework, you might need to change this. For Node, for instance, sometimes the builds go faster on a Mac host. The next four steps are to build our code, including restoring the NuGet packages. The following two steps are typically for Teams development. We are already zipping our manifest and our icons into a Teams app package in Visual Studio, but we need to do it here as well. Once we have our two app packages (so that we can switch them around), we need to publish them in the last step so that they get saved to use in our release pipeline. Once this is set up, after every commit, we are going to end up with three zip files: two Teams app packages and one with our build code in it. The Teams app packages need to be deployed to our Office 365 tenant, and our code needs to go to Azure. Let's configure this in our new release pipeline.

Create a new release pipeline and use the files generated from our build as artifacts. This pipeline will allow us to access the three zip files we created. As a simple release, we can deploy everything in one stage. This stage will have four steps, as you can see in Figure A-3.

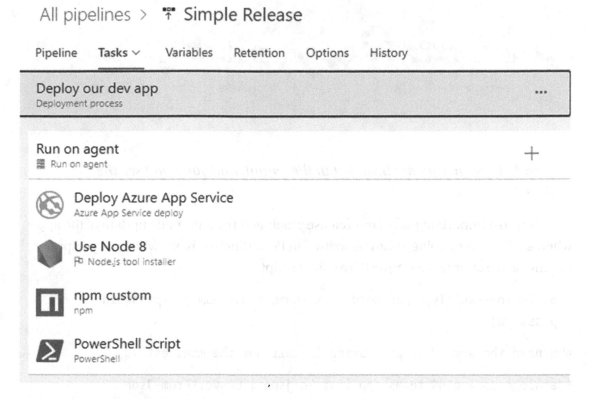

All pipelines > ⁺ Simple Release

Pipeline   Tasks ∨   Variables   Retention   Options   History

Deploy our dev app
Deployment process   •••

Run on agent   +
Run on agent

Deploy Azure App Service
Azure App Service deploy

Use Node 8
Node.js tool installer

npm custom
npm

PowerShell Script
PowerShell

Figure A-3. *The four steps of our simple release pipeline*

These four steps will consist of deploying to our app service, installing the Microsoft 365 CLI, and using the CLI to update our app in the tenant. At the same time, you can also use the CLI to install the app for the first time in a tenant. I usually prefer it to be a manual task. It can always be automated, but the first install of an app in a tenant, especially a production tenant, is something that I feel more confident about when it's a manual task performed by an admin. As you can see in Figure A-4, I already installed both the apps in my tenant, and you don't see the difference, because I gave them the same properties.

Figure A-4. *Both apps are installed in the tenant, and you don't see the difference*

The most important part of our release pipeline is the automatic update of the app when a release is ongoing. It can be written in PowerShell or Bash, whatever you prefer, but the next example is a simple PowerShell script.

```
o365 login --authType password --userName $(username) --password
$(password)

#We need the app id it got during install not the manifest id

$catalogApps = o365 teams app list -o json | ConvertFrom-Json
$existingApp = $catalogApps | Where-Object {$_.externalId -eq
"$(TeamsManifestIdDev)" }

o365 teams app update --id $existingApp.id --filePath "$(System.
DefaultWorkingDirectory)/_ProTeamsDev/proteamsdevapp/development.zip"
```

We first need to log in to our tenant with the CLI; in this case, I use a username and password, but you can also change it to certificate authentication. Also, as you can see from the script, my passwords and IDs are not hard coded, but they are added as variables and secure variables. Don't forget to consent the CLI the first time you use it; this means log in manually from your system the first time with this username before you start using it in a pipeline. Otherwise, it will not work. The next step is to get a reference to our app because we need the app ID to update the app, and the app ID in your tenant is not the same as the ID in the manifest. It's generated when you upload it for the first time. Then we can start to update our app with the last command. In this case, I am only updating the development app. I make the difference between the two apps by calling them development and production. But this is not good, because we will start switching them around between our test users and our general users. And then the naming would only just confuse us. But for this example, I named them development and production to let you see the difference. When running this release, you will find that the app back-end code gets updated and the app package in your Teams environment as well. Don't forget to update the version of the manifest every time you do an update. Maybe a good exercise for you once you start using this is to have a check somewhere that sees if you updated the version in the manifest, and otherwise just skip the update of the Teams app package. For our second app to get deployed, it's just a matter of creating a second stage that does the same thing only deploy to our second web application in Azure and deploy our production app to our tenant. You will end up with something like Figure A-5.

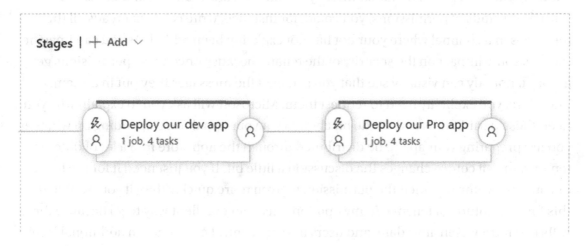

Figure A-5. *Deploy our development app and our production app*

Now we could even extend this part further. It all depends on how often you would want to switch the apps around. If you have to do it once a year, then adjusting the app policies in the Teams admin center manually would be sufficient, and automating this would have almost no return on the time you invest in creating it. But if you plan to do a monthly release cycle, then it would be well worth it to add a PowerShell script that switches the policies around. Recently, Microsoft has also announced new permissions and ways to add apps to specific teams, so you could even roll out your app one team at a time (`https://docs.microsoft.com/en-us/graph/api/teamsappinstallation-add?view=graph-rest-1.0&tabs=http`).

Protected APIs

Another thing that I should mention is the existence of protected APIs inside of the Microsoft Graph. Until now, we used the permission levels that we could grant when we did our app registration, like "group.readwrite.all" that will allow us to create a new Team in a tenant. But there are specific APIs in the Microsoft Graph that you cannot use until you requested them explicitly to Microsoft through a form: `https://docs.microsoft.com/en-us/graph/teams-protected-apis`. This request is another security measurement set in place to ensure that data stays private. These APIs are all about application permissions, so where you authenticate as an app and not as a user. With these kinds of permissions, you could, for instance, write code that reads all the messages in a channel where your bot has not explicitly been added. As you can imagine, this has some impact on the security of the tenant, because once these permissions get granted, nobody can visually see that you can read the messages they put in a Team. Therefore, you explicitly need to request them. Microsoft will ask you to explain why you need these permissions and a little bit about what your app does. Depending on whether you are preparing your app to be distributed through the app store into a lot of different tenants, this of course changes the discussion a little bit. If you just need it for the tenant of your own company, then the permission is given more quickly than if you want to do this for a multitude of tenants. In my opinion, this is an excellent way to go because these APIs can retrieve sensitive data, and users have no control over it. So an additional level of security is never negative. But in most cases, you can go with the alternative option, which is to have delegated permissions and to work with a bot that you add to a Team. A bot in a Team that does actions is more transparent for admins and end users.

PowerApps in Teams

This entire book was about custom development on Microsoft Teams. But don't forget that sometimes there are also other solutions to a problem and that the best answer is not always custom development. The effort you spend on creating a PowerApp and embedding that in Teams is usually far less than custom development. If it's not less, then you took the wrong path somewhere. Sometimes, providing a solution that only covers 80% of what the users want can be a great answer because you will spend only a fraction of the time and therefore cost on creating a PowerApp and embedding that inside of Teams. So if you have some time left, I do recommend that you play around with PowerApps and with their integration into Microsoft Teams. Creating solutions with the Power Platform in Teams can be a book by itself with all the newly released features. Therefore, we won't be spending more time on this, but it's something we cannot ignore. Another great feature is Microsoft Lists in Teams. Microsoft Lists (`https://support.microsoft.com/en-ie/office/get-started-with-lists-in-teams-c971e46b-b36c-491b-9c35-efeddd0297db`) is perfect for low-level or citizen developers who want to have a way to work with custom data inside of Teams. Even for experienced developers, these new features are not something to ignore, and you should always consider the pros and the cons when starting with a development project. Don't fear challenging more senior developers in the way they see things. This usually triggers exciting discussions and can only benefit your knowledge and theirs.

Summary

In this chapter, we discussed the advanced scenarios that you will come across when Teams development is going to be your day-to-day task. You now know that CI/CD will help you spend more time developing and less time on building and deploying your application.

Add your solution to the Teams app store

In this final chapter of the book, I wanted to give you some advice should you ever want to submit an app you create to Microsoft AppSource. AppSource is a generic name for the app store not only in Teams but also for Azure, Dynamics, Power BI, or PowerApps. I had the opportunity to get an app of mine added to the store beginning of 2020, and I wanted to share my experience with you. This way, you will have some insights into my personal experience on this. Sharing my story will help you understand the things to watch out for and what the procedure is all about.

Company

Should you ever want to publish your application, then you are going to do this through the partner portal. It's just the way the Microsoft Ecosystem works. Microsoft partners should create apps, and therefore the submission is started and maintained through the partner portal. If you don't own a company that is a Microsoft partner or you don't work for a company that is a Microsoft partner, then it's going to get very difficult to have your app in AppSource. If you work for a company that is a Microsoft partner and you are willing to create an app for Teams and submit that to AppSource, then I don't think your manager is going to have a problem with that. The visibility the company gets with having an app in AppSource is, if you look at the numbers on Teams usage around the world, enormous. If you have never seen the partner portal, then I provided a screenshot of it in Figure B-1.

© Rick Van Rousselt 2021
R. Van Rousselt, *Pro Microsoft Teams Development*, https://doi.org/10.1007/978-1-4842-6364-8

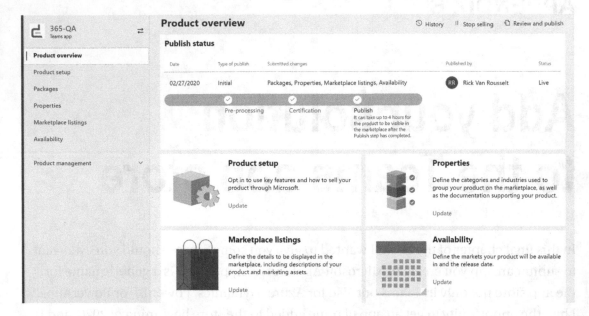

Figure B-1. *365-QA app viewed in the Microsoft Partner Center*

Submission

The first step you need to take after you are confident you know which app you are going to submit is to create a submission for the app in the partner center. You can submit various kinds of apps. There is also a possibility to submit an office add-in, a SharePoint solution, a Power BI visual, or a Teams app. In our case, we are going to submit a Teams app. After you selected a Teams app, it's time to start filling in a lot of information. The name is, of course, an essential part. There cannot be two apps with the same name in AppSource, so make sure that, on the one hand, you are original, but on the other hand, a name should also reflect what your app's goal is. Don't go naming your Teams app that has nothing to do with mail "Bulk mailer" or something. That would just be confusing to people when they see your app in the list of apps.

Another thing you should be aware of is that apps in AppSource are always free. That doesn't mean that you cannot charge people for using your app. It's just that it does not work like the App Store on iPhone or the Play Store on Android. You cannot just ask Microsoft to charge people, for example, $2 for installing an app. Microsoft doesn't do this. When you want to have revenue from your app, you will need to implement a system yourself into the app where you can charge users or where they can use it for a certain period for free. These in-app purchases as they get called do need to get verified, so you have to let Microsoft know how it works and what the cost is, and you are going to need to provide them with access to the full app so that they can verify the app before approval.

Next up is a CRM system. Having information about customers or potential customers might not interest you that much, but the sales responsible for your company is going to like it. When somebody installs your app, you at least want to know who did this. That information does get provided by Microsoft. Also, keep that in mind when you install a third-party app in your tenant. Your information is going to get sent to the creator of that app. The reason for this is that you can follow up with people installing your app to see if they like your app or not or to start a sales process. This data is not sent over directly to your mailbox, for instance, but will get sent over to a CRM system of your choice. The most well-known applications can be selected like Dynamics or Salesforce. If you don't have one of those systems (neither did I), then there is the option to choose an HTTP endpoint so that you can write an Azure function to insert the data in your CRM system or an Azure Table Storage. I took the last option; it was just a matter of creating a Storage Account in Azure and inserting the connection string. Once the data is in the storage table, then you can use a Logic app if needed to do something with it, like send an automated mail. The data you get is not that much, but it's enough for a salesperson to do their magic. As you can see in Figure B-2, they are just a few columns that get created, and some are even filled with always the same information such as Description or ActionCode.

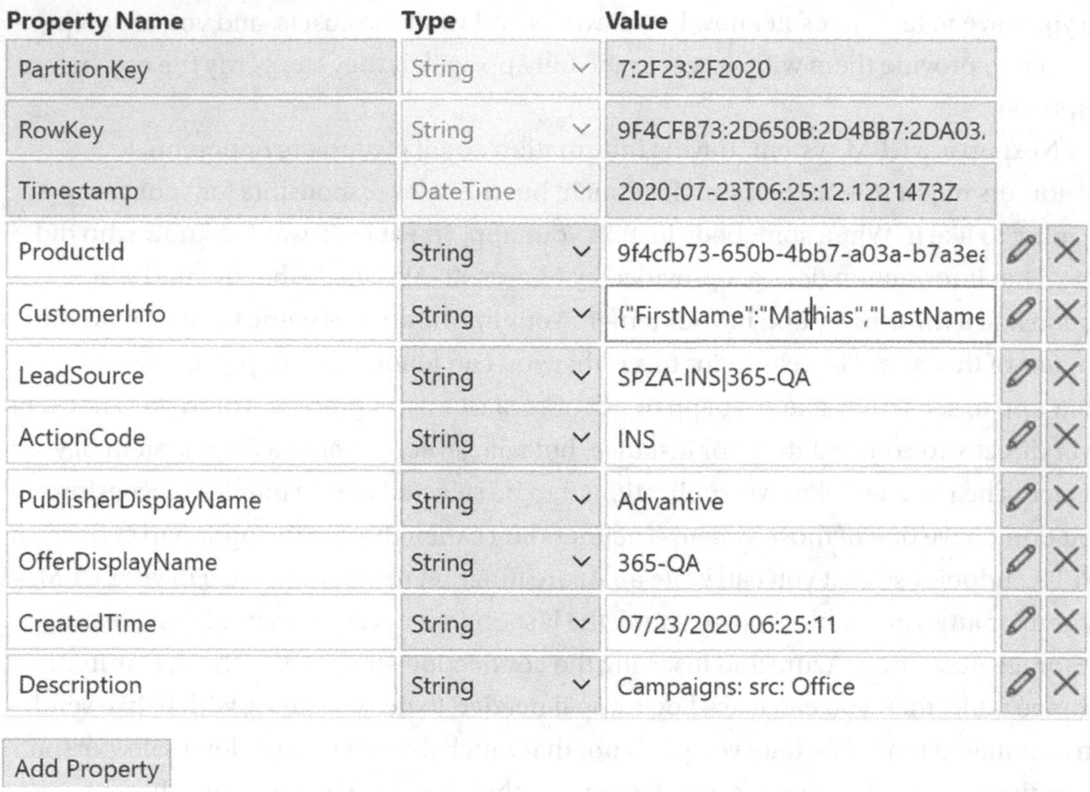

Property Name	Type		Value
PartitionKey	String	⌄	7:2F23:2F2020
RowKey	String	⌄	9F4CFB73:2D650B:2D4BB7:2DA03.
Timestamp	DateTime	⌄	2020-07-23T06:25:12.1221473Z
ProductId	String	⌄	9f4cfb73-650b-4bb7-a03a-b7a3e: ✎ ✕
CustomerInfo	String	⌄	{"FirstName":"Mathias","LastName ✎ ✕
LeadSource	String	⌄	SPZA-INS|365-QA ✎ ✕
ActionCode	String	⌄	INS ✎ ✕
PublisherDisplayName	String	⌄	Advantive ✎ ✕
OfferDisplayName	String	⌄	365-QA ✎ ✕
CreatedTime	String	⌄	07/23/2020 06:25:11 ✎ ✕
Description	String	⌄	Campaigns: src: Office ✎ ✕

Add Property

Figure B-2. *The information you get when somebody installs your app from the Teams store*

The most useful information is in the CustomerInfo column. It's JSON formatted with a person's first and last name, their email, company name, and the country where they are. So, it's enough for a salesperson, or so I'm told at least since that is not one of my favorite things to do.

Next up is selecting a category, and then it's time for the most time-consuming part of the process. At least for me, it was. You need to provide a link to a support page, a privacy policy page, and an End User License Agreement (EULA) page. Since I'm not a lawyer nor had any experience with software legal stuff, this was very time-consuming. You do want them to be correct, so I had to reach out to people to get those documents created and then to have them published on our company website. The support document was, although time-consuming, something I could do myself. If you do create one yourself, be sure that you let somebody else check it. After all, we developers tend to make our support documents rather simple because we expect other users to be such experts as we are in specific tools.

Review

Once all the paperwork is done, it's time to upload your Teams app package and to submit it for review. Or so you would think. But that's not the case for a Teams app. Teams apps must go through a separate approval process by a different team. So by this point in time, you should send a mail to teamsubm@microsoft.com and tell them what you are planning to do. This is of course at the time I'm writing this and could have changed by the time you read this book. With Teams adoption and therefore apps in Teams skyrocketing, they might need to change this process. They are going to need your app name, the ID from your submission in the partner center, and your manifest ID. I must say that the people running this service at Microsoft respond very promptly. I got a mail back the same day, explaining how the process is going to go and what additional information they required.

One of the additional items they need is your Teams app package. You would think that they can just download it from the partner center, but because the team that is helping you validate your app is not the same as the team running the normal validation of apps in AppSource, they don't have access to do that. They do require you to have already your manifest validated with the validation tool (`https://manifestvalidator.azurewebsites.net/`). Now that you know this link, you can already do this before you submit your app. The tool just checks the manifest for errors against the JSON schema. When you use App Studio or the extensions for Visual Studio or Visual Studio Code, those also do the same. It's a quick check, and I'm positive that with all the information you now know, you won't have any errors. The only difference is that this tool creates a report, as in Figure B-3. And this report you can send back to them along with your app package. The tool checks some of the different key points addressed in this page: `https://docs.microsoft.com/en-us/microsoftteams/platform/concepts/deploy-and-publish/appsource/prepare/detail-page-checklist`.

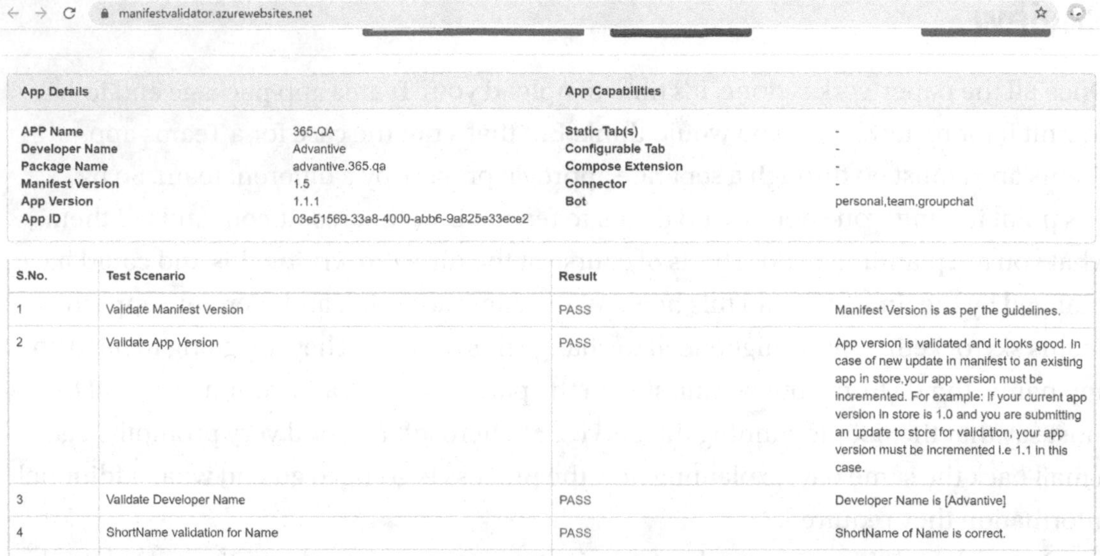

Figure B-3. *The manifest validator report for 365-QA*

The next item on their requirements list is a way to test and validate your app. You should add a document describing how they can test your app and a way to do so, to make sure that they get the best test experience. And don't forget they are starting at the first step, which is installing your app for the first time; I created a new tenant for them and provided the credentials. This is, in my case, something that I missed. My app worked, but I did not test what happens when you first install it. It slipped my mind; you start developing, you install it, update the manifest and the code a few times, but you never really uninstall and reinstall it entirely during development or even during testing. If you are going to submit an app to AppSource, then don't forget to test this step yourself. Looking at the test notes that I provided, it just consisted of a description of the app, the credentials to the new tenant, and a few use cases combined with screenshots that they could do. You should also check out this page: https://docs.microsoft.com/en-us/microsoftteams/platform/concepts/deploy-and-publish/appsource/prepare/submission-checklist. It describes all the steps you need to do and the things you should take into consideration.

Another thing that I wasn't expecting is that they asked for a meeting to demo the app. I like the commitment of this team. Looking at the number of third-party apps in Teams, they must do a lot of work, especially when talking to all of them just to understand the use case they are trying to solve. Having the opportunity to demo your app makes the entire process a lot easier; you can have all the screenshots and test notes in the world, but they cannot replace a ten-minute call where you explain what you are doing, why you created the app, and how it works. I appreciated the time and effort that the Teams app submission team invested, and this way, you can also expect that they did this with every app in the Teams store, ensuring that the apps available there are of decent standards and quality. After this demo meeting, they go to work and validate your app; in my case, I already had feedback after a day. The 365-QA app is also rather simple; there is no authentication required, and the use case is straightforward, so it probably was not that much work for them. But then it was time for the verdict. The following table is a direct copy/paste from the mail I received.

Please use the attached files with this email during app submission process via Partner center.

	Title	Description
1	Manifest	Please use the attached manifest in your app submission
2	Partner Center Description	1. Short description : Please follow the recommendations provided here. : `https://docs.microsoft.com/en-us/microsoftteams/platform/concepts/deploy-and-publish/appsource/prepare/detail-page-checklist#short-description` 2. Long description : Please follow the recommendations provided here `https://docs.microsoft.com/en-us/microsoftteams/platform/concepts/deploy-and-publish/appsource/prepare/detail-page-checklist#long-description` . Long description must be between 300 – 500 words
3	Partner Center Developer name	The Provider Name mentioned in the App Manifest must be same with the Developer Name in the Partner Center
4	Support Link	Please submit Support URL in Partner center which can be accessed by all the users to reach out to for any queries, ensure Support URL has contact details in it.
5	EULA	Terms of use page link with reference to the Teams app or all your products and services

(*continued*)

	Title	Description
6	Partner Center Screenshots	1. When you submit screenshots on Partner Center they need to be great quality, with very limited Teams UI/chrome and focuses only on your App's Capability. 2. The ideal screenshots should avoid excessive content as per the guideline. https://docs.microsoft.com/en-us/microsoftteams/platform/concepts/deploy-and-publish/appsource/prepare/detail-page-checklist#screenshots 3. It must be exactly 1366w x 768h pixels and no greater than 1024 KB. 4. See this sample link https://appsource.microsoft.com/en-us/product/office/WA104381505?src=office&tab=Overview - check images on the right side of the browser window.
7	Limitations need to be called out in Testnotes/AppSource Long description	If your app has any limitations/constraints, out of scope functionalities, please add them in the Long description.

As you can see from the response I got back, the most errors were esthetics. My descriptions were not according to standards, and my screenshots didn't match the exact width and height prescribed, which is challenging to get your screenshot or at least the parts you want to show to exact that dimension. But I can imagine that if they get all kinds of resolutions in the store, it's not going to look good. But at least my code and the functionality of the bot worked, and they didn't get any errors in that area. After you get this mail, you can hit the submit button in the partner center, including the email with the evaluation result, and after a few days, your app will be approved and starts to show up in the Teams app store.

Summary

This last part was all about giving you some insights into the app submission process. Because the process is a little bit different than with apps for other platforms, I did not want this part missing from this book. I hope that by providing this information, you will, once you get done building a cool app, share it with the rest of the world by placing it in the Teams app store.

Index

A

Action-based extensions
  adaptive card, 307
    ACMS, 330
    authentication, 330, 331
    botMessagePreview type, 332–334
    bot posts, 337
    OnTeamsMessagingExtension
      BotMessagePreviewEditAsync
      function, 334–336
    task module, 331, 332
  embedded web view
    Bot framework, 323, 324, 328
    fetchtask, 319, 320
    GetLocation, 324, 325
    logged-in user, 329
    Microsoft.Graph, 326–328
    OAuth connection settings, 324
    OnTeamsMessagingExtension
      FetchTaskAsync method, 322
    redirect URLs, 322, 323
    sign-in task module, 328, 329
    task module, 320, 321
  link unfurling, 337–340
  locations, 308
  static action-based extension
    action property, 313
    compose box, 317
    ComposeExtensions, 309, 310
    debugging, 313
    JSON, 315
    manifest, 310, 311
    OnTeamsMessagingExtension
      SubmitActionAsync method,
      315, 316
    options, 312, 313
    pop-up, 311
    task module, 317–319
    types of fields, 312
    value property, 314
  task modules, 309
ADAL.js, 127
Adaptive Card Management System
  (ACMS), 330
Advanced Teams development
  CI/CD, 361, 362
  Pipelines
    CLI, 369, 370
    development app and
      production app, 371
    Gitflow workflow, 368
    NuGet packages, 368
    protected APIs, 372
    stage, 368, 369
    YAML, 365–367
  PowerApps, 372, 373
  source control, 362–365
AppSource, 375, 376, 380

Printed in the United States
By Bookmasters